Illuminati Hunter

II

'Excellent Mr Harrison, or should I say Herr Drechsler? Exciting and funny is rare. But something tells me there is more.'

Heathcote Williams. Poet, Author, Activist.

1941 – 2017

Original book photographed 2012.

ISBN 978-1-914195-79-2

Book layout and design by Ethan Harrison. Production management by UKBookPrinting.com.

Foreword

After the successful republication of Illuminati Hunter, the original of which I found in a secondhand book shop, I was contacted by the great granddaughter of the owner of Necromancer, the English publishers that first printed it in 1913. To my surprise she told me that she had come across the two subsequent volumes planned for serialisation which never saw the light of day and, after a quick negotiation, they came into my hands. As with the first book, after this brief introduction, the following text, aside from the addition of the footnotes and the rear appendix, is an exact reprint of the next episode of these extraordinary and previously unreleased volumes.

There are several reasons which inspired me to republish this book. Mainly because, like the first, it is a marvellous read written in a surprisingly modern style that I am sure many readers will appreciate. But also, as with its predecessor, when I checked the details of the story on the internet I found that many of the claims, however unbelievable, were backed up by existing records or so close that it is impossible to believe they could all be coincidence. Hence the footnotes so you can see for yourself.

If the story contained within these volumes is true then it would throw an entirely new light on what is already an enthralling period of history. I am sure that you will find it fascinating, especially if you explore the E Book links or the website addresses in the paperback's appendix. I hope that you enjoy researching the background of this exciting adventure as much as I have and, of course, that you are thrilled by the incredible story itself.

E. Harrison 2019

ILLUMINATI HUNTER II

Merchant Kolmer & The Obelisk of Nempty

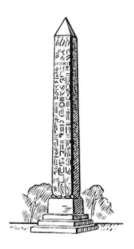

By Sebastian P. Drechsler

Published in Great Britain by Necromancer Press 1913.

Introduction

This volume is formed from a collection of memoirs discovered in 1898 at the University of Munich in Bavaria. Sebastian Pierre Drechsler was a student and eventually lecturer at Ingolstadt University between 1783 – 1800, before the faculty was closed down. He later went on to become Professor and then Director of History at Munich University until he retired in 1833. It is understood that the original memoirs were dictated by the scholar on his deathbed (circa 1852) and that he had not wanted them to come to the public's attention for 'some time' after he died so as not to besmirch his fine reputation achieved after many years working within academe. He was on record to have made claim that they would be valuable 'To those in the future who are already illuminated, or are ready to come into the light.' It should be noted that the transcript was dictated to an Englishman, a court stenographer by trade, who was not fluent in the Bavarian tongue but the far-sighted Professor had understood that his scribe's natural dialect was fast becoming the international language of the world and so by means of this translation would secure the text's widest readership when it eventually saw the light of day. This detail and the fact that it is a vocal record would explain the sound effects, British measurements, occasional vernacular and the constant personal observations of a humorous nature.

A. Jones Editor Necromancer Press 1913.

Sebastian P. Drechsler's Adventures 1785-1786

Baltic Sea

North Sea

JUTLAND

Louisenlund

St Petersburgh

PRUSSIA

Kiel

POLAND

RU

Hamburg

Berlin

SAXONY

Tuffengarten

HANOVER

River Oder

MOROVIA

Prague

Leipzig

River Elbe

Nuremberg

BAVARIA

Bayreuth

River Danube

Stuttgart

Ingolstadt

Graveyard

Passau

Landshut

Muniuch

Miles

For All The Blacksmiths.
Let All Your Children
Be As Stars.

As Above, So Below

'Quod est inferius est sicut
quod est superius'

I, Sebastian Pierre Drechsler, finding myself of bright mind but failing body at the grand old age of eighty seven in the year of our Lord 1852, do willingly commit these memoirs to paper. I solemnly give my oath that though, at times, much of the following text may sound unbelievable it is, in fact, a true and accurate account of the amazing adventures in which I played my part as a young man in my homeland of Bavaria many years ago. I also hope that if the text has survived long enough before coming to the public's attention, as I have intended, then the incredible tale that you are about to read no longer contains a very necessary warning for the world. But if that is the case then may God Almighty have mercy on your souls.

The strange thing about working for Professor Van Halestrom the Illuminati Hunter was that, on many occasions, I thought that our exploits were at an end and we had finally defeated the cursed Order which we fought so valiantly then, perhaps, I could return to living the life of a normal man. But time after time our enemies came back to wreak havoc and misery in our lives and the lives of others. The fight it would seem, as much as I prayed, did not want to die.

That is why I shall begin the next chapter of my memoirs on the last day of August 1785. For it was then that these dark forces came once more. Oh and how they came. But I shall take my time to tell my tale properly because it is important to tell it well. If only to pay tribute to those who were not as fortunate as me and who do not have the opportunity to tell it themselves. For they paid the ultimate price.

Chapter 1

The Crossroads

It was another rainy day in the fatherland of Bavaria. Apparently the dismal weather was due to the eruptions of a volcano in distant Iceland which, I remember very well, had been responsible for ruining that whole summer. But like any other healthy Teutonic young buck I was not to be put off by mere inclement weather, even if it was caused by an infernal volcano, and determined to enjoy my last free day before the start of my third year at Ingolstadt University: The esteemed institution where I was rather displeased to be, according to my history lecturer Old Herr Lipstad, 'a strangely over-active but under-achieving student.' You see in those days, though having the constant distractions of the evil Illuminati hanging over me and, of course, my studies, I was far more interested in lampooning idiots, admiring women and riding horses for, really, those were my favourite subjects. And that was what I was doing on that day: Riding.

I was a fine horseman back then; confident, strong, able and I possessed the biggest advantage of them all, the most wonderful horse; my four-year-old white mare Petrova. The best in any stable she could certainly fly and often did with me in the saddle. Around that time I had taken to perfecting the skill of pulling a staff from the ground while riding at a canter and, at a village called Ludigraben, situated on the crossroads two miles east of Ingolstadt, I would practice.

Having found my fellow students to be, on the whole, either hellish bores content to boast of their mythical sexual conquests in the city's bierkellers all night or toadying, pale-faced bookworms who did nothing all day but study, I had befriended Karl, the blacksmith's son who shared my passion for riding.

I suppose that, in a way, he had become my squire of sorts. He was thirteen, seven years younger than myself, and looked up to me as though I was his older brother. Suffice to say, this filled me with much platonic pride having no siblings of my own.

Throughout that wet summer, this pastime had become something of a habit of ours and, as usual, a small crowd of children and their mothers had huddled under the dripping trees along the road, happy to see young men performing tricks on their horses on a rainy afternoon in the countryside. Not much happened on a rainy afternoon in the countryside in Bavaria. Not much at all. Well, not usually anyway.

Oh, and one thing, before you get the impression that I was in anyway a heroic chap let me please assure you that, whilst being a strangely overly-active but under-achieving student, I was also a peculiarly vain and facetious coward until given damn good reason to be otherwise. And with these contradictions firmly set in place I somehow continued to make my way through life. Anyhow, I digress. Where was I? Oh yes, on my horse.

"Make sure you stand the stick up properly!" I called. Karl had knocked it over for the dozenth time on his ungainly old stallion Thunder.

"I can't do it!" he moaned.

"To be fair, Karl, it *is* hard."

This was true. It *was* very hard. It was raining, very muddy and his father's old workhorse would not have raised two sous from a French butcher. But I kept this to myself not wanting to hurt his feelings as his family was less privileged than mine. He stuck the stake back in the mud at the crossroads and trudged up the road pulling the animal behind him with his head hung low.

"Don't give up now!" I cheered, "Let me show you again!"

I gave Petrova a nudge in her flanks and flicked her reins. She knew what I wanted her to do and set off at a steady canter.

I hooked my heel in the stirrup on her far side and swept down off her opposite flank, gliding my right hand three feet above the ground like a Mongolian tribesman. After a wink at the spectating mothers I swung down and, at exactly the right moment, grabbed the stake clean out of the mud.

"Yahoo!" hooted Karl behind me, "I wish I could do that!"

"You can, boy! You can. Don't give up now."

I wheeled Petrova about, sending lumps of mud into the air as she found her balance.

"Practice, practice, that's what you must do, practice."

"I know, I know. Practice, practice," he sulked, "That's what you always say, but still I cannot do it."

"Now, now, you mustn't give up. Go on. Try again."

I enjoyed encouraging him. It was good to see him gain in confidence as I had done as a boy. I stuck the stake in the same place, making sure to leave it as upright as possible, before trotting back to his side and instructing him, "Now, keep your head down and try to keep old Thunder here in a straight line."

He huffed and puffed then pulled himself back into his saddle. After a moment he wriggled his nose, tugged the bridle with renewed vigour then gave a hearty kick to the old horse's belly and trotted off. This time he came off the horse's side a little lower and, though going a might slower than myself, was definitely on the right track.

"Go on!" I cried as an expensive black coach pulled by six black horses clattered out of the trees and slid to a halt at the crossroads, nearly causing a big wagon following behind to crash into its rear. An argument broke out between the coach driver and an unruly gang on the wagon but Karl resolutely carried on and, by Jove, the little chap pulled the stake out of the ground.

"Bravo!" I called and he looked back in happy astonishment but did not think to slow down as a tall man dressed in black flung open the coach door and joined in with the argument. Karl dragged his horse to a stop but as the old beast struggled to keep its balance, a clod of mud was thrown up and, by a million to one chance, hit the man on his cheek.

The rabble in the wagon fell ominously silent as the man slowly touched his face and fixed a wolfish stare on the boy. Crestfallen to have humiliated the gentleman Karl went to apologise but from behind his back the man brought out a whip and suddenly lashed it round the boy's neck with an ear-splitting 'crack!'

"No!" I roared but before I could act, he yanked Karl off his horse and powerfully heaved him through the mud up to the side of the coach. It all happened so fast that I was only starting to ride over, yelling, "Let him go you dog!" when - damn it - the bounder knelt down in the doorway and stroked the boy's hair in the most unpleasant of ways.

"Get away from him!" I shouted, boiling with anger.

The scoundrel did not even look up but continued eyeing Karl with revolting malice until I trotted up to the coach and his driver coughed, "Herr Kolmer."

Finally the bastard stood up and faced me but instead of apologising beheld me with utter contempt and rudely snorted through his nose. I was about to jump down and punch his teeth out when an ugly rat-faced character on the wagon's footboard pointed a musket at me.

Who the hell were this lot? I glared at the man in black but quickly reconsidering my position, held up my hands. I was not armed and there were at least two on the coach and seven more on the wagon. He grinned at my climb-down and, without taking his eyes off me, unwound the whip from Karl's neck with a clever flick of the wrist. He flashed the boy another perverted smile then fixed his eyes back on mine and such was his look of pure devilry that I could not take my eyes away from his as he closed the coach door and, after a cry from the driver, the caravan rattled away.

At last I tore my stare from his sickly grin and jumped down to tend to Karl. Though he was plastered in mud and had a bright red weal all the way round his neck, I believed that no bones were broken.

"Are you all right, lad?"

He nodded and rubbed his throat, gasping, "I did it, Herr Drechsler. I picked up the stake."

"Yes you did, Karl. Yes you did."

I glared back at the small procession rumbling down the road. I was determined to find out who this swine was and do something about him. I could not let these bastards get away with this. After all - my thoughts seethed in furious contemplation - I was an Illuminati Hunter. I had killed many men before. So, I could do it again. My concentration faltered. I watched Karl nursing his wounds. What should I do? Make no bones about it I wanted to kill that son of a bitch right there and then but I knew that picking a fight with him and his gang right now would be suicide. So, I would follow them and perhaps... I looked back at the convoy swaying into the trees. Of course, they must be headed for Ingolstadt.

I picked Karl up, cleaned him down and gave him a drink from my hip flask then helped him back onto old Thunder. We bid a forlorn goodbye to the alarmed village folk and trotted off. The more I thought about it the more I was certain that the despicable crew were headed for Ingolstadt. It was getting late and they must be looking for shelter. On taking up the road back home I inspected their tracks in the mud and noticed by its deeper markings that the covered wagon was much heavier than the coach. Upon looking closer I realised, 'Very heavy indeed.'

My theory was confirmed when we came to the city and found the wagon experiencing great difficulties crossing the lake of mud surrounding the eastern gate. The fiend in black was leaning from his coach screaming at his men to push the wagon through the swamp. We laughed when a couple of the brutes fell over covering themselves with filth before, with the four white shire horses being whipped to blazes, they managed to muscle the wagon inside the walls.

We walked our horses in behind them keeping our distance and mingling with other travellers on the road until the convoy pulled up outside The Eagle; a large hotel with stables and rooms for rent. I led Karl to the safety of some wagons on the other side of the street from where we watched the men dismount and was about to find one of the city's watchmen to report what had happened when the devil in black sprang from his coach and began shaking hands with a local councillor. I gawked in shock as the men embraced like long-lost brothers but my guts turned to lead when the Principal of the University, Herr Vacchieri, also strode up and enthusiastically joined in with the greeting, "Welcome to Ingolstadt, my dear Herr Kolmer!"

Saints alive! Who was this man? One thing was certain; it would be most unwise to accuse a friend of both the council and the university, of being a child abuser. I knew from much personal experience that picking a fight with a friend of the authorities could have grave consequences. Whatever anyone tells you not all Bavarians are good people and that is the truth.

I escorted Karl round the corner to the blacksmith's where I convinced his anxious father that, whoever this scoundrel was, I would be making a formal complaint through the proper channels. After stabling Petrova I made my way straight to the one person who I knew that could help. My master, employer, saving grace and philosophical guide who, over the past momentous year, had protected me from and trained me to fight against the dreaded Illuminati; the wizard-like Professor Van Halestrom. Of all people he would know what to do. I guessed that he would be at the university preparing for the start of the new term and, fortified by this prospect, I quickened my pace through the lanes leading to the university. At least I knew where the fiend in black was staying. And I knew his name: Kolmer. *[1]

---

1. **The Illuminati & Ingolstadt University.** Ingolstadt University was immersed in controversy throughout the end of the 18th century due to the activities of the Bavarian Illuminati. Adam Weishaupt, the founder of the Order in 1776, was Master of Canon Law at the university until March 1785 when he was sacked for his role in the infamous secret society which had, by then seen its ranks grow to over 3000 – see *Illuminati Hunter I.* Herr Vacchieri is not known to have been a member of the society though it is highly possible. He was definitely employed by the university during this period and is mentioned in a book called *Little Tools of Knowledge* (2001 University Michigan Press). The revolutionary zeitgeist associated with The Age of Reason which flourished throughout Europe's educational institutions during this period and prepared the ground for the American and French Revolutions, posed a threat to the authorities and this contributed to the university's closure in 1800. Interestingly, the campus also provides the backdrop for Mary Shelley's masterpiece *Frankenstein* (1812) set at the faculty in 1793 which is often seen as a metaphor for revolution; political, industrial, religious or otherwise. Though the author refers to Ingolstadt as a 'city' it remains a town to this day but during the late 18th century held such huge political influence, as many luminaries of the time were educated there, that this may explain S. Drechsler's exaggeration.

Chapter 2

The Merchant Kolmer

I strode through the university doors and up the shadowy hallway eager to find Van Halestrom and tell him what had happened. Deep down inside something told me that this Kolmer had a connection with the Illuminati but such was the fear that it induced in me I did my damnedest to ignore it. Two peaceful months had passed since I had last risked my life fighting the deathly Order and I had been enjoying the hiatus immeasurably. I flew up the stairs and along the corridor towards the Professor's study planning what I might say to him when I heard from over my shoulder, "Ah, Sebastian, just the man."

In a trice Van Halestrom appeared in his black robes from a door next to me and proceeded to walk briskly by my side. Discombobulated by his sudden appearance I tried to collect my thoughts but it was too late. "Come to my study," he offered.

"Excellent, sir," I panted. "I was going there now. There is a matter of some urgency I wish to discuss."

"I too have something I wish to share with you."

"But I feel that this information is of great importance, sir..."

"Equally mine is of some gravity," he interrupted as we reached his door. I went to speak again but he held up a finger. "Remember, Drechsler?"

I knew what he meant. He wished me to recite one of his tedious palindromes and I impatiently parroted, "Yes, Professor; Education, Education, Education."

He hummed contently and entered his study.

Good God. Sometimes he was an annoying old bird. But I was not done yet and continued pestering him as I followed inside, "My point will take no time at all to explain, sir..."

He spun round and stared down his beaky nose at me. "Neither will mine, Sebastian. So I will speak first." Seeing that he was determined I gave up. It was useless. Though chomping at the bit to tell him my story I knew that I would have to wait. After all, he *was* my master. He went to the fireplace and took down his pipe from the mantelpiece then lit it with his ingenious pocket flint box. After puffing out a dense cloud of smoke he began, "Today's lesson, Drechsler, is economics."

"Economics!" This was too much and I reeled in petulant despair. "Sir, what I know, or would care to know, about economics wouldn't fill a flea's codpiece. What does this have to do with anything?"

"It has much to do with everything, Sebastian. It is the Illuminati's plan to control the world's financial system and, therefore, the world. So listen you must."

Of all the things that I was not in the mood for it was a lesson in blasted economics and I reluctantly prepared to be bombarded with reams of confusing facts and figures.

As usual the Professor read my mind. "Relax, my lad. This fraud is so simple that a child could understand it."

Perhaps this was different. Maybe I *could* understand it.

He stroked his beard and began, "The Illuminati plan to set up a series of central banks similar to the Bank of England. These banks will print money out of thin air then loan it to the government at interest creating a spiral of debt that the government cannot escape which, in time, turns the people into slaves and the bank into the government, thus the *real* power behind the throne. Simple."

My cognitive functions rolled along until I grasped his point whereupon they promptly ground to a halt. I could not believe that this was the entirety of the plan. "But surely, sir... it can't be *that* simple?"

"Yes, Drechsler, simple but brilliantly effective. You see?" he flicked his eyebrows, "I told you a child could understand it."

He smiled at his little joke and I frowned to be the butt of it. His poor attempt at humour had broken my flimsy concentration and I stumbled, "But..."

"As the bank controls the amount of money in the system, by secretly printing enormous quantities to dilute its value, they can fleece the man in the street without lifting a finger. It is merely a subtle form of slavery that has been operating successfully in England since 1694. It is well known that those who hold the keys to Threadneedle Street hold the real power of the British Empire and the Illuminati wish to take over this enterprise by placing a series of their agents in charge before exporting the system around the known world. We have discovered that a high-level meeting is set to take place at an Illuminati stronghold somewhere in Europe at which the last touches will be made to the plot. This scheme, to bring man to his knees under the cult of false money, will be overlooked at the peril of civilisation because those who persevere to bring it about have the financial and political will to make their diabolical dream a reality."

As ever his conspiratorial thunderbolts left me speechless and I struggled to take in the ghastly business. *²

---

2. **Illuminati & The Central Banks.** Conspiracy theories regarding the Illuminati and the central banks have existed as long as the separate institutions themselves. As S. Drechsler states The Bank of England was established in 1694 and, since then, the pound has been devalued more than a hundred times giving his claims some weight. While it may be difficult to accept that the global financial institutions could ever be run in such a simple yet fraudulent manner, for some inexplicable reason, rumours of an over-arching centralised banking cartel controlled by remnants of the Bavarian Illuminati still persist to this day. To realise the true power of the world's financial institutions, then and now, perhaps consider the words of US state official H. Kissinger, 'Who controls money can control the world.'

Some quiet seconds passed before he asked, "So what did you want to tell me?"

I felt an empty expression cross my face. Such was the manner of his news that I had momentarily forgotten.

"You wanted to tell me something, lad?"

Of course! It all flooded back in a torrent. "Kolmer! I met a man today dressed in black at the crossroads. He attacked young Karl with a..."

"Whip," chorused Van Halestrom.

I stared at him dumbfounded as he glared toward the window and ominously murmured, "So Kolmer is here."

Hell's bells. Was I the only man in Ingolstadt who did not know who this swine was? Determined not to be the last to find out I begged, "Professor, who the hell is this blackguard? Everyone including the man in the tavern's dog knows who he is apart from me."

He was already by the window scanning the street for the cad. "He is Franz Kolmer; a ruthless devil from Jutland in Denmark, though he is a merchant and flies no country's flag: A crazed political radical and exporter of ancient artefacts mainly from Egypt. He is also deeply involved with several dark esoteric orders of which not much is known, but one thing is certain."

Much to my frustration, at this point he took a long puff on his pipe and leaned closer to the window. The suspense quickly became unbearable and I had to ask, "...Which is, sir?"

"Oh, he has the word 'Illuminati' branded on his very soul."

"Capital," I tensed. I knew he was not your average knave and, infuriated that my bad luck continued to be my faithful companion, I could not help but curse, "Damn it, sir, why has he come to Ingolstadt of all places and not gone somewhere else?"

The Professor came straight out with it, "He has every reason. His best student used to be Master of Canon Law here."

"No! Please... tell me it isn't so?" I stuttered, though God help me I knew that it was.

"It was Kolmer who indoctrinated Weishaupt into the dark arts."

"My God."

It could not be worse. Adam Weishaupt; my old lecturer and chief Illuminati villain, the madman who had tried to kill me so many times that I had lost count, whom I had helped banish from the university and the whole of Bavaria but six months ago was merely this man's *student*. God's dinner! I collapsed into one of the Professor's leather chairs.

"Where is he now, my lad?"

"The Eagle," I mumbled in a daze. My mind flashed back to the crossroads and the whip, and the look in his eyes when he stared at poor Karl, the way he stroked him. Good God. I remembered all my other battles with the awful Illuminati creatures and shuddered at the visions. I had barely got over the prospect of returning to university let alone this.

Van Halestrom put his hand on my shoulder. "Tell me, lad. Who was he with? What was he doing?"

I told him of the meeting that I had seen with the town's dignitaries and of the heavy wagon carrying its mysterious cargo. He took much interest in this and stroked his beard, mumbling, "I see, I see." Until, after I had told him of Kolmer's violence and my humiliating climb-down, he assured me, "You did the right thing, my friend, and by the sounds of it you're going to get the chance to get your own back." He moved to the fireplace and emptied his pipe.

"Well how is that going to happen?" I scoffed. And how *was* it going to happen? Although I was angry, locking horns with any member of the Order was a terrifying thought especially this vicious brute to say nothing of his army of thugs.

Van Halestrom breezily responded, "We will go there tonight to find out just what he is up to."

"What?" I choked, daunted by this frightening prospect. I could have told him exactly what Kolmer was *up to*: 'No good,' obviously.

But I knew that my concerns would be of little consequence as he was already rummaging through his desk, no doubt, collecting his things together for our imminent mission. I wondered, with much trepidation, if I was being unwittingly swept along into the next chapter of my adventures. Oh and how right I was to think such a thing. How right indeed. *3 *4

---

3. **The Merchant Kolmer, Illuminati Mentor.** S. Drechsler's recollections of this illusive character, whose past is shrouded in mystery, is highly noteworthy as he is the only eye witness to have ever seen him. Though very little detail is known about the merchant Kolmer he is recorded to have spent much time in Alexandria where he gained a reputation as an expert in ancient artefacts. As S. Drechsler states he was reputed to have initiated Adam Weishaupt, the father of the Bavarian Illuminati, into the darker aspects of Egyptian occultism based on the Manichean teachings which focus on the conflict between good and evil.

4. **Adam Weishaupt, Illuminati Leader & Professor of Canon Law at Ingolstadt University.** Adam Weishaupt founded the Bavarian Illuminati on May 1st 1776 (the same year of the US Declaration of Independence, the same date as the International Day for Communism, and also ancient pagan witch celebration). Throughout history there has rarely been another individual surrounded by more intrigue than the brilliant academic who could justifiably be known as 'The Godfather of Conspiracy' and has entered the popular cultural pantheon as one of modern history's most profoundly influential thinkers.

Chapter 3

The Eagle

That night as the bells of St Maria's struck ten o'clock I met the Professor outside the university and we rode together through the wet cobbled streets to The Eagle. I had never been inside the place myself and had always thought it quite the respectable establishment. The Illuminati, it would seem, had some taste. Van Halestrom had assured me that there should be 'no need for bloodshed tonight,' as he had put it. Even so, along with a large hat for a disguise, I had taken the precaution of bringing a pistol with me. I stared up into the blustering wind and rain praying that I would not have to use it. Anger, I have always found, can be an elusive master. When you have it no man wants to stand in your way but without it, when you often need it, it has the annoying habit of completely deserting you. My rage had dramatically subsided from earlier and, though I wanted my revenge on this bastard Kolmer, I did not enjoy the idea of walking into a tavern and shooting him in the face. But I suppose that was just the way I was brought up.

We tied our horses round the corner from the hotel and made the rest of our way on foot. The sound of rowdy voices wafted from the front windows as we crossed the street outside and the Professor murmured, "I will enter the stables at the side of the building but I also know there's an entrance through the saloon into the rear. This is the way you shall go and I shall meet you at the wagon." [5]

5. **The Eagle Hotel (Hotel Adler) Ingolsatdt.** This impressive hotel has been in the heart of the old city of Ingolstadt since the 15th century and will have hardly changed since S. Drechsler walked through the door over two hundred and fifty years ago. E Book readers can view the hotel here and a map of Ingolstadt's old street layout.

I did not like the sound of this. But as I looked at the stable doors I was certain that I saw breath condensing in the night air and I did not like the look of this either.

"Are you sure, sir?" I whispered but before I could argue he winked and skulked off into the shadows. I came up to the entrance and pulled down the brim of my hat then, with a deep breath, opened the door.

A wax-laden candelabra swung in the hallway alternately lighting a sign over one door denoting, '*Saloon*' and over the other, '*Night House Bar.*' I had no wish to enter the latter for it was from where the drunken voices were coming. But, as I turned to go through the first, the largest Frau that I had ever seen burst from it carrying a huge basket of laundry and with no modesty senselessly bundled me backwards. Alarmed to be travelling in the wrong direction and toward possible danger I tried to push back but I was no match for the enormous woman and, with one more gigantic thrust, she forced me into the bar. I stumbled into the room but was stopped on my heels by an ignorant catcall from behind.

"Ha! But you spend all your time reading, sir. What have books ever taught anyone?"

The clumsy washerwoman barged into me again but this time spilled her basket on the floor. My manners forced me to help her pick up the mess and she begrudgingly let me assist.

"You know nothing, fool!" snorted a second voice, "Why, if your brains were made of gunpowder you would still not have enough to blow your head off!"

A roar of laughter tempted me to see who was making all the noise. Curses! I should have known it. Kolmer and his gang were sat round a table covered with empty beer flagons and I whipped back my head so fast that I almost stuck my nose into the washerwoman's cleavage.

She scowled at me, grabbed the last shirt from my hands and waddled off with her basket as Kolmer scorned, "I'll tell you one thing, fool, if you were made aware of only half the secrets of the universe then *that* would surely blow your head off."

"Oooh!" whooped his ruffians, revelling in the taunt and loudly goading its recipient.

I reached the door and overheard the insulted man mutter under his breath, "Perhaps you're the fool." There was a sudden smash and I glimpsed Kolmer clutch the knave's throat so hard that his eyes almost popped from their sockets. "No one ever insults me dog!" he yelled and slapped the lackey round the face then pulled him up to his snorting nose. "Come the final revolution brother, you will be nothing. Nothing! Do you hear? Nor will your children or your children's children. You will bow to men like me, the true lords of civilisation. Not those lazy inbred aristocrats or their fawning politicians and ignorant generals. No, *brother*! Come the final revolution, it is you and your kind who will *forever play the fool*!"

Wonderful. He was good with children and he could have a good laugh with his comrades down the local tavern. He was, as the English say, 'an all-rounder.' Determined to leave their cosy little get-together, I was already halfway through the door when he called out, "You there, stranger! What do you say? Should I teach this dog a lesson?"

I could not believe it, for I knew he was talking to me. For God's sake, was there not someone else he could ask?

"Well, man?" he rudely barked, "What do you say?"

I tugged the brim of my hat even lower and mumbled over my shoulder, "Every dog needs a master and it seems you've the edge over this pack of hounds, so naturally you should take charge of 'em whichever way you see fit."

He seemed to appreciate my remark. So, not waiting to be

asked for a second opinion, I pelted through the hallway from where I heard him taking me up on my advice, though not as I had intended for he began beating his minion to a pulp. I burst into the saloon, through the empty room and, after a second to find my bearings, out the rear of the tavern and into the stables.

"That was too close," I breathed, glancing round the shadows. Amongst the collection of carts I quickly spotted Kolmer's black coach and beside it the wagon with its bulging canvas. After checking that there was no one about, I crept over but ducked down when I saw another cloud of breath by the doors. I wondered if it was a guard that maybe Van Halestrom had been unable to pass which would mean it was up to me to discover what was in the wagon.

I sneaked round the back and pulled up the heavy canvas. There was certainly something under there but it was too dark to see so I reached out and touched the object. Whatever it was it was cold, very smooth and, as I ran my palm over it I realised, made of stone. Judging by the bulge in the canvas it was about twelve feet long and, while three foot wide at its base near me, tapered to a point at the other end. So what could it be? I was snapped from my deductions by two voices coming from the tavern door, "He's a hard man, too hard. Look what he did to poor Heinz."

"But you need the money, Walter."

Thunder and lightning. They were coming this way. I peeped below the wagon but as I already had the canvas in my hand, I clambered underneath it and lay down next to the stone. I barely made it in time because the voices came over to the wagon and stopped right next to the back wheel.

"I tell you it's not right," grumbled the first, "Something bad's going to happen. I don't like this *thing* one bit."

"Well, let's hope we get paid first, eh?" muttered the second.

'What's this?' I thought, lying inches from the men like a corpse in a coffin.

But as I strained to hear what they were saying they both sighed deeply before emptying themselves on the cobbles and such was the deluge that I could not hear a word. When the torrent had eventaully subsided I thought that I overheard, "Master says we'll be here for a few days 'cos of the mud and he's got business to settle. Then we're off."

A few days, eh? I made a mental note to tell the Professor and as the voices returned inside I thought that I heard the first repeat, "I don't like it one bit. This things' cursed I tell you."

I wondered if he was referring to what he had just stuck back in his pantaloons, then it occurred to me that he meant whatever I was lying next to. So what was it? I was still in the dark about the monolith and reached out to touch the stone again.

"Hello, Drechsler."

Good God! I swear at that moment I almost swallowed my tongue and this was the only reason that I did not give myself away by uncontrollably bellowing, 'Help!' What madness was this? The blasted stone was talking to me.

"Hello, Drechsler?" whispered the voice again.

I quickly realised that it was Van Halestrom lying on the other side and gasped, "What in heaven's name are you doing here?

"I did say that I would meet you."

"I did not expect it to be *here*, Professor," I hissed, trying to control my jangling nerves. After a second I whispered, "So, what is it?"

"It's an obelisk, my lad."

"An obelisk? What does Kolmer want with an obelisk?"

"He believes it holds great mystical power and wishes to use this energy."

"For what?" I asked, staring at the thing.

"That is what I was trying to ascertain before your arrival. Now, if you'll permit me."

I heard his flint box spark and presently its soft glow illuminated the space under the canvas. In the dim light I could see the square shape of the stone and, as my eyes got used to the dark, I started to make out hieroglyphs carved along its side.

"It says here," murmured Van Halestrom, and I presumed that he was translating the markings, "The father... will find the mother and make... from this union, the son of... of... Oh... What is that word? ... Ow!"

He dropped the flint box when I presumed that it had become too hot to hold and we were thrown back into darkness. He rustled around to pick it up but a cough from the barn made us lay perfectly still. I strained to hear anything out in the gloom until Van Halestrom softly hissed, "We should go now."

We slid from the wagon like a pair of snakes and slithered through the shadows over to the stable doors. Seeing that they were open and there was no one around, we took a step into the doorway only to hear, "Who goes there?"

A startled thug materialised next to us but was far too slow to react and Van Halestrom was more than ready. The wily Professor knocked him out with one decisive punch to the chin and so fast that he was able to cushion the unconscious man's fall before quietly dragging him into a corner and swiftly covering him with hay. No 'bloodshed tonight' then, as promised.

"Time to go," he muttered, gesturing towards the open doors and within two ticks of a cuckoo clock we were scampering across the street with the squawking rabble in the bar fading behind us. Moments later we were mounted up and Van Halestrom called, "To the Castle Landfried! We have work to do!"

I geed Petrova after him through the city's streets and out through the northern gates onto the road for the castle.

I wondered why the Professor suddenly sought the sanctuary of his impressive mountain retreat but whatever the reason, as far as I was concerned, it was good news. At that moment I relished the prospect of the castle's stout walls around me, especially with lunatics like Kolmer and his men on the loose. Though this familiar route was quite challenging, particularly on a squally night such as this, we did not spare our horses once during the whole journey. Watching Van Halestrom up ahead I sensed him becoming more eager to reach our destination with every stride of his horse. The reason for his haste would soon become abundantly clear.

Chapter 4

The Obelisk of Nempty

We arrived at the castle soaked to the skin but not at all tired from our journey. After dismounting in the courtyard our horses were attended to by the sleepy stable lad and we ran up the stairs to the main door where Bacon, the pompous but wise, old English butler, hovered like a ghost in his night garments holding out a candlestick. It was sometimes easy to forget that he used to be the master of the castle and even Van Halestrom but his formidable countenance always reminded me of the fact. I sensed that he was displeased to be disturbed at this late hour as he greeted us with a little more than his usual air of condescension, "Good evening, *sirs*. I sense by your erratic demeanours that you will be staying up for some time?"

"That's right, Bacon. We have some work to do," replied Van Halestrom without stopping and striding up the main corridor, "To the library, lad. That's where we'll find the answer to the mystery."

We bounded up the staircase and swung into the library. I liked the library at the Castle Landfried. The grand old room was one enormous circular set of shelves packed to the very ceiling with hundreds upon hundreds of books. It was the most comprehensive collection that I had ever seen, amazingly, I believed even more so than the university. For, instead of solely scholarly works, here there was every kind of book that one could imagine. Indeed, if a piece of exotic information existed that was not contained within the castle's library then I considered it not worth knowing.

The Professor lit some candles and I busied myself preparing a fire while he used the wheeled ladder to bring down some volumes from the higher shelves. Soon the place was hospitable and he laid the books out on the table. Bacon brought in a steaming pot of coffee and coughed, "I trust, sir, you will be not be needing my services again before tomorrow?"

Van Halestrom excused him with a nod, "We may be some time, old friend. Thank you and goodnight."

The veteran servant slipped away and the Professor began leafing through a dusty old encyclopaedia.

I cast a ranging eye over the books and saw upon the cover of one, '*Intricacies of The Mystery School Religion*' and on another '*Hallowed Secrets of Ancient Egypt*.' I lifted the first and asked, "What is this all about, Professor? What's the significance of this obelisk?"

He squinted over the withered pages and explained, "The obelisk is the most important Illuminati edifice as it symbolises male potency and the phallus. Being the Illuminati, of course, they worship 'The Illuminated One' or Lucifer to you and me. So, in this case, it represents Lucifer's penis. It is usually erected in the Vesica Pisces; the space between two converging circles symbolising the female vagina and so, all together, signifying union and the sexual act: Procreation. Copulation. Intercourse. Coitus..."

"I see, I see," I coughed, "I think I understand."

This was a blatant lie. I did not have a clue what he meant by these embarrassing remarks. Sensing my ignorance he suggested, "I believe a small history lesson is required, Herr Drechsler. Remember your Egyptian gods?"

Well, this was an entirely different matter and he knew it. "Egyptian Gods?" I flapped, "Of course I can. Don't the Illuminati worship Horus, the evil Egyptian spirit who lights the top of the ghastly pyramid in my recurring nightmares. The very phantasm we sent back to hell last year?"

"The very same, my boy," he casually noted, "Well done.

Along with his mother, Isis; the vulva and Osiris, his father; the phallus, in this case they are the *unholy* trinity. Now, how's your geometry?"

"Geometry? What does this have to do with geometry?"

"Everything. It is the basis of the Illuminati's mystery school religion: Kabbalah. Remember Pythagoras' words: All is number?"

Economics, religion,, geometry, philosophy, mathematics, *biology*, whatever next? University was meant to start tomorrow. I frowned and tried to follow his ever-changing line of thought.

"I trust you are aware of Euclid's 47th proposition?"

I usually struggled to remember any geometry lessons but luckily this one significant theorem had endured. "Is it the formula for calculating the length of the hypotenuse on a right-angled triangle; $A^2 + B^2 = C^2$?"

"Excellent, lad, you are indeed a scholar. Now this is the part of the myth you probably know. Osiris was the father god of Egypt but Seth, his evil sibling, craved his brother's power and tricked Osiris to get inside a coffin which cut him into pieces: fourteen to be exact. Seth threw the pieces into the Nile but Osiris's wife Isis turned herself into a kite and found them then put her husband back together again and brought him back to life. Hence his title: God of The Underworld. Now the part you probably don't know. Isis could not find the fourteenth piece; Osiris's phallus. So, using her regenerative female powers, she created one made of gold with which he impregnated her and they had a son called Horus who went on to usurp Seth. Thus avenging his father and completing the eternal cycle. You see, lad? The myth explains the significance of the obelisk for it is how the symbolic male and female counterparts come together to make a third, the divine son. Or, as the Illuminati see it, Horus brought into this world."

I trembled merely upon hearing the spirit's name and gulped, "I think I see, sir, but what does any of this have to do with geometry?"

"Ah ha. This is where it becomes fascinating. Remember the secret wisdom hidden in the Kabbalah's mysteries is neither good nor bad but simply wisdom and this knowledge is contained in code and symbol. The Egyptian gods are signified by numbers and shapes; Osiris the father by the upturned triangle and the number three. You see - the tip of the phallus? Isis the mother by the sphere and the number four, this could be the moon, the earth or perhaps the womb, and Horus the son, by the pentagram and the number five, which symbolises man. Remember your geometry lad: $3^2 + 4^2 = 5^2$? The father *plus* the mother *equals* the son. It is the eternal cycle exemplified in mathematics. In this case, I believe the Illuminati are the male obelisk and they plan to copulate with the female Isis or Mother Nature to produce the son Horus, or as they see it, the usurper God: Lucifer." [6]

A shudder ran up my spine and he pushed the book toward me, pointing out, "You see, lad, all is code and symbol. The trinity is written in the stars. Isis or the Dog Star's appearance over the horizon in June came with the flooding of the Nile which replenished the desert. Thus her title: Goddess of Fertility."

He rose from his chair and climbed back up the ladder while I turned the book around. On the page was a set of Egyptian drawings depicting the struggle between Horus and Seth

---

6. **The Illuminati & The Obelisk.** The obelisks in Washington DC, Vatican City and the City of London have always given rise to conspiratorial interpretations. For instance, the existence of a line from the Millennium Dome to the pinnacle of Canary Wharf (also an obelisk) which, in turn, runs exactly to the Bank of England. Use Google Earth if you don't believe me. In these cases it is claimed that the obelisks, or phalluses, are intentionally aligned over water (to represent birth water) with a dome representing the womb (for instance the roof of the senate building) and, after that, the symbolic product of the union i.e. the child (Lincoln memorial) or, in London's case, the BOE.

and underneath an astronomical chart showing the triangular constellation of stars making the trinity Osiris, Horus and Isis, or Sirius the Dog Star. *[7]

From the shadows above I heard, "With this in mind, I believe the appearance of this obelisk can only mean one thing."

He carried on rummaging away without finishing, prompting me to ask, "And what is that, sir?"

"Fertility, my boy, a fertility ritual is in the offing, which naturally means a conception. Maybe it's the conception of a plan or maybe – a someone."

He descended the ladder blowing dust off another old volume and muttering to himself, "In here I think," and returned to his seat then opened the book. "Ah yes. Let me see."

"What are you looking for now, Professor?" I asked, still trying to keep up.

"I believe the inscription carved on the obelisk holds the key. Here we are; Nekhbet, Nefertem, Nemphelin. Ah, ha. That's the character... Nempty …Oh dear."

He mumbled to himself for a moment as if clarifying what he had read then frowned. "I thought so."

"What is it?" I asked with growing consternation.

---

7. **Illuminati Beliefs & Egyptian Symbology.** The Illuminati's belief system allegedly centres on the Ancient Mystery School Religion which, in turn, draws heavily on a combination of Kabbalist spiritualism, Neo-Platonism, Luciferianism and Ancient Egyptian symbology. Main characters include: The Eye of Horus (All Seeing Eye of Providence) the pyramid, cap-less or otherwise, (featured on the previous $1 bill) and the obelisk, which can be seen inverted at the top of £5, £10 and £20 notes. The celestial triangle combining the three stars mentioned by S. Drechsler (The Winter Triangle) symbolises the eternal Egyptian triumvirate: Osiris (Betelgeuse) Horus (Procyon) and, as described, Isis (Sirius the Dog Star) which rises above the horizon in Egypt on the summer solstice signifying the start of the rainy season and the replenishment of the lands representing the Goddess's procreative power.

He produced a notebook from his pocket and from between the pages pulled out a torn piece of paper with some scribbling on it.

"I took a rubbing off the obelisk. Always best to carry a notebook and pencil. Never know when you might need them."

Damn his notebook and pencil. What had he discovered? I was on the very edge of my seat as he read from a combination of the paper and the book and deciphered the inscription, "Let He, the father, be... with She, the mother and begat Him the most unholy child of …war. Nempty is a god of war."

A fresh blast of rain lashed against the windows and a moaning gust agitated the flames in the hearth. A storm was brewing outside.

"Right, Sebastian, there is a planet chart on the table. Tell me, on what night falls the next full moon?"

I turn the chart around and began scanning the calendar.

"… July, August, September... the 19th. On the nineteenth, sir."

"The nineteenth," he clicked his fingers, "That confirms it. In the mystery religion the number nineteen has great significance. It is the number of integer on Aristotle's magic cube which all add up to thirty eight." He could tell by my blank expression that I had no idea what he meant and explained, "Three plus eight is eleven, Sebastian. As ten represents the Kabbalistic God then one *above* Him is a heresy and, as nine is one *below*, it means fallen. But also, as the number one can be the Magician in Tarot then nineteen can be translated as 'The Fallen Magician.' Instinct tells me that Kolmer believes himself to be this character and is on his way to deliver the obelisk to an important fertility ritual set to take place on this date and that it is the Illuminati meeting I told you about earlier. You see, lad, the ritual, the date, the meeting, the bank, the money?"

"But you said war, sir? War on who?"

"War on everyone, Sebastian. From the poorest in the street to the richest in the land, the Illuminati plan to start a war with all the tribes of the earth. And their weapon is money or, more accurately, debt. "

"But surely, sir, couldn't all this be coincidence?"

"No, lad, to reach the next level of understanding you must learn that only the unintuitive interpret their lives as a set of coincidences. Coincidences are merely accidents and accidents *wait* to happen. They lack one thing: purpose. You, the ritual, the world, are no accident. You have purpose, lad. Never forget that. You don't *wait* to happen, you *choose* when."

He rescaled the ladder and I nervously sipped my coffee contemplating what all this might mean. I had not half finished the cup when he brought several more books to the table and piled them on top of one another until they almost reached my head.

"What are these for?" I asked, staring up at the teetering stack.

"They are to read, my lad. There is much you need to know: The Mathematics of Kabbalah, The Platonic Solids, The Vesica Pisces, The Flower of Life, The Tree of Life, Metatron's Cube..."

I watched the pile of books growing with an ever-increasing sense of desperation.

"What? *All* of them?"

"Why yes, lad. You are young and have the desire to learn, a keen intellect and an enormous pot of coffee," he inspected the pile and calculated, "So you should finish them by the morning."

"The morning? But I have university in the morning."

"You are young, Herr Drechsler, so in no need of sleep. Cook will tend to the fire and supply the coffee so you don't have to pause. I will be in the study making some notes." He took a step closer, "We do not have much time, Sebastian. Always remember the words of Sir John Dee, the father of British Intelligence,

'Knowledge is power.' So empower yourself, lad, empower." With this he strolled off bidding me, "Good luck. I will see you in the morning," and left me alone in the cavernous room.

I sighed at the pile of books and took down the top one called '*Sacred Laws of Geometry*' then brushed the dusty cover, opened it up and started to read.

Though at first I began to explore the texts hesitantly after a while I discovered many things which deeply intrigued me. At certain points I felt like a naughty schoolboy ogling erotic imagery for, such was the essence of the texts, this information would have been considered blasphemous only a few short years before. I especially enjoyed reading about Gematria, the method by which letters are ascribed a numeric value. Within these writings I found a sequence describing how the unpronounceable name of God was generated from the mathematics of a triangle and that the numbers for the word 'Father' and 'Mother' when added together made the number for the word 'Son,' which connected with what the Professor had told me. It was all extremely interesting and I felt as though I had been ushered into an esoteric world where some long-forgotten mystery prevailed that wished to be discovered. Such was my fascination that I was compelled to read on until the very small hours before finally succumbing to sleep.

Chapter 5

Back To The Grindstone

I awoke face down in a book and, as I pulled my head up, I noticed also a goodly amount of dribble. I wiped my chin to see a steaming pot of coffee appear underneath it.

"Good morning, Herr Drechsler. I see your studies were almost without end."

I looked up to find the Professor standing before me, bright as a button, dressed to a tee, hands on hips and surveying the cluttered table. I surreptitiously wiped the drool from the page as Bacon opened the curtains, filling the room with sunshine and causing me to wince.

"Something for me to tidy away, sir?"

"It's nothing, Bacon. The lad's been educating himself that's all. That's right isn't it, Sebastian?"

Van Halestrom pulled up a chair humming to himself and poured a cup of coffee. He was chipper that morning that was for sure. I eyed him with some envy as he helped himself to some cakes from the tray. My own clothes were still dank from the previous night and I shivered in my seat wondering what he was so happy about as my faculties slowly returned to me.

"So, Drechsler, I suppose you're ready for your first day back at university?"

Good Lord! He was right and me twenty miles away with no preparation. My mind was still swamped with geometric shapes and mystical charts.

"What time is it?" I clamoured, jumping up like a fly stuck behind a window.

"Relax, lad. It is but half past six and we will easily have enough time to get you to university. There is a hot bath ready for you, a change of clothes and, when you are dressed, a brandy for your coffee to smooth out those chinks in your armour."

I lowered myself back into my chair as it dawned on me that, as usual, he had thought of everything.

In no time at all we were rattling away from the castle aboard the Professor's carriage with faithful Petrova in tow. I was in much better spirits after my ablutions, some clean clothes and, as promised, a fortifying brandy warming my belly.

Van Halestrom chatted away beside me, "I believe we now have the upper hand on our friend Kolmer. Because of the mud and his lackeys unwittingly revealing his plans last night, we know he will be stuck in our fair city for some time. He cannot escape and, therefore, we have him exactly where we want him."

I was not so sure about this. It seemed like thinking that you had the advantage over a lion because you were alone with it in a cage. I tried to forget about the wretch. I was off to university and the fiend was definitely not going to be there.

The Professor dropped me off in the woods before the city gates and I proceeded the rest of the way on Petrova. We did this sometimes so as not to attract undue attention to our friendship. Meetings in the office were one thing but arriving in his carriage together on the first morning of term would have raised too many eyebrows. Students talk, to say nothing of the gossip between masters and this was an inconvenience we tried to avoid.

Though the roads were extremely muddy due to the weeks of rain, nimble Petrova still reached the university in time for the morning bell. I quickly led her round to the stables where some of the other third years had taken a couple of unfortunate freshmen hostage and were forcing them to clean their horse's stalls. This was still, to some of the old guard, a rite enjoyed by the senior members much like the fagging system that I have heard exists in the English public schools. Personally, I despised the habit. Of all things to be a slave master was the worst and I thought these 'good old boys' beyond the pale.

I hurried into the grand hall with everyone else and was surprised to see Van Halestrom at the side of the podium having heated words with Principal Vacchieri. After the agitated exchange Vacchieri waved the Professor away and walked over to the lectern.

'What's this?' I thought, as the other lecturers took their positions and Vacchieri cleared his throat before addressing us, "Welcome, Gentlemen. I trust your holidays were restful and that you have come back determined to work hard and, in many cases, a lot harder than last year." He cast a dour, bespectacled eye over us and soberly carried on, "The third year history students will be pleased to know that I have arranged a little surprise for them. The rest of you will be less pleased to find out that there are no surprises and that, for you, it will be business as usual." There was a lone cough from somewhere at the back and he finished, "So, without further ado, Gentlemen, I suggest that we quietly make our way to our respective halls and begin what, I hope will be, a far more illustrious term."

With this he dismissed us and left the stage followed by a line of masters. Well he might have had some revolting friends but you could not accuse the miserable sod of wasting time with unnecessary oratory. Van Halestrom was last to leave and tried to catch my eye with a concerned stare. Before I could grasp what was on his mind I was swept away amid the throng of students and carried off to my first lecture.

Still wondering what he was thinking, I entered the east auditorium along with the rest of the crowd and went to find a seat at the top in the shadows. Not being the brightest of students I was always uneasy about being picked out by the masters. Then I remembered, 'Weren't we going to have a surprise?'

Surprise was right. Herr Lipstad appeared below and called out, "As you have been told something special has been arranged for you this morning. You're going to have the benefit of listening to someone who knows a great deal about history. Unlike me they haven't been stuck in the dusty old lecture halls of academia but out there, in the real world, searching the lands of antiquity for ancient relics and bringing them back for us to marvel over. And this most learned gentleman has agreed to share his wealth of knowledge with us."

'Capital,' I concluded, 'the man sounds a great sort,' relieved that Herr Lipstad was not going to give the lecture as his were usually a mite dull. I wondered, with some anticipation, 'Who might this intriguing fellow be?'

Well I am no gambling man and have very good reason. For I would have bet my mother against Old Lipstad announcing, "I give you Herr Franz Kolmer," and the villain cheerfully bounding out from the shadows and taking his place behind the lectern. Good God! I nearly coughed up my guts and squirmed down behind those in front. What the hell was he doing here? To complete the nightmarish scenario the class erupted with warm applause as the vile bastard grinned round the hall and shook hands with Herr Lipstad.

Thunder and lightning! This was what Van Halestrom had tried to warn me about. Thank Christ I was not sitting in the front row, I would have soiled myself for sure. The blackguard was completely without trace of the previous night's excesses and, though I hate to say it, even had a twinkle in his wolfish eyes. I dreaded to think what was going through his mind as he flashed his white teeth at the wall of admiring young faces and I cowered down in the shadows wishing that I had brought the pistol from Petrova's saddlebags. After a moment the applause died down, Lipstad took a seat and Kolmer began.

Well he did and he did not. For, after a confident, "Good morning, Gentlemen!" he prowled back and forth grinning up at us for what seemed like an age. This was extremely unsettling and I made sure to keep a couple of my colleagues' heads in front of me all the time. He paced about for so long that I thought he was not going to speak at all until he suddenly called, "I see a lot of fine young faces out there!"

"I'm glad you can't see mine you bastard," I muttered.

After a poignant pause he carried on, "And your youth is the time to learn, Gentlemen: To learn what you will use in the future. Though history is important, today I want to talk, not only of the past, but of the future. For it is in the future that you will use what you have learnt today. Yes, Gentlemen, now is the time to learn because, as we all know, time waits for no man."

Well he could talk. You could not deny it and I peeked over someone's shoulder as he continued.

"Yes, time! The infinite!" he mused, "So what if there were a way of controlling time so that man could be infinite too? Well, I can tell you - there is!"

With this esotericism he undid his jacket and unfurled his hand with a self-assured gesture. He scanned the hall for a moment before resuming, "I have just returned from the Motherland of all civilisations. Not the land of the Greeks or the Romans but the land of Egypt. The ancients of this society were masters of their time. For theirs is the one true wonder from the ancient world that can still be seen today: the mighty pyramids at Giza. The great architects who designed these structures knew all about time, both the past and the future. They understood that if they could control the past then they could also control the future." He clicked his fingers like a conjurer and grinned, "Imagine the influence commanded by being able to predict a solar eclipse? Eh? For, to block out the sun was to be more powerful than God.

This is why these architects built the pyramids: to follow the stars set in the great clock of the heavens. Thus converting their divine energy from above down below and enabling them to control their civilisation for thousands of years. Yes, my friends. This is the very foundation of the wisdom of the ancients.'As above, so below, my friends: As above, so below."

It was an incredible transformation. Though there was still something lupine about him he was unrecognisable from the previous day and I leaned into the aisle to get a better view.

Over the next three hours he covered such a wide range of topics that it was hard to keep up, though, I was unnerved to find out, constantly enthralling. It was the man's enthusiasm that was so compelling. He was more like a sermonising preacher than a lecturer and I was shocked, if not a little disgusted with myself, to find his performance thoroughly enjoyable. After sharing amazing facts about the pyramids such as; star alignment, size, design, construction and details of the burial chambers, he neatly moved on to Alexandria, his second home, explaining how so much ancient knowledge had been lost due to the murder of the teacher Hypatia and the destruction of the city's library in 415 AD. Then he moved onto Plato's school of thought and especially the philosophy of men and women sharing their belongings, or the 'commune.'

Next he turned his attention to the future for in his opinion Plato had correctly prophesied the shape of things to come and this commune would be brought about by industry. He described how the great inventions of mankind would provide a wealth of capital which in turn would cause a revolution of personal freedom to sweep across Europe and then the world.

By the end he was like an actor relishing his role and passionately came to his crescendo, "Yes, Gentlemen! Before us lies, not only the opportunity to cast off the shackles of outmoded hierarchical religion, but the chance to march proudly into our bright new future. A future illuminated by the light of a thousand stars where society will be governed by its legitimate heirs not the nepotistic dynasties of the dark ages but instead a glorious pyramid arranged on the principles of merit and intellect. An order made from the energetic youth of today. And that youth, Gentlemen," by now he was gripping the sides of the lectern and staring intensely at us before he earnestly finished, "That youth is you!"

He took a theatrical bow, even putting the back of his hand to his brow for added pathos and - stone me - if he did not receive a rapturous standing ovation from around the hall. To my horror I found myself spontaneously clapping along before sitting on my hands while everyone round me rose to their feet. The clever swine was certainly a charmer and went down like pennies in a wishing well with the third years. Of course it was exactly what they wanted to hear and a speech full of the sort of revolutionary rhetoric that was responsible for getting the university closed down in 1800. But that is another story altogether.

After he had milked the applause, Herr Lipstad joined him and the two of them slapped each other's backs before leaving the hall surrounded by a gaggle of students no doubt eager to quiz the wandering scholar on any number of topics. Still more than hesitant about being spotted, I waited till the crowd had gone before slowly making my way down to the door.

After a cursory check outside, I stepped into the corridor only to find myself staring straight into Kolmer's eyes. He was talking with Herr Vacchieri behind the open door and smirked at me then bowed condescendingly low without taking his eyes from mine. I tried to hide my face and returned the gesture before hurrying off. Blast! I could tell that he had recognised me. What was I to do? A trembling voice inside my head kept whispering,

'Keep going Seb. Just keep going!'

So I did, all the way to the Professor's study like a terrified chicken. When I reached his door I checked up and down the corridor before urgently knocking and was not wholly surprised to hear, "Come in, Sebastian!"

I dived inside, quickly closed the door behind me and turned to find Van Halestrom seated behind his desk, steadily puffing on his pipe.

"I..."

"I know, Sebastian. Kolmer has come for us."

Chapter 6

The Chess Match

I had forgotten exactly how bad university could be. No sooner had we got rid of murderous Weishaupt than his conspiring Illuminati friends had started coming to the faculty to give blasted lectures before, no doubt, avenging their fallen allies. Damn it! When would my life become simple? I took a seat at Van Halestrom's desk and put my head in my hands.

"What is going to happen now, Professor?"

"I'm sorry that I had no time to warn you, lad. As you may have guessed, I believe Kolmer's appearance here is no coincidence. We are both known to the Illuminati and he must have been contacted by them or perhaps…"

"Perhaps? Perhaps what, Professor?"

"I fear I have some more bad news, Sebastian."

"More..?" I stumbled, "How could it be worse?"

His eyes narrowed and he came right out with it, "I fear Herr Vacchieri is also an agent of the Order."

"Thunder and lightning."

"I've had my suspicions for some time after receiving information about his attendance at various gatherings. Though, I'm not sure at what level he is involved, his recent behaviour leaves me in no doubt. He is Illuminatus."

"Dear God."

That was how it could be worse. These were certainly not the worries of a normal student. My knees started to knock as Van Halestrom carried on, "Whatever Vacchieri's connections, with regard to our positions at the university, his hands are tied. For, though he might suspect us, it would be foolish for a man who is already known to have links with an illegal organisation to do us any harm. No. For the time being he has to keep a low profile so he does not pose a direct threat especially if we keep our noses clean."

He squinted out of the window. "But Kolmer is different. I don't think he will do anything directly himself now he is known to the faculty and certainly not within these walls while he is still here."

My mind began to race calculating this new set of threats. "But I still have to go home, sir."

"If we stay on our toes eventually he will have to leave to deliver his cargo. Then I believe we will be back in the driver's seat. Until then we must be careful."

Careful was right. Ingolstadt was small. It was less than a mile between the city walls. I lived five streets away from the university and The Eagle was only five streets in the other direction. Kolmer could come round to pay me a 'visit' anytime he pleased.

"He must have worked out that it was us at the stable last night: two men, capable of defending themselves. It is obvious. The question is how much of a priority are we?"

I had another lecture in five minutes and was thoroughly unprepared for this avalanche of bad news. By God, I had been happily riding my horse twenty-four hours ago without a care in the world - or so it seemed. Considering our position I asked, "Are you sure we are safe from Vacchieri, sir? After all, he is the Principal here."

"Though they are both disciples, Sebastian, there are those who take orders and those who give them. I believe Herr Vacchieri comes into the first category and Herr Kolmer, most definitely, the second. You can tell by the way he speaks that he has been around those who are planning a dark future for the world."

He fixed his eyes on me and solemnly continued, "Oh yes, Sebastian, I listened to him from the hallway. 'A bright future in which man will be set free by the machines of industry and released from the shackles of the old religions,' is simply his way of saying mankind will be ensnared behind the yoke of the factory instead of the ox in the field and his new religion will be that of money and his gods will be those who control it."

"I see," I gulped.

The hallway bell rang indicating the start of the next lessons and I automatically rose from my chair. As much as I tried it was impossible not to contemplate my own part within such a future. *8

He gave me a resolute nod and, not forgetting my manners, I bowed before leaving his rooms in a state of spiralling vexation. Throughout the next six hours of study I busied myself calculating how many weapons I had back at my lodgings, plus the pistol in Petrova's saddlebags and moments after the last bell of the day, I was leading Petrova from the university gates into a drizzly Bavarian evening, trying not to seem too anxious whilst all the time checking that I was not being followed. After stabling her I scuttled round the corner to my quarters constantly fondling the pistol in my belt with my thoughts tossing hither and thither. I felt like one of the pieces in a cursed game of chess and prayed that I would have autonomy over my movements like an avenging queen and not be stranded like an impotent king.

8. **Illuminati World View.** The Illuminati's objectives were well-known even by this time: the destruction of all; religion, monarchy, family, nationality and property. Within contemporary historical context these objectives are most comparable to those of communism with the abolition of traditional social structures in favour of the state. Another political mode which fittingly describes this model is Malthusian collectivism, named after the philosopher Malthus, in which personal rights are given up in favour of the state. George Orwell's *1984* (1948) springs to mind.

Once back at my rooms I locked the door and made sure that my quadre bow was primed, loaded and ready along with several other weapons then laid them out on my bed. After this I checked the bars on my windows and the lock on my door and, with these precautions complete, sat on my bed feeling a mite sorry for myself.

I reached under the mattress and pulled out one of the straw heads which I had used for target practice at the Professor's castle. I stared at it remembering his words. "Always be decisive and deadly, Sebastian," and I took a knife from the pile and stabbed it through the straw. Struth! I sorely craved the safety of the Professor's castle or my parent's house back in Tuffengarten and perhaps, most of all, the feelings of hopefulness induced by my distant love and fellow Illuminati hunter, brave Lady Francesca. But she could have been in so many different places that it was pointless trying to guess where she might be. I let out a deep sigh and decided that it was better to be alert rather than mournful as this was probably the best way to stay alive.

And so it was. The nervous standoff carried on for days. At the beginning of the week the weather worsened to the point that the roads became impassable and I worried that Kolmer would never be able to leave. I cursed the rain and the endless mud whilst keeping my head down under my cloak as I toed and froed between my lodgings and university.

During these days I was haunted by a recurring nightmare in which Kolmer was chasing me through a shadowy maze of corridors in a creaking old house. When I eventually found the door to escape I opened it only to find him standing there with his whip in his hand and a devilish look in his eyes. Despite these nightly visitations by the end of the week my spirits had improved along with the weather and, for once, it stopped raining and finally the mud began to clear. On the Friday I began to relax.

Our adversaries had been in the city for five days and nothing had happened. Now, with the change in the weather, surely they would be on their way. With these reassuring thoughts in mind I even permitted myself a little whistle on the way to university and, after finishing my studies, went to see Van Halestrom for our weekly game of chess. We sat around his chess table absorbing ourselves in the game and a discussion about tactics with regard to the bigger picture.

The Professor moved a rook into the attack and observed, "Kolmer must leave soon. If my calculations are right the ritual can only be two weeks away and he will need time to reach his destination. He has been stocking up on supplies making the prospect of his journey imminent."

I countered his rook with a pawn.

"What happens when he leaves, sir? What then?"

He moved a pawn to defend the rook.

"We follow them, lad."

"Follow them? But they could travel hundreds of miles in that time."

Distracted, I took the rook with my pawn.

"No one else can do it so follow them we must. I have already made the arrangements. My clerk will send you a letter calling you home to attend a sick relative and as luck would have it," he winked, "I am set to attend some business in Frankfurt. Our bags are already packed and all other eventualities have been considered." He unceremoniously took my queen with his bishop putting me in checkmate. Blast. I was as trapped in life as on the board. He rose from his seat and chucked a small leather purse onto the table where it landed with a tell-tale clunk. I picked it up estimating that it contained at least forty coins - four hundred thalers - more than a year's wages for a normal working man. The Professor obviously thought this a serious job.

"This is a pivotal moment for the Illuminati, Sebastian. I'm certain Kolmer intends to deliver the obelisk to the important meeting of which I have told you. Now that the Order have been forced underground it is going to be harder to catch them. So we must take our chances when we can. This is our chance."

He lit his pipe and moved to his desk speaking in a more jovial manner, "So what do you say, lad? Are you ready to carry on to the next level of your education?"

He knew what I would say. Though I was a little surprised he had asked me, I had suspected that he might. If Kolmer was to be stopped we were the ones to do it. I fondled the pouch again but before I could answer he suggested with a wink, "I will let you mull it over," and left through the door leading to the clerk's office.

When I was sure that he had gone I tiptoed over to his desk and helped myself to his chair. I weighed the pouch again and calculated that there was enough money to see me through the rest of my education, even pay off my student's loan, at which time I could do what I pleased. Maybe buy a house where I could live with Francesca. Who knew? I gazed out of the window. Perhaps if we followed Kolmer at a safe distance we could avoid any unnecessary trouble and, if there was any trouble, Van Halestrom would be sure to end it. In the back of my mind there still lurked the distant prospect that, if I carried on in the Professor's brotherhood, one day I might inherit the castle as he had from Bacon and all that that entailed. Though this was the most far-flung, fanciful yet daunting notion it was impossible to ignore. A rare beam of sunlight shone through the clouds which, in my youthful innocence, I took to be a good sign and I slipped the pouch inside my breast pocket and gave it a pat. 'That's right,' I said to myself, I would go on the mission and carry on with my adventures.

Certain that this was the right thing to do my mind cleared. On the desk in front of me lay an enormous leather-bound book entitled '*Chess Masters' Strategy & Tactics*,' and, taking the opportunity to, at last, gain an advantage over the old bird I opened it in the middle and eased back into the chair.

There was a tap at the door but before I could say 'Who's there?' it flung open and a pair of crossbows flicked round the side and fired their bolts at me. I froze as the first punched into the book and ended up two inches from my nose whilst the other skimmed through my hair and smacked into the cabinet behind with a heart-stopping 'whack!'

Holy Mother of God! It was a miracle that I was not killed. Had I opened the book at the beginning the bolt would have pierced the cover and killed me for sure and if I had been an inch taller my head would have been split in two. One of the assassins grunted, "Run!" and I sat there for a handful of seconds in silent delirium before the Professor flung open the door beside me and demanded, "How many?"

I nervously glanced between the arrows and he did the math. He bounded across the room and checked outside but finding no one there, closed the door and strode over to his bookcase where he pulled back the tattered copy of Sun Tzu's '*Art of War*.' The hidden door of his secret cupboard swung open revealing his stash of weapons and, in the middle of the floor, a large canvas sack.

Speaking cool and steady he said, "I take it you have made up your mind, Sebastian?" I managed a half-hearted nod. "Good," he said and pointed at the bag. "You will need this. Now go home and get the rest of your things then meet me with Petrova at The Eagle as quickly as you can."

He swept back into the clerk's office and I put down the book which would not lie flat because of the arrow sticking through it.

I gulped and pulled myself over to the cupboard where I strained to lift the sack from inside which I heard the unmistakable clank of weapons. As usual it seemed as though the Professor, like everyone else, was two steps ahead of me.

"As quickly as you can, Drechsler!" he shouted.

There was no time to think and I found myself running down the corridors and off to my lodgings in a maelstrom of apprehension. After packing my quadre bow in its holster and everything else that I guessed I might need in the sack, I lugged it all round the corner to collect Petrova. The blacksmith had barely finished shoeing her so I paid him, loaded her up and asked if Karl was there so I could say goodbye to perhaps my only other friend in Ingolstadt. The blacksmith told me that he had not returned from school yet so I bade him farewell and rode Petrova over to The Eagle. When I arrived Van Halestrom was already walking away from the tavern shaking his head.

"They checked out early this morning," he said, "Now we know why they were so eager to leave." He pulled on his gloves. "Well, my lad, it seems as though the chase is on."

A shudder ran up my spine as I remembered the bolt punching through the book and I wondered what in Hell's name would happen next. If only I had known how far I had to go to find out then perhaps I might never have gone at all. For that was the day the journey began.

Chapter 7

The Journey

Looking back now I understand that this was a major turning point in my life. One week into my crucial third year of university, when I should have been studying hard in my rooms, I was gallivanting off with the Professor in pursuit of the Illuminati and potentially into all sorts of trouble. This was not the attitude my parents expected from their one and only son and I knew it. I want you to know that I did not take to these things lightly. Though I had already decided that I would go, in reality, I knew that it was one of the rashest things that I had ever done in my life. Riding out through Ingolstadt's northern gate behind Van Halestrom on that dull Friday afternoon in September 1785 I could hear my father's voice chiming in my head, 'You always were a chancer boy.' Yes. I knew it was irresponsible. Though I had been shot at I was still in charge of my senses and I could have said 'No.' So far I had got away with my rash behaviour but I knew I could not be a chancer forever.

Of course, Kolmer and his gang could have gone round the corner to hold their wretched ritual and we could have followed them, got a few shots off, Van Halestrom could have scribbled something in his notebook and I could have been back home by Sunday night happy as Ludwig and four hundred thalers richer into the bargain. Capital. But life, as I have often noticed, never does what you expect. Though I have also noticed that when a man thinks he knows what he is getting into but is then faced with a barrage of totally different experiences, most are usually vain enough to claim that, despite everything, their instincts were right all along and they knew all would be well in the end. I suppose that, one way or another, I am lucky enough to fall into this category and so found myself pounding after the Professor up the northern road.

He rode ahead of me with one eye on Kolmer's wheel tracks but still found time for banter. "Well, Drechsler. It seems reading has saved your life!"

The old eagle was right again. It must have been the first time that reading a chess book had saved someone's life but I still loathed his light-heartedness in such serious situations. I tightened my hands round the reins and looked up ahead, geeing Petrova on and yelling, "Where are they going, Professor?"

"Judging by the tracks Kolmer's coach and the wagon are travelling together and his two henchmen who just paid us a visit are trying to catch them up. I believe they are going at a fair rate. We must try to intercept them before they meet."

"But where?"

"North, lad. They travel north!"

With this he upped his pace, urging his chestnut mare on with a hearty, "Yah!" and I broke Petrova into a gallop.

You could travel a fair distance in half a day in a coach even accompanying a wagon and especially with a change of horses. It was already late afternoon with only a few hours of light remaining and knowing that they could be many miles ahead we charged on. The tracking was made easier because, to be fair, there was only one northern road with only the odd lane here and there leading off to small farmsteads. So, with the weather fair we made excellent speed. After four hours or so the tracks took us east past the city of Nuremberg which was lucky as there was a chance that we might lose the trail amongst the other markings. But with the last embers of sunset fading in the west, having only rested our horses once and never going slower than a canter there was still no sign of our quarry.

At a place called Beyreuth we stopped at a coaching inn to water the horses and to enquire whether Kolmer had been seen. The landlord was unforthcoming but my pulse leapt when a stable lad told us that he had seen the man in black earlier that afternoon ordering a fresh team of horses for a heavy wagon driven by a gang of ruffians. I tossed him a coin as Van Halestrom inspected the tracks in the road and reckoned that the two henchmen had also passed but had still not caught up with their master. So we pushed on once more, determined to keep going at least as long as they did.

That night was a long one. Even when it got too dark to ride safely we still continued at breakneck speed, only slowing for fear of ruining the horses and it must have been three o'clock in the morning when we finally made camp. Though this was a risk Van Halestrom was certain that Kolmer's men would also have to stop. After all, were they not human too? Settling down and bringing my blanket about me amidst the unyielding countryside I prayed to God they were before quickly falling asleep. But the old eagle was right once more and woke me in the chill of the morning handing me his telescope and nodding into the distance.

"There."

I pulled myself up with my blanket still wrapped round me and squinted into the lens. I had not realised when we had stopped but as the first light of dawn crept into the sky, I saw that we were perched on top of a small hill. As my eye focused through the gathering light I could make out a thin taper of smoke climbing from the forest on the horizon.

"It's them. On this road, five miles ahead, maybe less."

He grabbed the telescope from me and began collecting his things. I tugged at my blanket and peered into the distance grimacing, "How do you know it is them, Professor? How can you be so sure?"

He was already pulling himself into his saddle and rallied, "This could be our chance to catch them napping before they meet up with their comrades. We must be quick."

This was not what I had hoped to be doing at six o'clock on Saturday morning and I hesitated, feeling the damp chill penetrate my bones.

"Purpose, lad," he encouraged. Unfortunately this did not have the same effect as a huge pot of coffee, but when he called, "Don't forget to load your bow there could be action!" it had the same effect as several pots of coffee and even a brandy or two.

For, I knew exactly what he meant. He planned to kill them if he got half the chance. Suddenly the prospect of finding the men who had tried to murder me while they slept with the Professor by my side made me wide awake. I stowed my blanket in Petrova's saddlebags and pulled my crossbow from its holster. Feeling the cold metal in my hands I whispered, "Purpose," and checked the four arrows in their stays before throwing the weapon's strap over my shoulder and mounting up. I followed Van Halestrom out of the trees onto the road and with my heart beginning to race we resumed the pursuit.

Things were getting serious. We were closing in on them and my guts told me so. We made great speed with me trailing a few lengths behind and before long we were approaching the trees from where the smoke was coming. Being ever vigilant I was already carrying my bow, having no problem going at speed with the unwieldy weapon in my lap. However, when we pulled up four hundred yards short of the fire smoke, Van Halestrom spied through his telescope and declared, "They've gone! Come on, lad! They're on the move!"

We galloped on and quickly found the henchmen's camp not twenty yards from the track. Van Halestrom hastily examined the smouldering fire and called out, "Twenty minutes, maybe less! Off we go! We must catch them before they reach the others." He reared his horse and tore off in a shower of mud.

"Right then," I muttered. This was an entirely different prospect. Now we were going to find them when they were awake when I had wanted to find them snoring around the campfire in their stocking feet.

"Come on, Sebastian!" called the Professor and I dug my heels into Petrova's flanks and set off after him.

What a poor local would have thought seeing the two of us pounding along with our fearsome crossbows drawn and our cloaks trailing behind us in the flying mud as though we were off to rob a bank at the crack of dawn, God knows? But the spectacle did not last long because after a few miles we found them.

It was Old Eagle Eyes who saw them first. Lord knows why he needed glasses? He could have read a book if it was tied to a blasted albatross. I almost jumped out of my skin when he shouted from up ahead, "I see them!" Strangely, he hung his bow on his saddle's pommel and trotted onwards. Having my own self-preservation foremost in mind, I kept mine firmly out before me and followed at a safe distance. After a moment we came to a clearing and he dismounted. To my surprise the two men were sitting together leaning against a tree exactly as I had pictured but as I got closer, I gasped when I saw that their throats had been slit.

"Kolmer," puffed the Professor.

"But how can you be so sure?"

"Simple, lad, see these tracks coming from the north. They only come this far, then return."

I could see some hoof marks in the grass but did not understand how he knew that it was Kolmer.

"But?"

"One rider? Who knew they were on their way? Out here? Meeting them by chance?"

I recognised the men from the crossroads and choked, "But... why? They are his own men."

"Remember, Sebastian? He is a merchant and flies no flag for or *man* or country."

I peevishly shook my head letting him know that I wished him to be more precise and he tried, "Because they were late? Because they lit the fire? Because they had not killed us? Because he did not want to pay them? There could be many reasons."

I stared at the macabre bodies. How could the Professor know all this?

"C'mon, lad! We cannot rest. Kolmer must be close."

He leapt back onto his horse and set off again as though he knew exactly where he was going. I rode after him determined to find out what he meant by these wild claims. At least the bastards were dead so we did not have to kill them but how did the Professor know what had happened? I caught him up and shouted, "What's going on, Professor?"

Without taking his eyes off the road he called out, "They did not make the rendezvous!"

"Rendezvous?"

"They were supposed to meet Kolmer last night!"

"Where, sir?"

"Up ahead!"

"How do you know this?"

"Intuition!"

We were riding briskly now and it was becoming hard to keep up the conversation but I persevered, "You said... something about a fire?"

"Kolmer knew we might see it!"

"But how did he know we were still alive? Is it magic or... can he read minds like you?" He was galloping now and I called after him, "...How?"

"I will show you, Drechsler. Come on!"

Two miles further on, we reached a small village where Van Halestrom wheeled about in the square, intensely studying the tracks and droppings in the mud.

"By Jupiter! We were so close!" he cried, "Kolmer was here last night." He circled his mount examining the surrounding buildings one by one before exclaiming, "Over there!" He readied his bow and cantered over to an old barn door where he dismounted. After steadying himself he kicked it open and flashed the weapon about inside. "They were here!"

He disappeared behind the door so I trotted over and dismounted then stuck my head in the barn. I could not believe it, collapsed on the hay inside lay six exhausted black horses. How had Van Halestrom found the right barn so easily? He emerged from the shadows spying about like a hawk and murmuring, "There must be many helping them. But the horses are useless to us. They have been thrashed and maybe poisoned too. We must leave straight away."

With this he strode past leaving me in a state of perplexed confusion. Overwhelmed by this cart-full of information I was compelled to have, at least, one piece of the puzzle explained and I begged, "Forgive me, sir, but could you please tell me how Kolmer knew that his men had not killed us? Is it a spell? An incantation? I simply must know before going on."

He stopped in the doorway and nodded up into the eaves so I followed his eyes to a bird box from which a cooing pigeon was sticking out its head.

I scoffed in my most sarcastic tone, "Are you telling me this bird *told* Kolmer we are alive? Why, sir, maybe it flew from Ingolstadt and *tweeted* him the news?"

"Yes, Sebastian. The bird is a homing pigeon and trained to return to this place. Someone must have sent a message here. Simple."

He walked outside and I followed after him, wailing, "What? "Even the blasted animals are against us! Can... this be done?"

"Of course it can, Drechsler," he said, collecting his horse's reins and putting his foot in a stirrup, "Any history student should know the King of Persia and Julius Caesar used birds like this. Now we must ride."

With this telling remark he pulled himself back into his saddle and rode off leaving me staring worryingly into Petrova's eye. I mounted up and followed him hoping that she could not be turned against me too. We did our best to carry on but unsurprisingly, after another forty miles or so our horses refused to be pushed any further which dramatically slowed our progress. Though, it was not the animal kingdom that defeated us in the end but another part of God's great creation: The weather. After another twelve long gruelling hours in the saddle, taking us deep into another evening, it started to rain and as we reached the outskirts of Leipzig a dreadful storm set in.

Though we had ridden two hundred miles in less than two days, an incredible feat considering that we had done it on the same pair of horses, we were still not fast enough. For, as we reached the city walls the road became covered in a weave of muddy tracks making it impossible to pick out Kolmer's. The Professor dismounted and knelt over the myriad puddles and grooves, tracing the patterns with his fingers while the pouring rain melted them before his eyes.

"Surely it is impossible, sir?"

He did not answer but continued inspecting the churned mud while I shuddered in my saddle and watched the sodden crowds flooding inside the city gates. Now I was certain that the chase was over. It would be completely dark soon, the storm was getting worse by the minute and there were six roads leading away from this one junction alone any of which Kolmer could have taken. What could we do?

Van Halestrom rose from his haunches and turned toward the city, calling out over his shoulder, "Nothing is impossible, Sebastian. Come on."

Chapter 8

St Paul's of Leipzig

With the heavens opening and another dismal night setting in, two hundred miles from home, nursing several blisters on the most sensitive parts of my body, with the rain trickling down the neck of my dirty smelly clothes and a gaping hole where my stomach used to be, I was in no mood to argue. We came up to the city walls to join the huddled masses funnelling inside and it crossed my mind that Kolmer might well have sought refuge here, so I unfastened the catch on my quadre bow's holster and kept my eyes peeled, just in case, as we steadily flowed along with the swollen tide of humanity pouring in through the gates.

From the outside Leipzig seemed most impressive but I was most displeased by what greeted us on the inside. Though the city was twice the size of Ingolstadt, even boasting modern oil street lamps in some places, it was three times as squalid and I was horrified to see gangs of beggars teeming through the streets like packs of rats. Thankfully, Van Halestrom seemed to know his way round the warren of overcrowded lanes and within a few minutes he called out, "We are here," before leading us into the courtyard of a fine old church adorned with an inspiring steeple.

The Professor dismounted and was met by an attentive Pastor who after a short conversation led him into the church's vestibule. Presently a handful of choir boys ran out from the same door and into the bustling street. A minute later the Professor reappeared with the Pastor and explained, "We have sent word to the city gates to ask if anyone has seen Kolmer's caravan. Until then we should use this opportunity to get something to eat." He winked at the Pastor and introduced him, "This is Father Haval. He is in charge here at St Paul's."

The Pastor brought us in from the rain and saw to it that our horses were looked after then led us to a simple room with a fire. A servant soon delivered two bowls of broth along with a sizeable loaf and with these comforts to hand I quickly began to feel much better and even my blisters stopped hurting. Van Halestrom explained that the church's ministry were 'friendly to our cause' and had come to his aid 'many times before.' I wondered how this friendship had come about as the Pastor seemed to know Van Halestrom very well but what did I care? At that moment I was more interested in filling my belly and rubbing my feet by the fire. After an hour the Pastor returned and told us that the boys had found no word of Kolmer and the city gates would be shut in half an hour. Night had fallen and the storm only worsened.

The Professor paced round the room puffing on his pipe and stroking his beard. After a while he came to a halt and ruminated aloud, "Kolmer has planned his escape well; the route, the fresh horses, the messages. With all this activity there must be others who know his plans. That is how we shall find him. We shall fight fire with fire." He blew out a looping ring of smoke and asked the Pastor, "Have you any messenger pigeons, Father and also a quill and paper?"

The Pastor nodded and bid us to follow him and ten minutes later we were in the church's windy belfry looking out over the city's multitude of lights as the Professor secured a note to a pigeon's leg. *[9]

9. **St Paul's Church (Paulinerkirche) Leipzig 1785.** This impressive church built in the city of Leipzig in the 13th century was destroyed in 1968 by the communist regime of Eastern Germany. When S. Drechsler visited the church it was part of the university and boasted a stellar list of organ masters within its long history including, amongst others, Johann Sebastian Bach. Though there is no proof that the church had any secret societal connections, as the author rightly recalls it did possess an awe-inspiring steeple and belfry.

"Good luck, my little beauty," he said and nodded at the Pastor who released the bird into the stormy night.

The fragile animal fluttered out into the darkness and I shook my head in wonder. I did not care what Van Halestrom said or anyone else for that matter - even the King of Persia - the fact that this bird was going to fly all the way back to the Castle Landfried to deliver a message was an unfathomable miracle. Only heightening the wizardry I had been told that Bacon would 'know what to do' upon the bird's arrival. Sarcasm aside, to this day I find the habits of these trained birds astounding and their ability to fly hundreds of miles to a chosen destination a magic in itself.

The following morning Van Halestrom rose early and went out to see if he could find the trail again but the roads were submerged in many places and there was no sign of Kolmer or his wagon anywhere.

I relaxed then, certain that the fiend had got away. The men who had tried to kill us had been slain but we had failed to catch Kolmer, the mastermind behind it all, who by now could be halfway to St Petersberg. Well good riddance to him. As much as I cared he could have gone straight to Hell. On second thoughts he probably would have enjoyed that. I was merely happy that I would never see the vile character again. What could we do?

Rest. That was what I wanted to do and eat and bathe and rest some more. Though our quarters were Spartan they were comfortable, clean and free from draughts which made recuperation easier. The journey had taken its toll and I was still aching but by the end of the day I was feeling somewhat better so, after checking our horses, I took a stroll around the city. Though there were many impressive buildings lining its broader streets, in my opinion Leipzig was not the most pleasant of places. The beggars made me extremely uncomfortable and it shamed me to see the pathetic conditions in which they lived.

Feeling free to indulge myself after my labours, upon passing a dozing tramp I slipped a silver thaler into his hand. He did not stir but when I turned the corner I heard a mighty howl from behind. I prayed that he would not kill himself with drink that night and made my way back to the church feeling a mite fortified by my noble gesture.

On meeting the Professor he told me that there was no news and we took dinner together before I wished him good evening and turned in for the night. I was soon fast asleep and fell into a strange dream perhaps stranger than any other I have ever had. In this dream I was sitting happily by a lake on a beautiful summer's day, taking pleasure in watching my reflection upon the water when, to my delight, I spied an elegant swan gliding towards me. As the serene creature came closer it metamorphosed into my darling Francesca and I was instantly overwhelmed with profound feelings of love. But as she reached the shore and I went to embrace her she fought against me and her face turned into that of Karl the blacksmith's son. I stared in horror as he began to scream and weep tears of blood which poured down his cheeks and stained his white feathers. I jumped up in my bed gasping for air. Where had this dark vision come from? What could it mean?

Over breakfast the Professor told me that my nightmare was probably due to our arduous trip and my natural yearnings for Francesca. Having been away from her for so long these emotions were mixing with other tender feelings for my absent friend. I remained unconvinced and was certain that the vision contained some darker meaning. I passed the morning exploring the church where I listened to an organ recital including a rendition of 'Awake the voice is calling us' which soothed me greatly as it was an old favourite of mine from back home. In the afternoon I took the Professor's telescope up the belfry to have a look around.

The view from the steeple, being the tallest in the city, was spectacular and with the aid of the telescope I could see for miles. Over the mass of jumbled rooftops far beyond the city's southern walls began a seemingly endless forest and, examining this distant horizon, I spotted a solitary bird. I followed it for a while considering how fortunate it was to go wherever it chose until realising, with a jolt, that it was flying straight towards me.

I wondered out loud, "Surely it can't be?" but saints alive it was - and the bird swooped up to the belfry and flew in through the window. I was taken aback to have the creature flapping around before it took a perch where it sat cooing to itself. I was even more surprised to see the new message on its leg. Incredible! Could it really be from Bacon? After a few unsuccessful attempts I managed to catch it and rushed downstairs to find the Professor.

I burst into our quarters holding out the bird and Van Halestrom exclaimed, "Ah ha! Well done, Drechsler. I thought she would be back soon."

He beckoned me over to the table and made some space. I gave him the bird and he removed the note before reading it to himself and declaring, "I knew it. We have the information. Kolmer travels to Hamburg."

"Hamburg?" I cringed. It was at least another two hundred and fifty miles away and I considered the number of blisters that I would have when I reached this next distant location.

"Go and pack now, Sebastian. We will leave immediately. I have requested two extra horses from the Pastor which you will find in the stable. Collect your things and I will meet you there."

As usual, it all happened so fast that I had no time to argue and, before I knew it we were walking our small team of horses out of the church's courtyard with our saddlebags packed to the brim with as many provisions as our extra mounts could carry. Watching Father Haval wave goodbye from the church's gates

I already felt homesick for my simple room. Though I had only stayed there two nights I had the feeling that I was going to miss the humble little place. We left the city behind us and were soon back on the northern road. At least the weather had improved making the conditions a little better and, as the mud had receded, we made steady progress.

Whilst riding along Van Halestrom explained, "We do not have to push too hard now. Kolmer will not suspect that we are back on his trail so he will have slowed to spare his horses and avoid accidents. We will plan to reach Hamburg in four days' time."

"Then what, Professor?"

"Then, my friend, we shall see."

We travelled on into the evening and slept at a tavern that first night and were back on the road by sunrise. As we were no longer travelling at full tilt I took the chance to air some concerns which had been playing on my mind and confessed that I was worried my absence from university would get me into trouble.

He simply laughed and said, "My lad, as a third year student you only have a handful of lectures a week. As a man of growing academic stature are you not expected to educate yourself? Surely this trip is a fine opportunity to do so: In the real world, not reading about it from a book."

I was still getting used to his laissez faire attitude regarding my education and cursed quietly as he named the passing trees, "Pinus sylvestris, Quercas robur, Betula pendula. You see, today can be a lesson in nature."

The old bird eventually took pity on me and continued my education as we plodded on, discoursing on a great many topics from science to art and mathematics to religion. By the third day it was as though I had been studying hard for a month and, on the fourth as we neared our destination, I remember very well the philosophical debate that we were having because it was to have some bearing on the future.

At that time, though not being the most devout of Christians; drinking, lusting, swearing and committing other blasphemies on a regular basis, I still considered myself a man of God and, as such, found myself defending the philosophy of Jesus Christ to the sceptical Professor, whose ideas on theological matters seemed, even to me, downright heretical.

I believe our exchange went something like this; I had said, "How can you refute the words of Christ, sir; 'Do unto others as you would have done unto you'? Surely this wisdom is a blessing to all mankind. Why, if every man accepted the doctrine of The Golden Rule would not peace and justice prevail across the world?"

"If every man was of such a disposition then we would not need the philosophy in the first place."

"But surely, sir, it is the only way?"

"If only it were true, my lad, then what a wonderful world it would be. Unfortunately, I believe the Sermon on the Mount is but the mating call of the man who must forever be the slave to those who hath no morals. For there will always be those who prey on the gracious and the forgiving. Alas, my friend, it has always been the way. You have seen yourself the horror inflicted on those who get in the Illuminati's way; the plotting, the killing, the brutal sacrifices. Remember, it is the lives of innocent children that they take at their perverted rituals, insanely believing to trap their spiritual energy within an inverted pentagram. This is the madness that we are up against. What use are we as men if we merely turn the other cheek? Forgiving these monsters simply encourages them."

"Well, sir, if you do not believe in the word of Christ then what do you believe?"

"To be truthful, lad, sometimes I believe that the Christian faith was created to produce a world of pacifist sheep who unquestionably do their masters' bidding. For, even back then there were those in power who understood the advantages of having a compliant society over which they could rule."

I knew from experience how Van Halestrom's mind worked and what he was implying but checked to make sure, such was the weight of the claim.

"Why, sir, are you now suggesting that the entire Christian faith is but a creation of the Illuminati?"

"All I am saying, lad, is that it is best to keep an open mind about *everything*." *[10]

This was ridiculous. Though I respected the Professor's worldly knowledge on most things, sometimes his conspiratorial theories beggared belief and I went to contest these wild allegations, "But..."

He abruptly raised his hand and cantered off to a junction up ahead. I rode after him still a might riled by his contentious remarks.

"But surely, sir, Jesus' forgiveness is the saviour of humanity?"

His mind was elsewhere and for good reason. He leapt down from his horse and ran his fingers over a patch of rutted mud then gasped, "Kolmer! He was here yesterday."

---

10. **Illuminati Creation & Control of Christianity.** Some conspiracy theorists have long-contended the existence of various Illuminati plots, both historical and modern, to develope and control Christianity, and all other world religions, for their own ends. Certainly the Kabbalah, central to the Illuminati's Ancient Mystery School Religion, has very little in common with the New Testament and is, in the most part, diametrically opposed to the moral dogma taught within Christianity. Allegedly, the agenda, during Biblical times, was to 'turn things upside down' (See Isaiah 29:16) and, corrupt the real 'way' of Esu (Jesus). Through infiltration and scribal lies (see Jeremiah 8:8) these 'men who crept in unawares' (See Jude 1:4), 'creating a doctrine woven with lies.'

My heart began to trot even on hearing his name. Van Halestrom threw a glare up the junction and mulled, "But for some reason he has chosen another route. That's it. This road must be flatter and he wishes to preserve his horses. This is our chance to overtake him. We will hurry to Hamburg now so we can catch him when he gets there."

He pulled himself back into the saddle and called out, "Not far to go now, lad. Come on!"

And so it was. Sixty miles lay between us and the city. We broke our rides into a steady canter and completed the rest of the journey in a brisk six hours finally reaching the huge port on the river Elbe at nightfall. After questioning many on the road if they had seen the man in black but finding none and no tracks to follow either we held a vigil at the city's southern gate throughout the night. I wondered if we had done the right thing by going there when Kolmer's tracks went in the other direction but the Professor assured me that his information was accurate and that Kolmer would come.

By the evening of the second day I was growing ever more pessimistic and, much to my relief, Van Halestrom allowed us to rent rooms near our location where we could sleep properly and have our horses tended. We monitored the traffic at the southern gate in shifts and sometimes together but then, after the third day, I truly believed that we had lost them and mind turned once again to the time that I was missing from university. I had now been away for a whole week a duration which was only set to increase and reflected that I had never missed so much study time or been so irresponsible before.

My feelings of guilt and general downheartedness were not helped by our accommodation which comprised of a dark, slanting, dishevelled shack situated at the docks that was most obnoxious in several ways. Mainly, because it was filled with mosquitoes, prostitutes and rowdy sailors who seemed involved in a perpetual orgy with one another from dusk till dawn but also because it was mouldy, damp and stunk worse than a fishmonger's. This did not help my spirits to the extent that I was desperate to leave and by the time the fourth day dragged around, though I did not mention it to the Professor, I knew that there would come a time when even he would have to admit defeat and accept that the chase was over. Trying to get to sleep in the rattling boudoir that night I promised myself that I would confront him the following morning and considered the best way to broach the subject.

However, these plans were never destined to see the light of day. For the very next morning while I lay scratching in my bed he leaned over me and murmured, "I have found them. Their tracks lead north past the city. Perhaps two days ago. They must have had to go somewhere else first. We must leave now."

While happy to be leaving our unpleasant dwellings a fresh wave of anxiety engulfed me as we left the city. Attempting to subdue my anxious feelings I found little solace in the Professor's words, "Do not fear, my lad. We will catch them wherever they go." You certainly would not want Van Halestrom on your trail. He was like a hunting dog with the scent of his prey filling his nostrils. Nothing, it would seem, could make him give up. But later that day our progress was severely hampered once again when his horse threw a shoe and, although we had the spare mounts, towing the lame animal behind us slowed our pace to a crawl. We were now on the road to Kiel which was another fifty miles away and for once our usual banter subsided as the Professor fell into deep contemplation.

At a blacksmith's ten miles further up the road he eventually broke his silence. After much pacing around, puffing on his pipe and stroking his beard, he clicked his fingers and exclaimed, "That's it! I know where Kolmer's going. It is obvious."

He beamed at me, enjoying his eureka moment and obviously under the impression that I shared his insight. As usual, I was absolutely flummoxed and had to prompt him, "Where sir? Where is he going? It is far from obvious to me."

Chapter 9

The Ritual

"Louisenlund!" declared the Professor pointing his pipe at the stars, "Kolmer travels to Louisenlund. It lies twenty miles beyond the town of Kiel in Jutland, Kolmer's homeland. The ritual is to be held at a grand house formerly belonging to Frederick II, Landgrave of Hesse Kassel."

I had no idea how he knew all this but I did not like the sound of it at all. He saw my mortified expression and noted, "Ah yes. A man you remember well?"

"Remember is right, sir. Was he not the mad, axe-wielding General who chased us from Wolfsegg castle last year only to be killed by that monstrous dog?"

"That's the one," he nodded, oblivious of my displeasure. "Kolmer has come too far north for there to be any alternative. All that lies beyond Kiel is the Danish peninsula and the Baltic Sea. The house is situated on the coastline and is a Mecca for the Illuminati. The privileged Karl von Hesse Kassel, son of the General you were so lucky to meet, is a disciple of the Order and now the landlord. He is well-known for his Hermetic beliefs and fascination with astrology, alchemy and ceremony. Kolmer must be taking the obelisk there. The full moon will be in three days' time and I would bet my boots that's when the ritual will take place and that it will be sanctified by some gruesome act. This is our chance to cut out the heart of the Order once and for all."

"Right then," I sighed.

This was exactly what I had not wished to hear. We were going to mount an attack on an evil Illuminati ritual, at which God knows what wickedness would be occurring, and commit a cull of its elite. Hell's bells.

As the brutal truth struck home I worried that my parents might never see me again if I were killed in this distant place. Overawed with angst I resolved not to give any more of my hard-earned cash away to beggars before I had actually earned it. God was obviously unimpressed with my charity to be rewarding me so unfairly or maybe I was being punished for not giving every penny away before I was going to die? I considered the prospect of the violence ahead and bit my lip.

Van Halestrom finally recognised my concern and patted my back. "Do not fret, young Drechsler. You've fought them before and won. You can do it again."

This did not stop a volcano of fear erupting inside me and I watched the blacksmith pounding a red-hot horseshoe imagining it the sound of the nails being hammered into my coffin. Oh no Sebastian. What have you let yourself in for this time? *[11]

Looking back now I do not know if this was when Van Halestrom made up his mind what he was going to do. Perhaps he had already decided back in Ingolstadt when he first worked out what Kolmer was planning. Whatever the real truth, it still came as a shock. While I had always considered that there might be action I had pushed such thoughts to the back of my mind

11. **Illuminati Rituals & Louisenlund Holstein.** As S. Drechsler claims this grand 18th century mansion and its extensive grounds, owned by the Hesse Kassel family, was frequently used by the Bavarian Illuminati. The property survives to this day mostly unchanged and still contains from that period, amongst other anomalies, a mysterious pyramidal folly mentioned in the previous book pictures of which along with the impressive house can be viewed on the internet. Situated on the Baltic coast at Guby, Schleswig-Holstein in what used to be southern Denmark, it is now a private school. Hermeticism is a religious, philosophical and esoteric tradition which deeply influenced its Western counterparts, even the New Age movement, and was considered to be of great importance during both the Renaissance and the Reformation. The tradition claims descent from a doctrine affirming the existence of a single true ideology present in all religions given by God to man in antiquity.

and had secretly rejoiced every time we had lost our prey, relishing the possibility the chase was over and we would not have to confront them at all. Well, that dream was over. So much for getting a few long-range shots off and the Professor scribbling something in his blasted notebook. There was going to be a serious fight with yours truly stuck right in the middle.

Van Halestrom's horse was soon re-shod and we left the blacksmith's and camped outside. I remember staring up at the stars that night praying to God to protect me throughout the upcoming ordeal. By sunrise the next day we were back on the road again but with only another fifty miles to travel in two days our pace slowed to an amble. The land around the coast was as flat as a table and, knowing that we could easily get there in time, we skirted around the west of Kiel wishing to keep as low a profile as possible and provisioned ourselves from a few farms along the way. By noon the next day we came to a sign pointing north which read, '*Louisenlund 20 miles.*'

The Professor took out his telescope and, after briefly inspecting the woods ahead, recommended that we make camp in the forest. This came as no surprise as the forest surrounded us in every direction, stretching all the way to the northern horizon and the shimmering sea in the east. A few miles further on, we turned off the track and made our way through the pines. At last the weather was kind to us and bright sunshine lit the forest making for an unseasonably warm autumn day. In a glade half a mile from the coast we dismounted and unpacked our things. Thankfully, we did not sit around waiting as waiting for action was torture for me, and Van Halestrom suggested that we should busy ourselves with some target practice.

After letting off twenty bolts from my bow and, seeing them all ending up packed tightly together round a dead tree trunk, I felt slightly better. While we freed the arrows I asked him, "Tell me, Professor? How is it that you know of this place?"

"Simple, lad, I have been here before," he pulled another bolt from the sand and explained, "There was a man, a very bad man the supposedly immortal Comte de St Germaine. But nobody is immortal and I hunted him down here a couple of years ago and snuffed out his candle. Now he is no more."

I grimaced upon hearing this anecdote but did not ask about the circumstances in which this character had met his maker. *[12]

Van Halestrom went on, "Fortunately, this means I am familiar with the lie of the land. This will be our advantage." He began drawing a map in the sandy ground with onew of his arrows. "There is a large lawn at the back of the house where I'm sure the ritual will take place. We will approach from the west and take cover behind a small stone tower. From here we will wait for the best moment to attack then move in together. It will be better to maintain a distance from our targets as getting involved in a skirmish might favour our enemies as they will be there in greater number. We should try and eliminate as many of the leadership as possible before making our escape. Understood?"

My mouth became dry in anticipation. Though pleased to be attacking from a distance, the thought of the assault still made my knees shake. Remember, whilst I had been thoroughly trained in all manner of combat and already survived a few battles alongside the heroic Professor, it was not so long ago that I was a simple village lad more accustomed to shooting pheasants than hordes of people. So, at that moment as any other normal man

12. **Illuminati &The Comte de St Germaine.** S. Drechsler's hearing of this little-known but hugely intriguing historical character and his death, is inoteworthy. The Comte de St Germaine claimed to be immortal and was a member of several secret societies including the Bavarian Illuminati. He was an avid alchemist who was given a workshop at Louisenlund by his benefactor, Frederick II Hesse Kassel which is said to have been in a 'small stone tower' within the grounds. His death is recorded in February 1784 from pneumonia but if the author's claims are true then we now know better.

would have been, I was absolutely scared out of my wits.

Understandably, it was hard to sleep that night but I eventually dropped off and woke the next morning to find the Professor roasting a large rabbit that he had snared during the night. After this hearty breakfast I spent the rest of the day preparing my kit and checking the many weapons from my sack; two double-barrelled flintlock pistols cleaned and loaded, two throwing daggers sharpened and sheathed, two shot grenades fuses primed, my own flint box refuelled and checked, one sabre slung across my back in a scabbard, one quiver of fifty bolts and, of course, my awesome quadre bow greased and loaded. After putting on my black cloak, tricorn hat and neckerchief I was ready. It was now the end of the afternoon and I waited anxiously for the moment we were to set off.

At sundown the Professor nodded to me and we mounted up then walked our horses through the trees for a couple of miles until finding a convenient hollow in which to leave them. I whispered goodbye in Petrova's ear and the two of us made the last half mile to the house by foot. Creeping through the forest I could hear Van Halestrom up ahead reciting one of his poems. This one, I remember, fittingly morbid:

Who goes there? Nobody knows.
But it's the liars and thieves for whom the bell tolls.
Who goes there? No one but me.
For whom the bell tolls, it tolls for thee.

After a while he crouched down at the base of a pine tree and motioned me to join him. I knelt by his side and, though night was quickly falling, one hundred yards away past the tree line I could see a grand, white mansion with dozens of windows surrounded by an expansive lawn throughout which stood many flickering torches, lighting up our target like a theatre stage.

"We shall go around to the far side of the house," he whispered and headed off into the pine trees beckoning me to follow. Two minutes later we were lying in the undergrowth overlooking the other side of the house and, standing fifty yards directly in front of us on the top of a steep rise, the stone tower.

He nodded at its turrets and whispered, "Right. Off you go, lad. Don't worry. I'll be right behind you."

This was it. I checked my weapons were secure and that the coast was clear before bolting off towards the tower, keeping as low as possible. Half way there I glanced behind to see how the Professor's was doing and had to suppress a scream when I saw him fiercely grappling with a guard wearing a red-hooded robe. I gasped with relief when he skilfully got behind his assailant and, after a brutal twist of the man's neck, let his lifeless body fall to the floor. He waved at me to keep going so I sped off again.

"Where the hell did he come from?" I fretted, scuttling towards the base of the tower, trying to keep my kit from jangling and checking ahead for more sentries. When I heard Van Halestrom sprinting up behind I looked round to see aanother robed guard barely six feet away and about to run me through with a huge sword.

My God! Another one! I grabbed his wrist seconds before he could stab me but he slammed into my shoulder, sending us both tumbling down the side of the rise. We somersaulted several times on top of each other until landing in a tangled pile wherupon I wrestled myself free to fight him only to find an arrow sticking from his back. Holy Father! Van Halestrom must have shot him when he jumped on me.

With my faculties returning I saw that I was surrounded by a circle of burning torches and, therefore, fully visible to anyone watching. Already feeling extremely vulnerable my hair stood on end when I heard an ominous horn moan from nearby.

"Time to move Seb," I muttered and jumped up then glared down at the body at my feet. Cursing my luck, I began dragging the corpse away from the torches which I now noticed were set out in a five-pointed star. Shit! It was a pentagram. I had landed in the middle of the blasted ritual and I glanced over my shoulder to see Kolmer's shadowy obelisk looming up behind me. Damn it! Damn it! Damn it! I panicked and dropped the corpse's hands as I lost my balance and fell onto my arse. My pulse reached a frenzied blur when the ominous horn moaned again but this time much closer. Something was coming this way.

"Not now! Not now!" I hissed, frantically jumping up and hauling the body away. Where the hell was Van Halestrom when I needed him? I guessed that he must still be on the other side of the rise as there was no sign of him around the base of the tower. My feet slipped on the wet grass and the corpse's clammy hands pulled from mine but, with one more gigantic effort, I managed to drag it out of the light. I made it in the nick of time, because I had scarcely reached the shadows when a line of red-robed sentinels slowly appeared out of the gloom walking towards me from the direction of the house. With the last of my strength I finally heaved the corpse behind a row of ornamental bushes twenty paces from the obelisk and collapsed in a heap.

I peeped over the bushes as the line of hooded men reached the torches and slowly encircled the pentagram. When everyone had found their places the last man, who was carrying a large bronze horn which twisted round his waist then came up over his head into a huge bell, stepped forward and put the mouthpiece to his lips. A horrid moan emanated from the wretched old thing doing nothing to calm my tortured nerves. I tried to spot Van Halestrom at the base of the tower but from my position the ring of hooded men was in the way and the glowing torches made it difficult to see anything beyond. Curses! We were separated.

"Whatever next?" I whispered, surveying the unfolding scene. I would not have to wait long to find out and it was a sight that I shall remember until the day I die. *[13]

---

13. **Illuminati Rituals & The Pentagram.** Illuminati rituals are commonly suspected to include a pentagram which is inverted when the practitioners wish to summon or trap the negative spirits of sacrifices. The lure is an ancient type of horn either straight or curved the latter being the version seen by S. Drechsler. This curved version is designed to be carried when played and produces a distinct and threatening tone perhaps most associated with the Norse peoples; Vikings, Danes etc.

Chapter 10

The Waterfall

I lay trembling behind the bush staring wide-eyed at the sentinels surrounding the ring of torches and, standing above them all, the foreboding obelisk. The one with the horn blew another low, gut-churning note chilling the blood in my veins. I had a very, very bad feeling about this. He was obviously not about to play a cheerful fugue on it and invite the rest of his friends back to the house for a chat about music. He was summoning someone or *something* to come and join them. Right then the glowing full moon appeared from behind the clouds bathing the scene in a shimmering hue and eerily completing the unearthly spectacle.

I slipped my hand behind my back to release my bow but, to my horror, realised that the quiver had gone. I checked again. Shit! It must have fallen off when I was wrestling the guard. The crossbow seemed all right but with only four shots I was seriously under-armed. I peered towards the pentagram and spotted it behind the feet of one of the sentinels on the far side of the ring. Curses! With the Professor on the other side of the ceremony and me with hardly any ammunition our plan was in tatters. I prayed that he would not march out and start blasting away expecting me to join in. What a dreadful night this was turning into. The awful horn moaned again and I tightened my trembling hands round the bow as I prepared for matters to get even worse.

Right on cue, my eyes were drawn by the sound of a burbling waterfall not thirty yards away and my heart began to gallop when I saw an orange glow emanating from behind the cascade. I rubbed my eyes and looked again but there it was. I was certain.

"What black magic is this?" I whispered and ducked ever

lower as the glowing light grew brighter.

The horn sounded again and I wriggled backwards but pressed hard into the corpse lying behind me. I was seriously considering running away at that point but knew that I would have been spotted the second I broke cover. I noticed that the sentinels were all facing the waterfall and I gasped when I saw that the water was somehow dividing, creating a gap through which the orange light continued to grow. My God! Something was coming out.

In one heart-stopping moment the cascade parted like the Red Sea and from between the breaking waters emerged a strange priest bearing a glowing lamp and a gilded chalice and, emblazoned upon his white cassock, a red inverted cross. He was followed out by six hooded pallbearers carrying an open coffin on their shoulders and behind them, chanting a haunting incantation, another dozen or so robed men.

As soon as the solemn procession had shuffled into the moonlight the waterfall magically drew back together like a pair of curtains. How was this possible? I did not have the straightness of mind to work it out. The ungodly cortège reached the ring of sentinels who parted allowing the priest approach the foot of the obelisk where he put down the lamp. The pallbearers lay the coffin in the middle of the pentagram while the rest of the procession filed in and, after the last had found his place, the circle closed behind them.

The priest waved his hand signifying the chanting to end and a silence fell over the proceedings. All that could be heard was the spluttering of the torches and the cascading waterfall. I remembered what Van Halestrom had said about sacrifices and half expected a screaming child to be dragged out of the coffin and slaughtered in front of me. 'Please God don't let that happen,' I beseeched, vowing to close my eyes if such horror occurred.

The priest mumbled something inaudible and made a movement with his hand as if anointing the obelisk before turning to the others and holding out the chalice. One of them came forward and took the goblet then went to stand over the coffin. When this man adjusted his hood I glimpsed his wolfish features for a split second. It was Kolmer! I silently gasped and tried to watch as he bent down but lost sight of him as the others clustered round the coffin.

After a moment he stood up and raised the goblet to the obelisk, put it to his lips and drank. When he passed the chalice to the next man I thought that I saw something black on his lips but no matter how I moved about it was impossible to see what was happening. A couple of times I saw the goblet being passed around until, after a few minutes when I presumed they all had drunk, I was sure that I heard the priest mumble, "Nempty." This was confirmed when the congregation all solemnly joined in as one, "Nempty."

With this final oath completed the ritual appeared to be at an end. The priest retreated from the obelisk bowing reverently while the others turned and walked back towards the house. After the last one had left the red sentinels filed off behind them with the ghastly horn player bringing up the rear.

"Thank God," I whispered and let out a huge sigh of relief. My eyes fell back upon the open coffin lying in the middle of the pentagram. Apart from the torches flickering in the breeze and the splashing waterfall all was quiet once more. My heart leapt when I spotted Van Halestrom waving from the base of the tower. After checking the parade had gone he made his way down the rise towards the torches, so I pulled myself up from behind the bush and made my way over to join him. He picked up my quiver and nodded at the casket signalling that I should look inside.

I slowly approached the open box keeping my bow's sites trained on it but immediately lowered them when I saw the body of a boy lying face down inside. I rushed to the coffin and held the child's exposed wrist. Although it was still warm he was obviously lifeless. I looked closer and was nearly sick when I saw a tray full of blood beneath his throat. Sweet Jesus! I pulled back in horror with my hand over my mouth. They had been drinking the child's blood! Though I knew that it was useless I lifted the boy's head. I had to know who this poor soul was but when I turned his head round my world fell apart and my soul spiralled into the abyss. Beholding that sad innocent face I knew that my life would never be the same again. For staring up at me through a pair of dead blue eyes was Karl, the blacksmith's son. I could not believe what I was seeing but though it was tearing my soul apart, I could not help stare at his face - my poor, little friend.

An agonising rush of pain broke my heart in two and my eyes filled with tears. I stroked his blonde hair and went to shake him back to life but, of course, it was useless and his body wobbled pathetically in my hands. My mind raced to understand how he had come to be here? Then it dawned on me that he must have been in Kolmer's coach all along with us following only a few miles behind and the poor boy scared out of his mind. No! The pain was unbearable. I remembered how Kolmer had looked at him at the crossroads and my sorrow swiftly changed to seething rage. I went to roar with anger but the Professor clasped his hand over my mouth.

"Not yet, Sebastian." He fixed his eyes upon mine then threw a glance towards the house. I followed his line of sight and a chilling clarity passed through me as he carefully removed his hand. I wiped away my tears, grabbed the quiver off him, threw it over my shoulder and marched off. In an instant he was by my side but having trouble keeping up with me such was my eagerness to find those who had committed this atrocity. I felt like a bomb about to explode with my fuse burning down to the nub. The Professor realised this and grabbed my arm, bringing me to a halt. "Sebastian. We must do this properly."

He pulled me down to squat next to him and we surveyed our objective. In front of us a stone balustrade ran round the back of the building and beyond it the downstairs windows. The light of many chandeliers shone through the central one of these and, from inside, I could hear the faint cries of revelry. It was them - celebrating.

The Professor whispered, "I will enter through that window and you will come in through the door at the opposite end of the room. We must trap as many of them as possible before they scatter like cockroaches in the light." He squeezed my arm and looked into my eyes, "Do you understand, Sebastian?" I was too busy contemplating revenge to answer and he shook me, repeating, "Do you understand, Sebastian? I momentarily surfaced from my trance and nodded before he continued, "Remember, I will be there."

I nodded again and he squeezed my arm once more before letting me go. I sprang up and, noticing a path across the terrace leading to an archway at the rear of the house, I marched off. I crossed the terrace checking around for more guards and went through the archway into the house.

At the end of a darkened corridor I stopped upon seeing that it opened out into a large circular hallway. From behind a pair of doors on the far side I could hear the sound of laughter. I poised my finger on the bow's trigger and took a step out of the shadows but jumped back when a door barged open a few yards away. I was bewildered when a completely naked servant wearing nothing but an outlandish mask appeared from the door carrying a silver tray on his shoulder.

He padded across the hallway towards the banqueting room so I waited until he had passed then crept out behind him with my weapon at the ready. He came up to the door and raised his hand to knock but stopped a yard short to check the contents of his tray. I ducked down behind him biting my tongue and hoping that he would not turn around and ruin the surprise for the others. I tried to control my breathing while he scratched his backside inches from my face and when he was satisfied that he had what he needed he stepped up to the door and gave it a knock. I pulled myself up to his shoulder and waited for the reply with my heart pounding in my ears. An eternity seemed to pass while we stood there listening to the cheers and laughter before, at last, somebody shouted out, "Come in!"

Chapter 11

Judgement and Destruction

Whatever the diners had ordered they were going to be truly unthankful for what they received. I was going to make sure of that. The servant pushed open the doors and I followed him into the bright noisy room. Beyond him I could see at least twenty naked men seated at a long table greedily indulging in a lavish banquet and all wearing the same perverse masks over their eyes. Considering the circumstances the scene could not have been more disgusting if Satan himself had been toasting the proceedings at the head of the table and, as I looked closer, I saw blood on some of the diner's chins. I had controlled myself up till now but could do so no longer. They had killed my harmless friend and now they were celebrating with a damnable feast. They carried on stuffing their faces as the oath erupted from the depths of my being, "Die you filthy scum!"

I kicked the unsuspecting servant in the back, smashing his face into the table and throwing food, blood and crockery everywhere. There were gasps and shouts of uproar but such was my sudden appearance the diners were all too stunned to move and stayed seated. I put the business end of the bow in the face of the closest man at the end of the table and shot into his mouth. 'Zut!'

A blast of blood splashed over the wall at the side of the room and he crashed backwards in his chair. The fellow next to him was not too shocked to put up some kind of resistance and angrily bellowed, "Who the hell do you think you are?"

"Illuminati hunter," I hissed, launching an arrow into his neck. 'Zut!' It struck him in his Adam's apple and he fell onto the tablecloth clutching at his spewing throat and trying in vain to scream.

"That's for Karl, pig dog!" I cursed as pandemonium broke loose around the room. Turning on the next naked fiend I fired into his flabby groin at point blank range and nailed the fat bastard's crotch to the chair. 'Zut!'

Ignoring his horrendous screeches, out of the corner of my eye I spotted one of them jumping up next to me. I fired into his chest and he crumpled behind the table with blood splattering from his wobbling mouth.

The surprise was not over by a long chalk and a cloud of glass crashed over the panicking demons as Van Halestrom burst through the window at the far end of the room. He thumped onto the table and, with his bow at the ready instantly shot two men in their chest as they pulled themselves from their seats, before spinning on his heel and firing again at another pair opposite. The first uselessly held up his plate which shattered as the bolt pierced his guts but the second was slyer and ducked under the table as the next arrow smashed the back of his chair in half. The clever bastard bounded back up and I immediately recognised his black beard below his mask. Kolmer! I threw the bow's strap over my shoulder as he pushed a small banded casket across the table to an unmasked ally who picked it up and dashed out of the doors behind him. My mind momentarily faltered. What's this? What's in the box? I had no time to consider it and pulled out a flintlock pistol as several of the others frantically piled out of the room. One of them threw a bottle at my face which I had to dodge before gunning him down with both barrels. 'Boom!'

"Curse you!" I roared as the top of his head blew off and he slid to the floor pulling half the service with him. Seizing his chance Kolmer leapt onto the table and snorted down at me before diving through the doorway after the rest.

"They're scattering, lad!" yelled the Professor, skewering another naked victim as the others poured from the room like cockroaches scared by a candle. I dropped the gun and pulled out a knife as I ran after the melee of panicking men while one of them on the other side of the table armed himself with a ladle.

"You'll have to do better than that!" I spat, stopping to hurl the knife into his chest and he splashed headfirst into his soup bowl with a blood-curdling scream.

I flung myself through the double doors and entered a dim, echoing room where a gaggle of squealing, naked young women were huddled round the fireplace. I guessed that they were the prostitutes for the perverts' dessert course and they shrieked again when a fearful cry reverberated from the banqueting hall as the Professor killed another one of the beasts.

The women were of no consequence to me. I wanted Kolmer. But he would have to wait. As I strode past the whores a sentinel appeared from a cellar door up ahead and seeing me immediately drew his cutlass and charged over. With my rage at boiling point he did not stand a chance. Without stopping I drew my other pistol from my bandolier, cocked it, aimed and blew his brains out when he was but three paces away. He flew up in the air and crunched down onto his back as another sentinel came up from the same doorway. I fired my second barrel hitting this one square in his chest and he reeled backwards on top of the reinforcements coming up from below. I dropped the gun as I ran over to the door then barged it shut with my shoulder and brought out a grenade from inside my coat.

Keeping a cool head while many voices shouted from behind the door I produced my flint box and lit the fuse. With the bomb vigorously fizzing away I kicked in the door's bottom panel and threw it through the hole. Seconds later a powerful explosion almost blew the door off its hinges followed by the screams and awful cries of many. It sounded as though the whole garrison was down there and good riddance to them all! The bastards could go straight to hell and burn forever.

Another one of the naked monsters ran past the weeping prostitutes and out the opposite door. I refocused. I had to find Kolmer. I chased after the man down the corridor but when I came to the bottom of the central staircase and he was nowhere to be seen, I took the opportunity to reload another four bolts. Within moments I was ready and, straining my ears, thought that I heard a floorboard creak from above me. So, letting my intuition guide me, I pelted up the stairs.

At the top I ran along a corridor lined with doors the fourth or fifth of which was slightly ajar so, with the bow firmly under my chin, I flicked it open with my toe. There was no sign of anyone but as I went to go, I was sure that I heard voices coming from inside. I jumped back to my position but now could only make out the muffled commotion downstairs. Then I definitely heard the voices again. I slipped into the room and tiptoed toward an open door which was letting in the moonlight. I was within a couple of yards when a shadow passed across the doorway and I heard a woman say, "What's all the noise, Fitzy?"

I froze in the dark as an Englishman's voice replied, "It's only Karl enjoying himself, Dora, my dear. You know what his parties are like. Now, why don't you come back to bed? After all, our masters will be most displeased if we do not provide them with their bastard."

What the hell was this depravity? The calculating lasciviousness threw me for a second and I held my breath to hear the conversation.

"Please don't be like that, Fitz," simpered the woman.

"Why not? What's wrong with being a bastard? I'm a bastard. Most of my brothers and sisters are bastards. Even my own father's a bastard and, while he might not recognise me as his rightful son and heir, it does not prevent my blood from being of the most regal stock. At least *our* bastard will have the illusion of a great title when he assumes his position of power. And won't that be a fine day for the Jordan family eh? When their progeny becomes the true ruler of the nation?"

"Is it really true, Fitzy: The *true* ruler of the nation?"

"Everyone knows the man who holds the keys to Threadneedle Street holds the real power of the realm."

Threadneedle Street? My God! They were talking about the Bank of England. It was the devilish conspiracy the Professor had told me about. Overcome by intrigue I pulled myself closer to the doorway where I could see the silhouette of a woman standing by a moonlit window. Fighting the urge to march straight in and shoot them I remained where I was, compelled to hear the rest of the extraordinary conversation.

"Still, sir, it's not what a girl wants to hear before she gives herself to a man. However lowly a family she's from she still wants to be romanced. Y'know? Flattered."

"Ah but, Dora, such is your beauty you will come to the attention of many a blue-blooded man such as me. All I wish is that I am fortunate enough to sample your gorgeous delights for one sweet, glorious night. And that night, *my dove*, is tonight."

"Ooh," she cooed, "That's better, Fitzy."

The shadow disappeared from the window and I heard the rustle of sheets and the sound of kissing. Amongst the gasps and giggles I heard the man muse, "Not everyone receives the privileges that have been bestowed on you, my sweet. You may have the best legs in theatre but you are very fortunate to be here tonight in such elevated company."

I had heard enough and strode into the room. He saw me coming and ducked behind her as she straddled him on the foot of the four-poster bed.

"What the hell do you think you're doing?" he clamoured but his cowering did him no good and I shot him in the knee, causing him to screech in pain and throw the woman to the floor.

I stood over the end of the bed, prosecuting, "On behalf of the free and good of this world I commit you to death. May God have mercy on your pathetic soul," and pulled the trigger. 'Zut!'

The arrow pronged into his forehead but he stayed upright for a moment with blood streaming down his face before finally toppling backwards onto the sheets. He deserved nothing less - to be killed in front of his lover in cold blood. I stood at the foot of the bed glaring down at his twitching corpse until after a moment my eyes fell upon the snivelling woman by my feet.

She caught my stare and pleaded, "Please don't hurt me, sir. I'm just a simple actress from Dublin. Have mercy on me, sir. I'm just a poor girl who has lost her way."

She threw her arms round my leg, weeping profusely but without thinking, I raised the crossbow to her head. She panicked, "I'm a mother already, sir. That's why they picked me. Please, sir, have mercy, sir. Please!"

She implored me with her eyes and, after what seemed like an age, I wrenched the bow away. It was no good. I could not do it. Even after what I had seen. I could not commit this brutal act. I kicked the sobbing bitch away and she gasped and let me go.

I was torn from my morass by Van Halestrom shouting from somewhere outside, "Sebastian!"

I ran to the moonlit window and looked out over the front lawn to see him in a sword fight with three hooded sentinels and, somewhat behind them shouting orders, one of the Illuminati elite who had managed to cover at least some of his modesty with a military jacket. Disregarding my fear of heights, I threw open the window and stepped onto the ledge then leapt onto the portico below, before quickly jumping down the rest of the way and landing with a soft crunch in the shadows at the base of the building. I had been so quick and camouflaged by my black clothes and the darkness that the sentinels had not seen me and carried on engaging Van Halestrom. I readied the quadre bow and marched into the moonlight shooting the first in the back and the next in the guts before he had time to react.

They both screamed in misery and fell to the floor as Van Halestrom cried, "Ah! There you are, Drechsler!" and charged at the remaining guard with a flurry of sweeps. The coward in the jacket did not wait to see what happened next and sprinted away across the lawn. The Professor lunged at the sentinel, pushing him back with a swipe and yelling, "After him, Sebastian! He runs to find Kolmer! I have just seen him."

Kolmer! Given another chance to get him this time I could not let him escape again and I tore off after the man in the jacket. But, to my despair, the moment I set off the moon moved behind a cloud and he disappeared into the darkness right before my eyes.

"Not now. Not now!" I spat, running across the lawn and frantically searching the horizon. I soon came to a terrace leading to the beach with nothing in front of me but the great expanse of the Baltic Sea and, to the east and west, the woods stretching down to the gently breaking waves. But as I scanned in both directions I could not see him anywhere. Where had he gone?

I steadied myself on an ornamental metal sphere and strained my eyes along the beach then as the moon came back out I suddenly spotted a naked man one hundred yards away pelting towards the distant trees. I tore off like a shot from a gun. If it was not the man in the jacket then maybe it was Kolmer? I could not tell as one distant pair of buttocks flashing in the darkness looks much like any other. One thing was certain, whoever he was he was fast. I was still carrying all my kit but my prey, unhindered by any weight, was stretching the distance between us. Damnation! If it was Kolmer I could not lose him now.

I cast off my hat and cloak, even releasing the scabbard holding my sabre trying to keep up, but it was no good, he was vanishing from view. I had but one chance. I stopped and quickly loaded a bolt then took aim as the man disappeared in to the shadows. I estimated his position as best as I could then pulled the trigger. 'Zut!'

He must have been two hundred yards away by now and I waited for the impact dreading that I had missed. Another second passed and I had all but given up hope when I heard a distant screech. Good Lord! I had got the bastard. I bolted off across the beach preparing to avenge myself and praying to God that I had got my man. *[15]

---

15. **Illuminati & The Number 11.** It is an intriguing coincidence that the eleventh chapter of this book is called 'Judgement and Destruction' as the number 11, along with other interpretations, also signifies that to the Illuminati. As S. Drechsler states these other interpretations include the 'Master' and 'Magician.' In the Kabbalah God is represented by the number 10 (male and female opposites) as there are ten sephirot (emanations) in the Tree of Life. Therefore, the number 11, being one *above*, is seen as an 'affront' to Him and the number nine, because it is one *below* ten, represents 'fallen.'

Chapter 12

Tragedy and Retribution

I ran towards the trees with my heart pounding like a galley drum at ramming speed and slowly began to make out a pale body lying in the moonlight. As I got closer I thought that I saw an arm move and prayed that there would be time for my quarry to meet his judge, juror and executioner. But when I reached him and lifted his chin with my boot I realised that it was not Kolmer but another man with a similar build and fashionable bushy whiskers. Curses! The bolt had struck him between his shoulders and he was bleeding heavily from his mouth. He let out an unintelligible groan as his eyes rolled around and he coughed up more blood. I knelt by his side and, noticing a bronze amulet round his neck depicting a serpent entwining a cross, I tore it off. My bloodlust intensified as the bastard moaned again and I raised my bow. Why should this wretch live when poor Karl had had his life taken away from him? Burning with blind rage and primordial anger I smashed the butt into his face. But once was not enough. I dropped on him and straddled his body then smashed the bow down again and again until his head turned to a splattered pulp before my eyes.

"Stop!" yelled the Professor, clasping my thrashing arms from behind. I struggled against him but he increased the pressure, insisting, "It is over, Sebastian! You must stop! Now!"

At last I desisted and rolled off the corpse before bursting into tears and crawling away. I am not sure how long my blubbering lasted; maybe twenty minutes passed while I moaned and howled obscenities at the moon. Though the murderous moments in the house seemed to last an age, with their horrific detail etched onto my mind forever, the following hour was a blur of nightmarish anguish interspersed with rare moments of clarity.

I remember staggering back to the house to search for Kolmer and any of his surviving friends even though the Professor had assured me that all the remaining Illuminati agents were dead. On finding only corpses in the grounds, I turned my attention inside the house but discovered only sobbing servants there some of whom incoherently ranted at me for killing their masters. Such was my stupor after the battle that I could not hear their voices. While one of them cursed me - in English I think - I recall catching my reflection in a gilt-framed mirror and saw that my face was covered in blood. I stumbled from the house and collected a horse along with some rope from the stables and managed to lasso the obelisk and topple it onto the lawn. After this Van Halestrom warned that we must go as it would be dangerous to stay any longer. We collected Karl's body and finally left the house of horror behind us.

Sometimes you experience things in life of such magnitude that, even as they happen, you know they will never leave you. I knew, without doubt, that that night was going to be such a moment. I feel there is no risk of being considered melodramatic when I tell you that I knew I would never be the same and I truly believe that I never was. Though I had witnessed many horrendous acts working for the Professor; killing men, seeing them die, even watching Jan, my oldest friend, slain by one of the Professor's arrows, I had managed to take them in my stride. But this was different. Jan was a man and capable of making his own decisions. He knew what he was getting into when he joined forces with the Illuminati. The louse had also tried to kill me proving that there had been something unwholesome about our friendship from the beginning. So much for old school friends, however much they make you laugh. I had also seen Klaus, the Professor's trusty driver, murdered in front of me which in many ways was far worse. For, though I had known him only briefly, he was a man of great integrity and I considered him a true friend.

Karl was different. He was an innocent thirteen year-old boy and for many reasons I could not help but feel responsible for his death. In the throes of self-pity I truly believed that it was my fault. He would have never become involved if it had not been for me. Though we had killed many of the devils - fourteen in all and at least ten guards to boot - Kolmer, his abductor, had got away and this one fact was as painful as having red hot needles stuck under my skin. Though we did not know if he was wounded Van Halestrom was certain that he was not dead and I knew that my pain would not cease until I was certain that he was. I promised myself that one day, somehow, somewhere I would find the devil and kill him. I was positive that my unhappiness would not end until I did.

These were not the only matters of profound importance to consider. It quickly occurred to me that we would have to see Karl's father again. What would I say to him? We could not take the body back to Ingolstadt. The injuries on the boy would raise awkward questions, questions about the manner of his death which would surely place the Professor and me under suspicion. The best thing to do was to plead ignorance but this did not sit well with me. I was on good terms with his father and worried I would not be able to maintain the deception.

Early the next morning we buried Karl in the forest in a simple grave. I made a cross from some branches that I found and we committed the body to the soil before conducting a short service and reciting the Lord's Prayer. We were most despondent in these dire moments and there was not much talking between us at all. We quickly set off and were soon back on the road eager to put as much distance between ourselves and Louisenlund as possible. We skirted around Kiel aware that rumours of two men causing a slaughter may have already reached the town and from there it was only sixty miles to Hamburg which we also avoided, sleeping out under the stars as the weather permitted.

We were not so lucky after that and for the next few days the heavens opened emptying a deluge of such biblical proportions that it almost washed the road away from under our horses' hooves. Needless to say this made the journey an even more depressing affair, if that were possible.

During this time the Professor left me alone with my rampaging thoughts of tragedy and retribution. I presumed that he was also deeply moved by what had happened. It is a testament to our downtrodden spirits that during this part of our journey we hardly spoke a word. I was happy with this arrangement preferring at that time to bottle up my feelings. Though I sensed what I had overheard in the moonlit bedchamber was pivotal to the ritual, the sacrifice and the whole Illuminati plot, such was my solemn introspection that I kept it to myself.

Strangely, Van Halestrom had not read my mind either as was his usual habit. I wondered if he had lost the power to see into people's thoughts and the future. He certainly had not known that Karl was on board Kolmer's coach and had also failed to read my strangely fateful dream. Perhaps even he was fallible. Riding through the pouring rain on that long journey home the whole world seemed fallible.

So it was with some relief that four days later Pastor Haval welcomed us into the vestibule at St Paul's church as night drew in over Leipzig. We were soon eating our first cooked meal for days in front of the fire in our sparse but homely quarters. While we tucked into our stew I decided that this would be the time to tell Van Halestrom what had transpired in the bedchamber and I recounted the conversation that I had overheard between the aristocratic bastard and his slutty concubine. When I had finished he wiped his mouth with a napkin and pulled out his pipe.

"Extraordinary, lad. Then it *was* a fertility ritual. I knew it. These personages, Fitz and Dora you say, were intended to create an illegitimate child who could be compromised at a later date by their Illuminati masters when placed in a position of power at the bank. In time we shall find out who these characters are."

"But I don't understand, sir. The child would not have been able to assume his role for years."

"Then understand the far-sighted nature of the Order's plans. Remember, Sebastian, this dark creed has been conspiring for thousands of years against humanity." He got up to stretch his legs and concluded, "But you say you got him before they could copulate? Then we have dealt them another hefty blow. Well done, lad. Well done." *[14]

I was still far too distraught for celebration but recalled something that I had found in my pocket which I had forgotten until unpacking my belongings. "Also, Professor, there is this." I held out the bronze amulet that I had pulled from the neck of the man on the beach and Van Halestrom came and took it from me.

"Very interesting, very interesting," he postulated and tapped it with his pipe, "I trust you know what the symbol means?"

Though submerged in a miasma of self-pity and regret, several years of scripture lessons had not escaped me overnight and I dutifully recited, "It signifies Moses saving the Israelites from the serpents in the wilderness. Book of Numbers 21:9 'And Moses made a snake of copper and put it upon a pole, and it came to pass that, if a snake had bitten any man, when he beheld the snake of brass, he lived.'"

---

14. **Dora & Fitz Illuminati Surrogates**. S. Drechsler mentions hearing Dora's surname 'Jordan.' Interestingly there was a famous actress from Dublin called Dora Jordan who fits this description and could well have been this character. This well-known celebrity was described as having 'the best legs on the stage' and later went on to have twelve illegitimate children with William IV. The name (prefix) Fitz literally means 'Royal bastard' persuading me to believe that the other individual might well have been a grandson of James II. Unfortunately as details of these children are scant, it is impossible to know for certain.

"Very impressive, Drechsler. But I'm afraid the Nehushtan, as it is known, means something entirely different to the Illuminati. The Kabbalist word for the serpent of Moses is 'Nachash' or 'the shining one.' This word has the Gematric value of 358 and is numerically equivalent to the word Messiah, allowing the Illuminati Kabbalists to draw a perverse connection between the two. In their eyes the brazen or bronze serpent becomes the Messiah. It is pure serpent worship or Luciferianism. Here look at this."

He got out his purse then picked a coin and held it up, explaining, "You may be too young to have seen one of these. This is an old Bohemian thaler. On one side is Christ crucified and on the other the serpent wrapped around the cross with the inscription 'Num – 21'; a reference to the book of numbers. You see, the Illuminati enjoy hiding their symbology in plain sight. They believe displaying their demonology on the populous' money gives them occult power. Why this man was wearing such a thing remains to be seen but perhaps it has something to do with their future plans. You have done well, Drechsler. You should be proud." *[15]

---

15. **Illuminati & Monetary Occult Symbolism.** This famous coin would have been old when Drechsler saw it but certainly existed and as described. Interestingly 'Thaler,' Bavarian money of the period, is the word from which 'Dollar' is derived and also, tellingly, in the context of S. Drechsler's account, the serpent wrapping the cross is thought to be the symbol which inspired the dollar sign '$.' Though it is impossible to say whether the claims about this coin's design are true there can be little doubt that similar occult symbolism is contained within the current US $1 bill. There are hundreds of videos and texts available on the internet explaining the various interpretations of these coded messages. A wealth of information also exists suggesting many other denominations including; UK, Australia, EU and several other countries, not to mention other US bills, also contain hidden esoteric messages.

Seeing that my dark mood did not lift he assured me, "Sebastian, it was not you who put the child on board the coach and took him away. Remember that. And if it had not been Karl it would have been another boy from another family. They are the wrongdoers, not you. Do not punish yourself. Punish them."

I heard his words but they did not get past the locked door of my mind and I shrugged in silence.

I found my grief impossible to overcome and was still deeply troubled when we finally reached Ingolstadt three days later. So wrapped in my thoughts was I that I rudely forgot to say goodbye to the Professor on the road and while he made his way back to the castle I carried on to my lodgings in the city. I had four hundred silver thalers in my pocket, enough to buy a house, but I would have rather been penniless and off to practice riding tricks with my young friend.

My mood was no better when I eventually returned to university the following day. Unsurprisingly, I took little in but was not so oblivious that I failed to notice my fellow students giving me a wide berth. It certainly seemed that my alibi of attending a dying relative was authentic. I was obviously grief stricken so, accordingly, my lengthy absence was not viewed with any suspicion and everyone respectfully kept their distance with only the bravest coming forth to extend their condolences.

As soon as the day was over I went straight to my regular tavern to get blind drunk before staggering home to bed where I was haunted by awful nightmares. The nightmares persisted as did my drinking and by the end of the week I was in a dreadful state. Though I made it to my first lecture in ages I had only done so after consuming a bottle of wine for breakfast. This was a sin that I had never committed in my life. 'Only liars and scoundrels drink in the morning,' my mother had always said and I knew, without having to ask, that my father agreed with her.

I knew of many people who had taken to the bottle and had noticed the dreadful effects that it had on those poor souls who came to rely upon it. I noticed it on their breath, how it aged them and, on occasion, sent them into unwarranted fits of delusional anger. Of all things, I did not want to end up like that. But due to my troubled mind and because I could find no other way of subduing my raging melancholia, the next Monday morning I was still drunk and shivering in the draughty university library with an empty stomach and a cold autumn wind going up my back because I had gone there without a proper coat.

By the evening I was stocious again at the tavern and was woken by the innkeeper while asleep at my table. He told me to go home and I shot him a glare before pulling my flimsy jacket around me, grabbing my half-finished bottle of wine and lurching out into the street. Falling through my front door I did not even get to bed before passing out again and drifting into another nightmare. In this vision I was in the dock of a courtroom while the judge brought down his hammer and Karl's pale body was paraded in a coffin to the horrified jury. The sentence of death was passed and the hammer struck again as I waited for the Grim Reaper to come and take me away.

I awoke in a fearful sweat with the judge's hammer still banging in my head. My God! Had the dream come true? I quickly realised it was not the judge's hammer but someone pounding on my door and I wondered if the Grim Reaper *had* come to take me away.

"The Grim Reaper wouldn't knock you fool," I muttered and pulled myself up then fumbled over to the door. After another impatient rap I flung it open only to find - My God! - I *was* in a dream.

Chapter 13

Some Dreams Do Come True

I have lived long enough to know that, though some nightmares definitely come true, thankfully so do some dreams. When I opened the door to my lodgings on that chilly October night I wished wholeheartedly not to wake from mine. For standing there in all her shining beauty, resplendent in a white fur hat and coat was my saving angel, Francesca Kropotkin.

"You!" I gawped.

"It will be a sad day when your deductive skills desert you to the extent that you no longer recognise me, sir," she laughed, showing off her dazzling smile.

I did not care about her sarcasm or her surprise on finding her beau bleary-eyed, unshaven and stinking of wine with his hair sticking up like the Bavarian mountains. I did not care about her driver's consternation when I swept her off her feet and twirled her around like a long-lost bride returned safely home. I did not care about her hat falling off or about her protestations when I pushed my rough face into her hers, protestations that soon gave way as we came together in a long, passionate kiss.

When our amorous embrace had eventually ended she happily sighed, with her feet still off the floor, "I would have come sooner had I known how much you missed me, sir."

"You will never know how much I miss you, my lady," I replied and carried her over the threshold.

The embarrassed coachman lugged her many bags inside and asked uncomfortably, "Will you be needing me anymore, Madame?"

I was already carrying her into the bedchamber and she giggled, "I think I have everything I need, Hans."

I closed the door with my heel and heard the front door slam.

My lady was a perceptive woman on the whole and she was correct in her estimations of that evening's pleasure, for I provided everything that she needed and she too gave back in great abundance. Her sudden appearance that night was exactly what I needed. Indeed, I believe that nothing else could have had the same effect on me as the healing powers of her feminine touch and it was never made more apparent to me than on that night. After we had pleasured each other extensively we talked for hours. This is why I loved Francesca so much. Such was the nature of the matters that I wished to discuss almost anyone else would have fainted at their slightest mention. But she listened patiently as I explained everything that had happened over the past month; Kolmer, the hellish events at Louisenlund, Karl, the sacrifice and everything in between. As I recounted the tale, which involved shedding some tears for the boy on my part, Francesca seemed to understand and did not think me any less of a man.

After I had shared my thoughts it was as though a great weight had been lifted and the next few days were as fine a time as I have ever spent. The two of us bathed together and feasted before, after permitting myself a shave under her instruction you understand, she allowed me to promenade her through the streets that Friday evening. It was superb showing her off to the townspeople as they ambled by. Such was her beauty, complimented by her stylish furs that not one soul passed us without gazing at her in awe.

She too had been busy since I had seen her last and had survived several run-ins with the rancid Illuminati herself. While we happily strolled along she boasted, "I too have killed many of Lucifer's prostitutes since I last saw you and enjoyed murdering every single one. Some like this - Some like that."

She mimed slitting and garrotting throats as an alarmed passer-by choked on his roasted chestnuts. This was another reason I loved her so dearly. Her dainty features completely belied her wild bravado. I was positive that there was not another woman like her in the world.

"Now they have been routed from Bavaria they are spreading like ants whose nest has been destroyed."

"Cockroaches," I suggested but she carried on unabated.

"They see Russia as a problem as it is run by a feudal system of ancient families controlled by the Tsars. The governments of Europe will be easier to topple because they all rely on a centralised power structure. This is what the Illuminati seek; to unify regions together always centralising, centralising before crashing them together in war. But the idiot Slavs find it impossible to come together about anything, even what to eat for dinner. So the Order has something different planned for Mother Russia. My father is very concerned about the future of our country."

"Ah yes, your father, I have heard much about him and have painted a fair portrait of the man in my mind."

"Then, with my own brush, I would add the word 'fool' to his forehead," she laughed. "He is very well, thank you and will be much obliged for your kind words. Perhaps you should meet him one day?"

It was difficult to imagine this happening as he lived over a thousand miles away.

"It is rather a long way, my sweet."

"Only the same distance you have recently travelled."

This was true but I still blanched at the thought as she chatted away, "Tell me about your parents, Sebastian. Maybe I should meet them too?"

This was as likely as me visiting her father every weekend to give him harpsichord lessons.

"I'm not sure that is a good idea yet, my darling."

"Why not? Am I too outspoken for your parents?"

Of course, this was exactly the reason that I had not told my parents about Francesca. I knew that I would need a great deal of time to explain a woman, such as her, to my reserved mother and father so I lied to spare her feelings, "Of course not, my sweet."

I should not have bothered. She knew what I was up to and teased, "If you are to make an honest woman of me, Sebastian, then one day I shall have to meet them. After all, I am the daughter of a Duke. Is this not enough for the parents of Herr Drechsler? Would they not like an aristocratic grandchild?"

For once I could not tell if she was joking. She knew that I wanted children and often taunted me with the idea. Though, I did not mind. I did not mind anything she did.

It was bliss to have her stay with me over the next week. She was there when I returned home from university in the evenings and I was transformed by her company, even finding the motivation to catch up with my studies. By the day of her departure, though I was deeply saddened to see her go, we had enjoyed ourselves so much together that I felt relaxed enough to say farewell. After a long and meaningful embrace outside my door, with tears in our eyes I bid her a happy auf Wiedersehen. She waved and blew kisses from the carriage vowing that we would see each other soon. Upon returning indoors I was overwhelmed with affection when I found a note on my dresser that read;

For the first time I feel I can use the word love when I talk of my feelings towards you, Sebastian Drechsler. So I leave all my love with you to look after. Francesca Kropotkin.

It was true. It was the first time that she had used such words and simply looking at her beautiful handwriting gave me a well of strength inside.

Returning to university the next day I was in excellent spirits. Though I was still mortified by the tragic events at Louisenlund I had resolved to wrap my vengeful feelings into a tiny ball and keep it inside me like a piece of grit that would, in time, turn into a shining pearl of retributive destruction. After my lecture I discovered a note inside my locker that read; '*Playing a game with an old master in my room at one o'clock. Maybe you would like to watch.*'

Well it was obvious that the Professor wanted to see me but who was this old master? Surely he did not mean Herr Kandinsky from the university chess club? The old fossil was so ancient that these days he was getting hard to understand. There were no other old masters of whom I was aware. Who could the Professor mean? I would not have to wait long to find out.

Chapter 14

The Black Door

By the time I had reached the Professor's rooms I was bristling with intrigue. Who could this man be? I had never seen anyone else in Van Halestrom's office apart from his clerk and I had rarely seen him. Nevertheless, it was upon the clerk's black door that I knocked. An instruction communicated by a black oblong drawn on my note, another ploy that we used to maintain the secrecy of our meetings.

The clerk opened the door and inspected the hallway behind me before bidding me to enter and leading me through to the Professor's study. I found Van Halestrom at his chess table taking tea with a rather pensive looking priest.

Seeing that the chess pieces had not been moved, in my innocence, I thought that I was still in time to see the match. Though, I was to find out that a very different game was about to be played.

I bowed respectfully and the Professor acknowledged me, "Ah ha, the very man. My dear Abbé, let me introduce Herr Drechsler, the student I have been telling you about. Sebastian, this is a very good friend of mine, Abbé Augustine Barruel."

The priest greeted me with a reticent nod and I took his hand.

"Sit down, Sebastian. Pour yourself a cup of tea. The Abbé here is from the Jesuit Order in France. He travels from that troubled country to Moravia and has interrupted his journey to see us." Van Halestrom turned to his guest, prompting, "Abbé, please continue with your news. You were telling me that the prevailing mood in your country was one of strife."

Barruel fingered his saucer before beginning in a flurry, "As I say, the situation in beloved France grows graver by the day.

Unrest is being provoked by tentacles of the Illuminati who exert their revolutionary influence through the Jacobin Club and the Philalèthes Brotherhoods. These so called *societies* are nothing but devilish covens opposed to all those who serve the cross. I fear they plan conspiracy against the Jesuits and the Church as they did in '62 and that soon I shall have to flee the land I love once more." He eyed us and took a tentative sip of tea before resuming, "I am aware that the Bavarian authorities have, at long last, turned on Adam Weishaupt and his cronies to cut out this godless canker before it spreads across Europe. But the seditious power has merely been driven elsewhere and is already infiltrating the highest echelons of French life. Why, it is not uncommon for men of the most important office to behave without reason. I… I have tales of such open treason that it would be blasphemous to mention their detail."

He put a dainty handkerchief to his lips and brought himself under control. After a moment the Professor offered, "Sebastian, I have taken the liberty of showing the Abbé the interesting pendant you recently came across."

I deduced by the way the Professor had brought up this subject that he had not told the Abbé the precise manner in which it had fallen into my possession. He obviously had good reason so I played along with an innocent nod and he asked the priest, "Would you tell us what you know about this, Abbé?"

Barruel glowered at the pendant which I noticed next to the chess pieces and he flustered, "This despicable symbol is everywhere, previously only in the capital's darker streets but lately in the corridors of its finest salons. It is worn by those who wear the red cap of revolution and is the mark of the money manipulators lurking within the Order. The brazen snake entwining the cross symbolizes Christianity strangled by the Luciferian serpent. These insurgents claim to seek liberty when, in truth, they only seek liberty from God. I know it. I have tried to warn my peers, but they merely scorn my conspiratorial theories of revolution in France, even when they have proof that the same plotters thrived in your decent country. Well, we shall see who is wrong and who is right. Yes. We... shall see."

He had to stop himself again and sat there with his cup almost rattling on its saucer. The Professor slipped me a discreet look and refilled it. "Now, Abbé, I believe there's something you wanted to ask me?"

For the first time Barruel appeared reluctant to speak and regarded Van Halestrom with some caution before answering, "It is true that I seek information, sir; information of a very sensitive nature. As you know I make it my business to know as much about the Illuminati as possible and, as such, it has come to my knowledge that a series of... most unfortunate incidents recently befell their elite membership at a retreat in Jutland."

He obviously meant our slaughter in Louisenlund but Van Halestrom appeared blissfully ignorant and shrugged, "I'm sorry, Abbé, but I have heard nothing about this."

Barruel watched his eyes carefully and added, "I have also heard such was the ferocity of these incidents that only a few survived to tell the tale, including the landlord, a merchant, an actress and a certain Xavier Zwack."

The Professor shrugged again and smiled, "While I believe it is good news for all who seek the destruction of the Illuminati, it is from your lips that I have heard it first."

"I see," nodded Barruel, casting a wary eye over me and adding, "Yes, it is good news. Good news indeed." His eyes fell back to the chessboard. "One more thing, Herr Professor. May I take the amulet? To show... my friends, you understand?"

He gave a flimsy smile and Van Halestrom passed him the pendant. "Of course, take it to show your friends. That's right."

Ten minutes later, Barruel gave us one last uneasy look before closing the study door behind him and I urgently whispered, "But why, sir?"

"We don't want everybody to know what we are about, Sebastian. You saw that he already has his suspicions, I believe he made that clear." I nodded in agreement and he suggested, "Anyway, I think the Abbé has been a little economical with the truth himself." He moved to the window gesturing me to join him and discreetly pulled back the curtain. From our vantage point we could see a smart coach parked in the street.

"It's Barruel's coach, Sebastian. Tell me what you see?"

"I see a priest's coach, sir."

"Look again. Which way is it pointing?"

"...South?" I figured, "But what does that mean?"

"That Barruel travels to France, he does not come from there."

"Surely, sir, you cannot tell where he's been from this alone."

"You're right, Sebastian. On its own it might be inconsequential but the fact that his driver tipped the stable lad with Moravian coins makes it more than likely. For some reason he was not being altogether truthful with us."

"Why would he do this, sir? Is he... *Illuminatus* too?"

"There are many pressures on all of us during these troubled times, my friend. Men are scared and have good reason to be. No one knows who is their ally and who is their enemy."

Barruel reappeared in the street below and glanced up in our direction before boarding his coach.

"Pray, sir, why did you give him the amulet?"

"I did not want him to think that it was important to us. Though, somehow I feel it may have been in the days to come."

We watched the coach pull away and another thought crossed my mind. "Tell me, Professor, why do you call him The Master?"

"I have every reason. He might not have impressed you today but make no mistake, Herr Barruel is an extremely diligent and determined man. He writes very well too. You should read his work. I believe that, some time in the future, he will produce something *masterful* and of great merit which may be very useful to our cause. That is, if he survives that long." *[17]

He let the curtain fall and regarded me with a happy smile. "Now, Sebastian, you seem to be in an altogether better mood. This is excellent news as I have another task for you."

This did not sound like excellent news to me and I protested, "But, sir, my studies."

"Your studies will not be affected in the slightest as you will only be working for one night at the weekend. This weekend as it happens and, as usual, you will be paid well."

"But I have enough money to buy a castle already, sir," I chivvied, alarmed to hear of more plans involving myself and danger.

He dismissed my concerns with a wave of the hand and rolled out a map on his desk. "Do not fear, Sebastian. This task is simple. You will merely be looking after a few friends of ours who are currently involved in some legal proceedings." He stubbed a finger on the map. "Here, in the village of Rottenberg."

---

17. **Abbé Barruel (1741-1820) The Original Conspiracy Theorist.** This French Jesuit Priest and publicist could be genuinely described as the first conspiracy theorist. He fled to Moravia in Bohemia due to anti-Jesuit sentiment in France but returned in 1773 and went on to complete his magnum opus *Memoirs Illustrating the History of Jacobinism* (1797) expounding the theory that The French Revolution of 1789 was instigated by secret societies including the Jacobian Club and Philalèthes Brotherhoods which, in turn, were heavily influenced by the Bavarian Illuminati. This masterpiece is still highly regarded today and considered to make a convincing political argument.

He lit his pipe and explained, "You will be escorting professors; Grünberger, Cossendy and Renner to Frau Hoffmeister's safe house. Once there you will wait for me."

"Will I be working alone?"

"No. Francesca will be helping you."

"Francesca?"

My heart skipped a beat upon hearing the news but I was thrown when he gave me a knowing look over his spectacles and mentioned, "I trust you enjoyed her recent stay?"

What was this? What did he know of my liaison with Francesca? Before I could demand why he saw fit to pry into my private affairs he carried on in his casual manner, "I knew you would appreciate her visiting. That is why I sent for her. Anyway, it seems to have done the trick." He turned his attention back to the map and continued, "Now, this is the rest of the plan..."

Discovering that Francesca had come to see me under his instruction and not her own volition threw me into a foul mood. Wench! When all along she had let me believe that she loved me she had really been providing a service for her master. Was Van Halestrom her pimp? How I managed to not fly off the handle I do not know, but such was my injured pride that I dared not reveal the extent of my feelings in front of Van Halestrom. Adding to my woes it transpired that the three men I was to look after were, in fact, Illuminati defectors who were to give evidence against the Order at a vital inquiry with me unwittingly becoming their shield. 'Some court proceedings,' my Bavarian arse.

Suffice to say, I stormed away from his study under a cloud of jilted anguish and left the university, not only cursing the entire female race for their abominable scheming but Van Halestrom and the damnable Illuminati to boot. So lost in my thoughts was I that I did not see where I was going and blindly walked into someone coming the other way round a corner.

I was about to tell them to pay more attention when our eyes met and I froze like Lot's wife. For standing there in front of me was Karl's father, the blacksmith. I had not seen him since his boy went missing and now he was only two feet away. His eyes brimmed with inconsolable pain before he barged past me. Seeing his ruined countenance turned my guts inside out and I went to call after him, but remembering Van Halestrom's advice that it was better to be quiet because of Kolmer's connections with local officialdom, I obediently kept my vow of silence and scuttled home in an awful mood, praying that one day I would have the courage to confront the poor man and tell him what had really happened.

I spent that evening in my local tavern having myself several stiff drinks then rose early the next morning eager to visit a church and cleanse myself before my next mission. It may sound selfish, but that Saturday night as I saddled up Petrova, though consumed once more by remorse for Karl and his father, it was not these thoughts that most preoccupied me. Even the prospect of my next potentially dangerous mission gave way to other considerations. Considerations which barged their way into my consciousness with such vigour that not even a visit to a church and a tavern had removed them. I might have not even noticed if the Devil himself had jumped out from the shadows because, at that moment, it was that confounded woman who constantly paraded through my tormented mind.

Chapter 15

Hear No Evil, Speak No Evil, See No Evil

I mounted Petrova outside the stables round the corner from my lodgings as the bells of Ingolstadt struck nine. Dressed like a highwayman in my black breeches, cloak, neckerchief and tricorn hat I certainly looked the part and, with my dramatic bow strapped about me plus a large lantern to light the way, I certainly felt ready for such a role. But as I turned Petrova onto the cobbles I knew that whatever the night held in store, until I had confronted Francesca about her conniving ways, I would not feel right at all. I had been tortured by one particular haunting memory of her covered in bubbles whilst sitting at the other end of my bathing tub. I shook my head to cast off the vision and stared out beyond the city's towered gates, murmuring to myself, "C'mon Seb. You have to concentrate tonight."

This was true. Riding across country at night in the rain can be dangerous for any rider, regardless of their experience. Potholes, ditches, obstructions of every kind lurk in the shadows. Even wild beasts can be a threat. Yes indeed. There are many hazards on the lonely road that lie in wait to catch out the unwary horseman.

The swollen Danube roared noisily under the southern bridge as I rode out into the drizzle and reviewed my journey one more time. I had allowed myself three hours to travel to Rottenberg, calculating that this would give me enough time to find it in the dark and the foul weather. I was to meet Francesca there at midnight with her coach in which we would take the three professors; Grünberger, Cossendy and Renner to Frau Hoffmeister's farmhouse where Van Halestrom would join us. "Simple," as he had said. What could go wrong? The image of Francesca's naked shoulders drifted back into my mind and I shook my head again.

The going was slow but steady and, after what I estimated was about two and a half hours, my lantern shone on a twisted sign at the side of the road which read, '*Rottenberg*.'

I trotted through the hamlet and, eaxactly as the Professor had described, at the end of the main street hidden behind a tree with branches that reached out like witches' fingers, I found the house. I walked Petrova in but could not see anyone about so I dismounted and had a look around. In reality, the house was a derelict pile of tangled timber and sagging roof tiles which eerily reflected my lantern's glow. For a second I had a sense of déjà vu, but how could this be? I had never been to this place before.

I let Petrova's reins slide from my hand and, as I squelched in closer, thought that I saw a light shine in an upstairs window but when I checked the side of the house was covered in darkness. I came up to the front door and quietly called out, "Professors? Are you there?" but there was no reply only the sound of trickling water and the faint gust of wind in the trees. This was not a good sign. I had expected my charges to be ready and raring to go. Seeing the door was ajar and that Petrova was where I had left her, I steadied my bow, held out the lantern in my other hand and pushed the door open with my boot.

At the end of the hallway hung a rickety old door and I crept up to it trying not to go through the rotten floorboards. I eased the door open with my shoulder but jerked back as a trickle of water splashed from the ceiling. I waited till it had stopped before edging into the pitch-black room, whispering, "Professors? Where are you? I've come to take you away." *[18]

18. **Illuminati Defectors; Professors Renner Cossendy & Grünberger.** As S. Drechsler claims, official accounts record that these three professors were important witnesses at an inquiry set up to investigate the Illuminati in 1785. They had recently defected after not receiving 'special alchemic powers' promised to them by the secret society whilst also becoming disillusioned with its objectives and, as such, became targets for reprisals.

On lifting my lantern I was startled to find a pair of pale-faced, old men cowering on a battered chaise longue and clutching each other in sheer petrification. I could not help but gaze at the odd couple's ghostly faces until one of them wailed, "If you are going to kill us just get it over with! Get it over with!"

I realised that my appearance with the frightening quadre bow had alarmed them and tried to reassure the trembling duo, "No, sirs, I come to take you to sanctuary."

Without letting go of his colleague the other snivelled, "Do you hear that Johann? We are to be saved. Saved."

The eccentric pair continued their embrace while the first whimpered, "I am Professor Cossendy. We thought you were going to kill us. We thought we were going to die. We thought... Oh..."

His companion interrupted, "I am Vitas Renner. Professor Vitas Renner." He craned his neck trying to make out my face behind the shining lantern and fretted, "Our protectors left us here an hour ago. Since then we have been alone. We feared the worst. There are Illuminati agents everywhere plotting to do away with us."

"You need worry no more, Gentlemen, for help is at hand. Now prepare to leave immediately, and tell me," I peered around the room, "Where is the third member of your party?"

Their pale faces both looked aloft so I went to the stairway at the side of the room and climbed to the top. Upon seeing candlelight flickering underneath the door ahead I crept over and gave it a knock. "Professor?" I hissed, "Are you in there?"

I heard some shuffling about so, without waiting to be invited, I opened the door. Whatever I had expected to find was not what greeted me. For hunched in the middle of the room was a startled grey-bearded old man dressed in a black cloak, holding a glass phial over his skullcap. He stuck out his hand and exclaimed,

"Stay back you devil!" Then, with this warning, he poured the contents of the phial over his head and a fearsome expression crossed his face as he boldly declared, "Ha! Now the great power of alchemy will turn me invisible and you will never see me again!"

An awkward moment passed while we stared at each other in the lantern light until I felt obliged to point out, "Believe me, sir, all I can see is you."

He brought down the phial and frowned at it. "Maybe you are meant to drink it?" He faced me and wailed, "They promised us great powers, but they lied. They lied!"

I had neither the time nor the inclination to find out what he meant or aid him with his bizarre experimentations, and urged the old coot, "We should leave now, sir. I come to take you away."

He scanned the room as the news sank in, murmuring, "But what about my things?"

I shone the lantern around the room seeing scores of books, bottles and charts scattered across the floor and also I noted, drawn under his feet in chalk, a pentagram.

"Only what you can carry yourself, sir, we must be quick."

This was true. For at that very moment I heard Francesca shout from outside, "Quick, Sebastian!"

"We must go now," I said, but the mad old scholar knelt down and began picking up a huge pile of papers then rolled up some charts. I was not prepared to wait for him to gather his entire laboratory so, as he opened a case to pack it with the rest of his possessions and eyed a huge glass flask that obviously would not fit inside, I threw the bow's strap over my shoulder, grabbed him by the collar and rudely pulled him from the room.

"You're hurting me, youth. Unhand me this instant! I am Grünberger, supreme alchemist."

"Believe me, sir, the moment you are in the coach I shall let you go."

I pointed him down the stairs and followed on close behind. At the bottom, upon seeing that the others had already left, I pushed the fussing man towards the front door.

"Sebastian!" shouted Francesca again and her sense of urgency reminded me where I had seen this place before. It was the house from my nightmare in which Kolmer had been waiting outside. Good God! I am ashamed to say it but when we came to the door I pushed Grünberger out first. It was a small sin based on superstition but if Kolmer was there he could kill the mad professor while I ran away. Thankfully, there was no one there to ruin my honour and I squelched through the mud after the old duffer with my bow in one hand and my lantern in the other. Though the lantern was practically useless for the coach upon which Francesca sat was covered in enough lamps to light the Vatican.

"Where on Earth did you get *that*?" I blared as I hauled myself towards the ostentatious coach. But before she could answer an arrow smashed through the window of the open door and thumped into the contrivance's side with a powerful 'whack'!

"We are going to die! I know it!" screamed Grünberger, throwing his papers up in the air and floundering up to the coach. I dropped my lantern and bundled him through the door.

"Hurry, Sebastian!" cried Francesca as another arrow fizzed by in the dark.

"Go! Go! Go!" I yelled and whistled Petrova to my side then quickly jumped into her saddle. I watched the coach lurch away to see three horsemen bearing down on us with drawn crossbows. Francesca bravely forced the coach through the wall of riders but Petrova reared up as they galloped in closer and, as I struggled to control her, one of the riders fired his bolt at me. By God, if it had gone an inch either way it would have struck Petrova for sure but instead it ricocheted off my quadre bow, making me drop it in the mud. The horsemen had to turn awkwardly on the slippery ground which allowed Francesca to escape and me to bring Petrova under control.

I was only a couple of lengths from the bow which lay sticking up next to my glowing lantern. The closest rider smirked when he saw it then spurred his horse to chase after the coach. We both set off together and I swept down over Petrova's side with my hand inches from the ground. I had one chance. If I missed I would have to come around again.

"C'mon, Seb, do it for Karl," I muttered as the bow came closer and, at the last moment, I swept it up. Yes! I swung myself up on the saddle and dug my heels into Petrova's flanks.

"Ha! C'mon, girl!" I pointed the weapon at the rider alongside and pulled the trigger. 'Zut!' He did not even scream but clutched his throat and fell away into the darkness.

"Yes! Take that pig dog!" I roared but as I did - Curses! One of the other riders galloped past me. Holy smoke he was going fast and, knowing that I would have to use both hands to catch him, I hung the bow on my pommel as the third rider also overtook me.

"Damn it! C'mon my beauty!" I yelled and pushed Petrova to a gallop.

Though Francesca was driving out of her skin the coach was no match for the first horseman and he quickly caught her up. The other, seeing me overtake him, barged his horse into me but I forced Petrova past and left him floundering in our wake. The coach had to clumsily turn a corner and the first rider drew alongside, pulled himself up on his saddle and leapt onto the roof. I furiously tugged on Petrova's reins, getting close enough to hear one of the professors wailing, "He's on the roof! He's on the roof! We're all going to die! We're all going to die!"

I was about to catch them when the coach plunged down a steep hill and at such a pace that, with the darkness and the mud and the uneven ground, I could scarcely keep up. Onward the candle-lit coach rattled down the narrow lane until banging over a small bridge at the bottom and swerving round a bend. Coming round the corner I saw the lane widening up ahead so I goaded Petrova into another surge. I quickly drew alongside and grabbed the baggage rail but as I dragged myself on board I saw the villain on the roof only inches behind Francesca with a knife in his hand.

"Behind you!" I raged and at the very last second she turned and grabbed his wrist as he tride to stab her.

"We're all going to die! We're all going to die!"

"Damn it! Be quite man!" I bellowed, hauling myself aboard as the brute pinned Francesca down with his knee and wrenched his knife hand free.

"Do something, Sebastian!"

Hell's teeth! I flung myself along the roof and slammed into his back, sending the two of us toppling past Francesca off the footboard then, in one awful moment, down onto the hitch. We frantically grasped at the harnesses as the horses' hooves flailed inches from our faces but I managed to hang on first and kick him in the guts. He lost his grip and I glimpsed the look of death in his eyes as he fell under the pounding hooves. I somehow managed to cling on and, with his screams ringing in my ears, shimmied back along the hitch.

"Give me your hand!" yelled Francesca, throwing me hers and dragging me back to safety. I heaved myself back into the seat only to see her eyes expand as she screamed, "Behind you!" and I turned to see the third rider leaning from his horse bringing down his sword. The blade slashed into my shoulder and as I fought to keep my feet he pulled himself up on his saddle and jumped onto our footboard. He brought up his sword again but I barged him down into the seat and clashed my face into his. We wrestled for the blade and, out of the corner of my eye I spotted a ring on his finger depicting the serpent wrapped round the cross.

"Pig dog!" I roared and head butted him backwards with blood pouring from his nose. I got ready to do it again when a deafening 'Boom!' rang out next to me and I watched aghast as his head exploded in a halo of crimson brain matter.

"My God!"

I pulled back in revulsion from the decapitated body as Francesca coolly muttered from behind, "That's the end of that bucket of shit."

I whipped my head around to find her holding a smoking blunderbuss in one hand and flicking the reins with the other. Good God! I would think twice before taking on Francesca Kropotkin. Doing my best to ignore the smouldering corpse, I checked that Petrova was still faithfully trotting behind and wiped the blood and brains from my clothes. We clattered on through the countryside until, after another mile or so, we came to a small village.

"We're going to die! We're going to die!" Wailed the professors and Francesca gestured over the coach's side.

"Perhaps you should calm down the chickens and collect Petrova while I get rid of our friend here."

She brought the horses to a halt next to the wall of an overgrown chapel and I jumped down, shouting in through the coach window, "Control yourselves, Gentlemen! There is nothing to fear."

As I said this, the headless corpse tumbled into the road on the other side of the coach and they all clambered over to stare at the grotesque cadaver and scream as one, "We will die! We will die!"

I collected Petrova and tied her to the back of the coach as an old woman in rags shambled out of the shadows, waving her hands about and moaning, "You can't leave him here. There will be plague. Plague there will be. He must be buried. Be buried he must."

I unchivalrously waved my hands back at her and pulled myself up into my seat but the persistent crone came into the lamp light round the footboard, wheezing, "Give me five thalers and I will bury him for you. Yes, yes. Bury him I will."

"Five thalers?" I quipped.

Francesca scowled impatiently. "Pay her, Sebastian. We need to go. There may be more agents around."

Another volley of the professor's hysterical shouting echoed around the sleepy village and I begrudgingly searched my coat then tossed the old hag some money. She caught it in her filthy hands then set about going through the corpse's pockets. Francesca lashed the horses into action and within moments we were clattering back along the twisty lanes as she urged the horses on, "Yah! Go on you devils!" onward to the house of Frau Hoffmeister.

Chapter 16

The Stone

Francesca and I watched Van Halestrom sitting by the farmhouse fire as he listened to the three professors who all chaotically babbled away to him at once. He looked from one to another, nodding this way and that until finally the cacophony became too much to bear and he raised his palms, pleading, "Please, Gentlemen. One at a time. I only have one pair of ears." At last the men fell silent and Van Halestrom patiently asked, "Once again, Herr Renner. Who was your Illuminati contact?"

Renner bit his lip before blurting, "It was Zwack. Zwack came to me first. But there were others. I..."

"Zwack came to me too," interrupted Grünberger, "He promised us powers, alchemic powers."

"They promised me powers as well," gasped Cossendy, "They sent me coded messages. Look! I have them here." He pulled some bits of paper from his pockets and waved them about.

"But, Johann," wrangled Grünberger, "You have interpreted the code incorrectly."

"No I have not interpreted the code incorrectly, Herr Grünberger, it is you who has interpreted the code incorrectly."

"I will not stand for this!" blustered Grünberger.

"Gentlemen, if you please," adjudicated the Professor. There was a pause while the men all glared at one another before Van Halestrom asked, "You said you heard of the recent ceremony in Jutland? Can you remember, sirs, exactly what you heard?"

Now instead of blabbering the three men held their tongues as though their very lives depended on it. Van Halestrom looked amongst them and suggested, "To be fair, Gentlemen, I probably know more than you ever will yourselves. I only wished to hear what you had *heard*. That is all."

Renner bit his lip again and went to speak but Grünberger stopped him, "Are we not in enough trouble already, Vitas? Surely we must think of our families."

Renner ignored him, confessing, "All I heard was that the meeting was about money and... the cross and the serpent."

"You have said enough, Herr Renner! I have a wife and children."

"I have a wife and children too," echoed Cossendy.

"What does it matter that they know? Do you not think everyone will know soon? Are these not the same questions we will have to answer at the inquiry?"

"Of course not, you fool," fumed Grünberger, "The authorities have no interest in these matters. They merely want to know what the Illuminati plans for the future."

"This *is* what the Illuminati plans for the future," spat Renner, "I say again: these are the questions we will be asked at the inquiry. So why not answer them now?"

Grünberger stewed at him and crossed his arms while Renner answered more softly, "Also, we knew the ceremony was important because... the stone would be there."

Van Halestrom leaned forward in his chair. "Tell me, Professor Renner, of what stone do you speak? Do you mean the obelisk?"

"No... Not the obelisk."

"I'm warning you, Renner," growled Grünberger, shifting in his seat.

Renner defied him and finished, "The Cintamani Stone, the sacred stone from The Dog Star."

Grünberger threw up his hands while Van Halestrom's eyes opened wide and he delved, "I have heard much about the stone of which you speak, but only from learned men such as yourselves who have condemned its powers to be imaginary and fanciful."

Now, instead of keeping tight-lipped Grünberger reared up like a fighting cockerel and crowed, "Then these *learned men,* of which, you speak, *sir*, know nothing about the true nature of the universe. Why, The Cintamani Stone is clearly sent to us by the gods to bring mankind together as one. It comes straight from the greatest star of them all: Sirius, the brightest in the constellations. It is common knowledge to all those with the *true* understanding of science that the stone can prolong the life of the living and give life to matter that possesses none. It is the supreme alchemic source of the Order's power and it would have been mine too if... only... I..."

He faded off but Van Halestrom pried, "So who brought the stone to the ritual?" Now, all three of them looked truly terrified and tensed in their seats. The silence continued until Van Halestrom sighed and put his hands on his knees, venturing, "Will you tell me this then, Gentlemen." He stroked his beard and asked, "Was it a man dressed in black?"

Grünberger scowled at Renner so fiercely that he answered the Professor's question without saying a word. It had to be Kolmer. My mind flashed back to the banquet at Louisenlund. Of course! 'That's what was in the box.' Van Halestrom winked at me sensing that I was catching on. Clever old bird. He had tricked them into telling him exactly what he needed to know. Grünberger caught on too and frowned at Renner who defiantly turned away in his chair.

Van Halestrom looked between them and clapped his hands. "Well, Gentlemen, it has been a long night already and I'm sure you are weary from your journey. We will talk further tomorrow but for now, the Frau has prepared beds for you."

He stood up as the three men shared uneasy glances and slowly rose from their chairs. Frau Hoffmeister duly appeared bearing a candle and escorted them upstairs.

Francesca and I joined Van Halestrom round the fire as he filled his pipe and muttered, "Well, well, well, *The Stone*, eh? That might explain Kolmer's detour."

Though I understood how he had tricked them into revealing what he wanted to know, I had no idea about this stone. Francesca seemed to share my ignorance and before I could ask for an explanation, she beat me to it, "The Cintamani Stone, Professor? Is that not..?

"Yes, my dear. It is."

"My God," she gasped, putting her hand to her mouth.

Exasperated to obviously be the only one in the farmhouse apart from Frau Hoffmeister who did not know of what they spoke, I begged, "Will someone please tell me what's so important about this blasted stone?"

The Professor faced me with the fire casting shifting shadows across his features and answered, "It is a mysterious, ancient relic holding profound spiritual importance for many creeds and going under many names: The Cintamani Stone; The Stone of Destiny; The Philosopher's Stone; The Lapis Exilus and, even to some, The Holy Grail. It is said to come from Sirius, the Dog Star and to bestow upon whoever possesses it awesome alchemic powers, including the power to give life. But, perhaps more importantly, there is another myth; that the stone once sat in Lucifer's coronet and that, during a fight with the Archangel Michael it was broken into five pieces before falling to Earth where it would give the one who controlled it the power to bring Armageddon to the world."

We looked apprehensively at one another in the firelight as he carried on, "Whether real or imaginary, my guess is that the Order attempted to harness these forces for their ritual in Louisenlund. Though, such is the reverence the Illuminati has for the stone, something tells me it holds a deeper significance.

Whatever it is, there is one person who knows for sure: Kolmer."
*19

---

19. **The Cintamani Stone & The Illuminati.** This infamous relic, the pre-cursor of The Sorcerer's Stone has a fascinating history. Pieces of it are ru-moured to have been fashioned into the Holy Grail, as well as one of King Solomon's rings and, also, placed in the Kabba; the black cube residing in the Al-Masjid al-Haram mosque in Mecca, central to the Muslim faith. As S. Drechsler states it is also known as The Lucifer Stone and fabled to possess immense wish fulfilling powers. In regard to these memoirs, The Cintamani Stone has a remarkable connection with Nicholas Roerich, a Russian artist, diplomat and self-proclaimed mystic who, along with Henry Wallace, the then US Secretary for Agriculture, and President Roosevelt, oversaw the de-sign of the one dollar bill in the 1930's. Wallace, who was deeply involved with the occult and later became US vice president, referred to Roerich as his 'Guru' and arranged for his 'master' to take several missions to the mystical Shamballa, said to be in Tibet and thought to be the home of the stone. It is revealing that its later history became so involved with a man who had such close proximity to The Great Seal, cap-less pyramid and All Seeing Eye used on the one dollar bill as this also seems to be its connection within this story. This is either an extraordinary coincidence or maybe there is another more telling interpretation to these events.

Chapter 17

The Sun behind the Sun

That night was as uncomfortable as any that I have ever had. Well, almost. It was certainly one of the most frustrating. Due to the three professors hogging Frau Hoffmeister's spare beds, Van Halestrom, Francesca and I had to sleep together under a solitary blanket on the draughty farmhouse floor in front of the dwindling fire. Owing to Van Halestrom's snoring and Francesca's greediness with the blanket I hardly slept a wink and, because the two of us were never alone, neither did I get the chance to confront her about Van Halestrom's vulgar matchmaking. My frustration only worsened when she left early that morning without saying a word and gave me only a solitary peck on the cheek before riding away.

"You'll see her again soon, my lad," hummed the Professor joining me on the porch as I despondently waved her goodbye, "We're all busy during these turbulent times." It was too early in the morning to ask him how, if he was so busy, he seemed to find the time to arrange my personal affairs. "If you don't mind, Sebastian, I need you to stay here looking after our friends until Bacon relieves you later. Then it's back to university for you."

Busy was right. I had much to do already and wondered how I would fit it all in. I watched Grünberger, Cossendy and Renner pacing around the garden clucking to themselves like the chickens. After hearing what they had said the night before I was still greatly puzzled by the mysterious business and quizzed Van Halestrom, "Sir, could you please explain the significance of this Cintamani Stone and Sirius to all that is happening?"

"Of course, lad, it is simply this. Sirius, the Dog Star, or The Blazing Star as it is known, is the very basis of the Illuminati's occult beliefs. Remember the word *occult* simply means secret.

While the sun warms the physical world Sirius's incomparable brightness in the night sky illuminates the spiritual plane. For those with occult knowledge this symbolises that there is, in fact, another god *behind* God: The all seeing eye of Lucifer.

I trembled at his interpretation, remembering the burning eye from my recurring nightmares shining at the top of the ominous pyramid.

"But..."

"Try to think of it like this, Sebastian. In ancient Egypt the priest would tell the peasant toiling in the field that the sun was the eye of God, when he himself believed that God was, in reality, the Spirit *flowing* from the sun. What the priest had not been told by his elders was that they secretly worshipped another sun: the sun behind the sun. The Blazing Star of Lucifer that burns behind the Eye of God." *[20]

I was simultaneously chilled and flummoxed by these complexities within complexities and quipped, "Sir, it always seems that when trying to understand the Illuminati each curtain drawn merely reveals another."

---

20. **Illuminati & The Blazing Star.** As S. Drechsler states Sirius or The Blazing Star - 'the sun behind the sun' is of utmost importance within the Ancient Mystery School Religion worshipped by the Illuminati. Within the Hermetic belief system the brightest star in the heavens is symbolised by the pentagram. While the sun warms the physical world the blazing light of Sirius warms the spiritual plain and its radiant beams symbolise deity and omnipotence (The creator is everywhere) and of omniscience (The creator knows and sees all). Hence the 'All Seeing' Eye of Providence. The Blazing Star also holds unrivalled mystical prominence within Freemasonry which many historians and conspiracy theorist alike, contest has a secret Illuminati connection. Sirius, situated at the bottom of the inverted pyramidal asterism called the Winter Triangle, is known in Egyptian mythology as Isis, the mother, with the other two stars Betelgeuse and Procyon, respectively Osiris the father and Horus the son. The ancient family trinity can be viewed on the Star Tracker app.

"That's it, lad. Now you're catching on."

This riddle stopped me in my tracks. What could he mean? He looked me square in the eye and explained, "Understand this, Sebastian. To move to the next level you must accept that there will always be another level. It is of profound importance to not merely *think* this but to *know it* as truth."

Sometimes his lessons were beyond my capacity to understand and I gawped at him.

"Sorry, Professor but it seems that whenever I think I'm getting somewhere, I realise how much further I have to go."

"Ah ha, you see. You *are* getting it."

Curses. I was all at sea. Searching for something buoyant on which to cling, I hesitantly ventured, "So, remind me, sir, at what level am I now?"

He hoisted an eyebrow as he had done numerous times to remind me that I should never ask this question and, only when I had achieved the necessary level would I no longer need to ask. Damn it. It was all too confusing and I nursed my injured arm.

"Your wound is deep, Sebastian. You must let Frau Hoffmeister bandage it."

"It is nothing, Professor."

"If it were nothing, Herr Drechsler, you would not be nursing it, it would not be bleeding and we would not be having this conversation. Get the Frau to look at it."

I bowed my head and mumbled, "Yes, sir."

He cast an eye over the professors wandering about.

"Also there is another worrying concern."

"What is that, sir?"

"I fear we have a traitor in our midst. Only a few knew of our mission to collect the professors but it seems that our enemies were well informed."

For the first time it dawned on me that what had taken place the previous night was an ambush which made our survival all the more fortuitous.

"We must be more careful to protect our plans in the future. The professors will need to be protected at least until they can testify."

"And when will that be, sir?"

"Matters of law move with all the speed of an encumbered snail, even if the future of the state hangs upon it. But we'll have to see what we can do about that. Hopefully, it will be soon."

He filled his pipe and I watched Grünberger reading a book as more of the previous night's mysteries came back to me.

"One more thing, Professor..."

As usual he read my mind. "Let me explain, Sebastian. I believe the Cintamani Stone was brought to the ritual because Sirius also symbolises feminine perfection and 'the divine spark' and the Order wished to somehow exploit this essence to breathe life into their creation. To animate what is inanimate: To become gods. The ultimate alchemy if you will. Do you see, lad? What we witnessed was a fertility ritual. The obelisk was Osiris the male. The stone, Isis the female. The waterfall was the birth water and the blood spilt, the sacrifice to sanctify the ghastly rite. The plan to take over the Bank of England is the child born to it and the bastard soul who will do it for them: The Star Child Horus, Lucifer himself."

I tried with some difficulty to take in all the devilish significances. He was right though. It was these esotericisms, along with the proximity of Francesca's tantalizing body that had been on my mind all night as I tossed and turned on the farmhouse floor. However, I still felt there was more that I could not grasp. "But did not Grünberger claim that the stone was sent by the gods to bring the world's civilisations together as one?"

"He did, lad. But try to realise that one man's togetherness is simply another man's slavery. Also, he did not say *which* gods had sent it." He scratched his head before going on, "As I said, I feel the stone's presence at the ritual has some other deeper significance but alas, I cannot fathom it. I believe that we must solve this riddle before understanding the entirety of their plans. For, as we were so successful in destroying their first attempt, I fear that we must be ready in all ways to do the same again."

I frowned and sighed, "As usual, Herr Professor, I feel there is much I need to know."

"Then as usual, Sebastian, I feel that you are beginning to understand."

He smiled and went to pat my shoulder but remembering that it was injured, clasp the other. We watched Renner and Cossendy pacing around the garden muttering to themselves while Grünberger leant against a tree reading his book. He saw us looking and turned away hiding the open pages behind his shoulder.

Van Halestrom observed, "It would appear that not all information can be trusted to those who believe they know best what to do with its possession eh, lad?"

"That part of the mystery, sir, is perhaps the only one I feel I understand."

And that was the last we said about the business on that day. Indeed, such were the climactic events of the night in Rottenberg that once again I wrongly assumed my adventures might be at an end. Little did I know that, far from bringing everything to an end, we had shaken a hornets' nest of retribution and before too long would find out exactly how badly. Van Halestrom left and I was soon relieved by Bacon whereupon I went back to university to read my books, count my money, nurse my wounds and try and live as normal life as possible.

Now, when I remember those far off days and my fight with Kolmer, it seems that what happened next did so the very next day, but, as in any true account, what really happened was the passage of time. Not that anything changed much over the following weeks. I did try to live a normal life and buried my head in my books but more in an effort to forget about Francesca and to hide from Herr Vacchieri and, in the same anxious manner, started visiting an inferior blacksmiths on the other side of town. The distant volcano continued to erupt, the rain continued to fall and I continued to look over my shoulder. Van Halestrom eventually returned from organising the professor's inquiry so my training sessions resumed and, though I failed to rid Francesca completely from my mind, at least it seemed my university career was on a more even keel as opposed to hanging by a thread.

Nevertheless, this state of affairs was not set to endure and, even though over the past months I had dared to dream that my struggle was over, in May of 1786 everything changed again. And I remember it very well. Because it was when my story reached a new fevered pitch from which it would not desist until its bitter end. Where once more my fight against those who threatened the freedom of every man, woman and child in the known world consumed my life. Oh yes, and the mystery of the Illuminati revealed itself even further. Further than I ever could have imagined.

Chapter 18

The Spurs

The day started so well. For once it had stopped raining and I was galloping Petrova past a meadow of fresh summer flowers to the Castle Landfried for my next lesson with the Professor. On that particular morning I remember that I was wearing a fine new cloak which I had splashed out on in an effort to cheer myself up and I recall it heroically billowing about me as I swept along. Best of all I had also bought a new pair of riding boots boasting the most ostentatious spurs that I had ever seen. In hindsight I blush at the memory of them but in the obliviousness of my youth I thought them extremely dashing and considered myself like a brave Frederick the Great; the sweetheart of every Bavarian maiden. In reality, of course, I looked like a total idiot with more money than sense and scant idea of fashion. But as these matters were of a slightly subtle nature they were simply inconceivable to me so I happily thundered on my way.

I arrived at the castle and threw Petrova's reins to the stable lad before hurrying up the stairs and, expecting to meet Van Halestrom, was dismayed to find Bacon waiting at the top giving me a disdainful look and tapping his thumbs.

"Good afternoon, sir," welcomed the old butler and glanced at my feet, "I see you have bought yourself some new boots."

"That's right, Bacon, just the job eh? Where's the Professor?"

"I'm afraid, sir, he won't be instructing you today as he has been called away on urgent business. I will, therefore, be the recipient of that dubious pleasure. So if you and your boots would like to follow me, sir, maybe we can begin."

Trust my luck. Condescending Bacon was the last thing that I needed on this rare sunny day. Though, never wishing to overstep my mark within our fellowship, I obediently followed him down the hallway and into his study. Upon entering it struck me that I had never been inside before and I was surprised to discover a neat room with no furniture except for two chairs at a simple table on which lay some books bathed in sunlight falling from a small arched window. He gestured to one of the chairs which I took and I picked up the top book from the pile.

"Ah, *Hermetic Philosophy*," I remarked, "The very text I am reading with the Professor."

"I am quite aware of your reading lists, sir. After all, it is *I* who sets them hence, rather obviously, its presence here today upon my humble table."

Gadzooks. Another secret. It was Bacon who set my lessons when I had thought that it was the Professor. I would not have been surprised if everything that they had told me since we had first met was, in fact, a tissue of lies deployed to obscure some greater mystery. The old codger very deliberately held out his hand so I passed him the book and shrank back in my chair. It was going to be a long morning. He took the book, turned over an hourglass on the table, cleared his throat and, as I prepared for the inevitable tedium, he began to read.

I soon discovered that my fears were totally unfounded. For it quickly became apparent that Bacon was the most excellent teacher. He read purposefully but with great timing and poise, stopping when he thought that I might not understand and offering further explanation where he felt necessary. It was most enlightening and I felt the detail sink in as the time passed with great speed.

Approaching the end of the lesson Bacon moved onto Hermetic spiritualism and I had taken to staring contemplatively out of the window. Not that I was ignoring him but being so engrossed by the subject, as I gazed amid the tops of the distant clouds I felt myself understand the ideas on my own terms and fused them with my personal experiences.

It was then as he methodically continued, "The most revealing Kabbalist interpretation of the intrinsic relationship between inner and outer worlds is expressed in the maxim: As above, so below," that a key unlocked a door in my mind allowing it to swing open and the light of understanding to shine inside.

Bacon sensed the change in me and put his head on one side. "Do you understand, sir? The idea being asserted here is..."

"Yes, Bacon," I interrupted, having a eureka moment of my own, "I think I understand very well, in fact, I think I understand very well indeed." I recalled Kolmer using the expression at university and, in a flash of clarity, my cognitive functions suddenly fell into place. I muttered to myself, "As above so below: To replicate the heavens upon Earth. The eternal cycle written in the stars; The mother, the father and the child. On... earth as it is in Heaven. It's even The Lord's Prayer. It seems so obvious now, so simple."

Bacon closed the book offering with an air of caution, "Perhaps, sir, what at first seems obvious may, in turn, not be simple." "So what's next?" I asked, seeing that the hourglass was not yet empty and eager to hear more.

"I think you have understood enough for today, sir. We shall let that sit for now. There will be time in the future to hear more." *21

---

21. **Illuminati & 'As Above, So Below'**. This seemingly simplistic, yet subtly complex Hermetic maxim is, perhaps, the central pillar of the Ancient Mystery School Religion associated with the Illuminati and, without doubt, the most defining philosophy of the gnostic traditions. A compelling case could be made that, in its contemporary form, there is no place better to contemplate this mainstay of esoteric thought than Chaos Theory or fractals: the inner and outer worlds being in essence the same and only separated by matters of scale. As S. Drechsler's account mentions the same foundational overarching philosophy can also be found in The Lord's Prayer 'On earth as it is in Heaven.'

Somewhat surprised by his relaxed attitude, I rose and let him lead me from his room back to the front door where he bade me good day with an uncharacteristically good humoured smile.

I collected Petrova and rode away from the castle putting everything back together: Kolmer, the fertility ritual, the obelisk, the money, the serpent and the cross, the scheme, the sacrifice, the tiny specks of light above controlling the masses below. I felt this insight had laid, for me, a new foundation upon which I began to build my next layer of understanding. Though, somehow the significance of The Cintamani Stone still lay shrouded in shadow and Bacon's words chimed through my consciousness, 'What at first seems obvious may, in turn, not be simple.'

While I pondered this riddle I trotted past a row of crofters' cottages a mile before the turning to Ingolstadt and thought that I heard a voice cry out, "Help me!"

I pulled Petrova up and scanned the buildings to see from where the call could have come. There was no one about and I wondered if I had mistaken the cry for that of a distressed animal or maybe the wind in the trees. But as I wheeled Petrova around, I noticed that there were no animals about and no wind whatsoever.

"Help me!" bleated the cry again and I was sure that it was coming from a barn at the end of the row. I cast an eye over the building and, seeing footprints in the dry mud leading inside, I dismounted and walked over.

I stuck my head inside the door and called, "Who's there? Are you all right?"

I swung open the door letting the sunlight cast my shadow across the dusty floor. Edging forward my eyes grew accustomed to the gloom and I was sure that I could see someone's feet in the shadows at the back.

"Help me!" whined the call again and I took another step then heard someone move behind me. 'Whack!'

Something hard smashed into my ear and I collapsed onto my knees whereupon I was kicked in the back and sent thumping face down in the dust.

"Fool!" Scorned a rough voice from behind and its owner crashed down on top of me pinning my arms to the floor with his knees. I spat out a mouthful of dirt and struggled to throw him off as a second man emerged from the shadows at the back of the barn. He raised the brim of his hat revealing a mouthful of twisted, yellow teeth and jeered, "*Help me*," then spat on the floor and snarled, "Kill him. Then we can go."

Shit! I had fallen into a trap and was going to die for sure. In the dust ahead of me I saw the shadow of the man on my back raising his arms over his head with a huge knife in his hands.

No! There was no time to think and I jerked up my leg and stabbed a spur into his back. Even through my boot I felt the rowels pierce his spine and he screeched in pain then dropped the blade inches from my face. His weight shifted on top of me and I threw him off then grabbed the knife and sprang to my feet as the other thug came over. Seeing his wounded companion writhing on the floor his expression changed to angry surprise and he unsheathed his sabre. I squatted down as he came at me and in one decisive move, leapt forward and viciously kicked him in the balls. They burst apart on the end of my boot and his face contorted with torment as he dropped to his knees. Remembering to strike once and purposefully, I lunged forward and stabbed him through his throat then pulled out the knife as a shower of blood squirted onto the floor which he pitched into with a gasp. Without wasting a second I jumped on his friend, yanked his head back by his hair and slit his throat from ear to ear while his harrowing screams turned into a disgusting gurgle.

Something snapped inside me and I sawed the knife back and forth so hard that I almost went through his gullet before jerking his forehead in the crook of my elbow and snapping his neck with a sickening crunch. I dropped his head and stayed there straddling him and panting with exertion as his blood mixed with the dust.

I pulled myself up and, taking one last glance at the carnage, recognised the man in the hat as one of Kolmer's henchmen from the crossroads. I spun round half expecting the man in black to be standing behind me but I was alone apart from a solitary fly buzzing in the shadows. I stumbled from the barn raising my trembling hand to block out the sun as a roaring noise filled my ears. All at once my legs gave way and I fell onto one knee and vomited. It must have been the shock of the violence but, after taking some steadying breaths, I wiped my mouth and pulled myself to my feet then mounted Petrova. Aware that there might be more assassins lurking close by I reared her before tapping my bloodstained spurs into her flanks and galloping off.

Somehow I had survived the trap but I was profoundly shaken. I could not live like this. Knowing that at any moment I could be killed or that I may have to murder those who came after me in the most brutal of circumstances. I would turn into an animal. The look in the henchman's eyes as the knife plunged through his neck slid back into my mind. Holy Father! How was I still alive? Thanking God for my immodest sense of fashion, I put my head down and gave Petrova hers.

Two miles down the road I saw another rider approaching fast and, regarding his hardy nature, I squeezed the handle of the knife in my belt. But a hundred yards further on I relaxed when I recognised Van Halestrom's familiar form waving at me. When we came up to each other he inspected my dusty, blood-splattered clothes and asked, "How many were there?"

As usual his perceptiveness overwhelmed me and I stammered, "Two, sir... But how...?"

"They came after me too, Sebastian. I was lucky to escape, though my assailants were less so. Come now, to the castle. We must check that Bacon and the others are safe."

He galloped off with me bringing up the rear and soon we were back at the castle where much to our relief we found Bacon and the staff well and untroubled. Van Halestrom recommended that it would be best for me to stay that night and, being most ill at ease, I did not argue but gratefully made myself at home.

Over dinner that evening he explained, "Someone close to us is not who they seem. I fear these attacks will persist until either Kolmer is dead or we have removed the traitor from our midst. Until that time we must be extra vigilant. I swear we will never use a horseman again to deliver our messages. I put my oath on it. From now on we will only use the birds." His eyes narrowed and he frowned. "In all my time fighting the Order this is the most threatened I have ever felt, but if it's a fight they want then it's a fight they shall get eh, my lad?"

He defiantly raised his glass and toasted, "Are you with me?"

I picked up my drink and noticed that my hand was still shaking but timidly shared the toast, "I am, sir." Before gulping it down with as much fear as I could swallow. Things were getting serious. Very serious indeed.

Chapter 19

The Mockingbirds Sing

The next months were memorable for many reasons. Not least, because the threat of deathly menace had returned to my life, but also strangely for the weather. For, I remember to this day, the summer of 86 was very hot indeed, sweltering, no less. I clearly recall the steam coming from the piles of mud around the city as the sun finally came out and we were treated to a good old-fashioned Bavarian summertime. Not that I was able to enjoy it. Nightmarishly, I failed my Canon Law exam, no doubt because of the stress and had to retake it over the holidays but not only this, the university was also awash with gossip and rumours of Illuminati trials, arrests and plots as more news came to light in the press. The pressure was overwhelming. How I managed to keep both lives going is a miracle in itself. Constantly hearing about the Order whilst knowing they were actively trying to kill me made my studying a living nightmare. I sweated and read and looked over my shoulder then penned another manuscript and sweated and read some more.

It could only have been three short months after I had to fight for my life in the barn when Van Halestrom informed me the Illuminati inquiry, at which the three professors were to give evidence, was to take place in Munich right away. He had used his influence to forgo the usual bureaucracy and so, without delay, I would have to leave to guard them during the proceedings. Unsurprisingly, because of this unexpected duty my studies were further disrupted and, along with not seeing Francesca for a miserable six months and everything else mounting on my young shoulders, this brought on a new sense of vexed moroseness in me. It seemed that my exciting new life meant the total abandonment of my old reassuring one which was a development that, in my naivety, I had not foreseen.

All in all I was a nervous wreck by the time I reached Munich in September to meet the professors. The intervening time since our last meeting had left them looking even more haggard and gaunt. As usual Grünberger did most of the talking though much of it was bordering on the hysterical and paranoid. For once I did not blame him. I too was feeling the strain. Everywhere I went stories of Illuminati reprisals and threats filled the taverns and newssheets of the land.

Whilst escorting them to the courts onboard Van Halestrom's carriage for the first day of the inquiry Grünberger fretted away beside me, "They will send men to this place to come after us. I know it. Everyone knows it. Everyone knows that we are here. It is common-knowledge that the inquiry is to take place in Munich. I fear for our lives knowing that we are targets of the Order. Why could the proceedings not have been kept a secret? Why does everyone know?" *[22]

Renner sighed in the corner, "With men like you around chattering all day, Grünberger, secrets are impossible to keep."

He pulled the brim of his hat over his face and hunkered down next to Cossendy.

"Fear not, Gentlemen," I assured them, "I will see to it that nothing happens to you. I give you my word."

---

22. **Illuminati Court Cases 1786.** Several similar court cases involving the Illuminati took place during this period. After discovering the Illuminati's intentions of usurping governments and destroying the aristocracy the authorities were determined to control the secret society, punishments for the membership of which had existed since their exposure the previous year. Though other details of this precise trial are nonexistent, amazingly, the professor's testimonies are recorded in the publication *Grosse Absichten des Ordens der Illuminaten, dem patriotischen Publikum vorgelegt von vier ehemaligen Mitglieder* (*Great intentions of the Order of the Illuminati, presented to the patriotic public by four former members*) Joseph Lentner, 1786. (German speaking) E Book readers download available above for those who wish to verify the author's claims.

Grünberger's forehead creased and he cautioned, "What if your word is not enough, young man?"

I tried to look as stalwart as possible though, to tell the truth, I was as apprehensive about the forthcoming days as they were.

My task was to protect the men as they travelled back and forth from our tavern to the courts. However, whilst I had been happy to discover that the inquiry was to take place in the city's impressive government buildings where I thought we would be safe, upon dismounting and entering the halls I noticed that, though there were scores of councillors, judges and other officials milling about, no one was armed and it seemed that matters of security were not taken seriously at all. The administration appeared to be alarmingly unaware of the Illuminati's tactics so I vowed to stay as vigilant as I could.

Though this was not as easy as I had planned, for I quickly began to suspect that my fears were unwarranted. The hearings dragged uneventfully on as many other witnesses were brought in front of the magistrates to give their testimonies. Most of these were of no interest whatsoever and, on the whole, along with the immeasurably boring legal proceedings, the entire affair was as tedious as watching another man's horse eat. So, with my charges not due to take the stand for weeks, I soon fell into a general state of lethargy.

It was on the second week that I started to pay very close attention. For, as I sat trying to concentrate as Grünberger was finally sworn in, the doors at the back banged open and a troop of extremely roguish looking gentlemen maundered inside. While they passed and took their places a few rows ahead I eyed them with deep suspicion. Their rakish clothes were obviously not those of the court employees and one of them, in particular was dressed in such finery, with a grand feathered hat and a fine gold braided coat, that I was convinced he was of noble bearing.

The others deferentially let him sit first as a bailiff came over reminding them to remove their hats as this was the protocol of the court. When the men idly obliged the lavishly dressed individual momentarily turned his head and revealed his profile.

Good God! It was the devil to whom Kolmer had given the box over the table in Louisenlund. I instantly hid my face, pretending to rub my chin. Damn it! Grünberger was right. The bastards could simply breeze into the hearings. How had they done this? They must have had great influence with the authorities. My mind raged. What should I do? There were five of the dandies including the high-born devil himself. Renner and Cossendy were still none-the-wiser and sat twiddling their thumbs in the row directly ahead.

'Play your cards carefully Seb,' I told myself and tried to stay calm. I could not run straight out of the hall as it would look suspicious. I would have to hope that the swine did not turn round and recognise me. While I sat there nervously talking to myself, Grünberger glanced up at the men and his eyes filled with dread and his voice began to waver as he answered the magistrate's questions. After a moment Renner and Cossendy noticed them too and became similarly flustered and I cowered down in my seat waiting for the right moment to escape, before sheepishly creeping outside when no one was looking doing my best to hide my face.

I paced up and down the hallway frenetically trying to work out a plan. Damn it all! When would my nightmares end? I would have to get word to Van Halestrom to come and help me. But how? I decided that I would have to send a message by horseman. It was the only way. Though he had told me to only use the birds and the note might take three days to reach him it was my only option. I cursed myself for not bringing one of his pigeons as I had been too busy with university work before I left. What an idiot. If only the Professor could read my mind now.

I managed to borrow a quill and paper from a passing clerk then deliver a note to the postmaster's office in town before returning to the court. I was in the nick of time to find the proceedings adjourned for the day and the three professors skulking away from the building. I waved them towards the carriage not wishing to be seen myself and the three of them scuttled over in a general state of hysteria with Grünberger fussing at the front, "Why did you leave us? You gave us your word."

"I knew no harm would come to you in the hall, sirs. I'm sure that you were safe at all times." As I said this the group of conceited rakes exited the building and glared right at us. "Come along now," I hurried, "We cannot stay here all day."

"Did you not see who was in court?" demanded Renner as he clumsily pulled himself aboard.

"It was him. It was him," panicked Cossendy. "He is one of them. He will kill us for sure!"

"In we get, sirs," I encouraged, seeing the distinguished demon himself join his men and stare intently at our carriage. With the three flustered men aboard I banged on the roof to tell our driver to leave and we set off with a jolt. Thank God we had got away without him seeing my face. But as we trundled back past the courts he glimpsed me through the window and I saw his eyes expand with angry recognition. Damn it! Damn it! Damn it!

"Who is that man?" I gasped, uselessly trying to hide my face.

"He is Xavier von Zwack," bleated Cossendy, "Government lawyer and such trusted friend of the courts that he does not even bother to defend allegations of his Illuminati membership. They call him Cato. This is what we feared would happen. What do we do now? What do we do?"

I peeped at Zwack through the back window as he came into the middle of the street surrounded by his gaggle of men who all stood ominously watching us rattle away. Shit!

Renner nuttered next to me, "Will your word save us now, boy?"

We returned to our tavern where I hurried the professors inside and forbade them to leave without my strict permission. When they were all safely ensconced in their rooms I went to my own and loaded a couple of flintlocks then sat by the window scanning the street outside. My worst fears came true when, an hour after dusk, two of Zwack's men reappeared on horseback. One of them saw me peeping out the window and – Bugger the saints! - If the cocky swine did not give me a sly nod. Pig dogs! They knew we were here. I yanked my head behind the curtains. How had they done this? Maybe they had someone follow us from court. That would have been easy. After a moment I peeked out again and saw that they had dismounted and were chatting on the street corner and having a smoke. At least they did not look as if they were going to burst into the tavern. I prayed to God that they were not that brazen. Then I remembered the curs who tried to assassinate me at the university. They had not waited to be told to come in either.

I sat on my bed in the shadows cursing my luck and fiddling with my flintlocks. After a while I decided to go downstairs to check that the doors and windows were bolted and hopefully find the proprietor to ask him if he knew somewhere else we could stay. I stuffed the flintlocks in my belt, pulled my shirt over them and crept from the room. Judging by the silence of the landing the professors had stopped wittering for once and were all quietly tucked up in their beds, so I carried on downstairs. But after checking the bolt on the front door and searching about I could not find the owner or his servants anywhere, only a lonely candle flickering on the counter in the reception. Gadzooks. Why could I never find someone when I needed them? I quivered in the lonely hallway mumbling to myself and frantically trying to work out what to do next.

"Oh. Hello, Sebastian."

Hearing Van Halestrom's voice behind made me jump so high that I painfully banged my head into the eves and spun round to see him emerging from the shadows. "What in Heaven's name are you doing here?" I gaped in utter disbelief.

"Something told me you needed me."

"Well, it wasn't me," I hissed and rubbed my head. *Had* he read my mind - from fifty miles away? I had only sent my message three hours ago.

Before I could ask he took his gloves off and began, "I come with good news. Renner holds the balance in the inquiry as he has a signed letter from Xavier Zwack inviting him to join the Illuminati and this is the crucial evidence needed for Zwack to face charges. Herr Zwack is a man of formidable power within the Order and also a government magistrate so his downfall will be a great victory for us and a decisive blow against the Illuminati. It seems that we have them on the run."

"Well that would be music to my ears, sir, had they not run right to this very place." I gestured to the front door and whispered, "There are already a couple of his men waiting outside."

He looked over my shoulder and shook his head, "Ah. I don't think we have anything to fear from them."

"But they are outside right now - watching us. Surely if they fear Renner's testimony they will try to harm him."

"I do not believe that will be the case."

"Why? Why not? Why do you not believe that will be the case? Explain this to me."

He frowned. "I also have some *bad* news."

As he said this Renner appeared from the privy and shuffled past carrying his chamber pot, bidding, "Ah. Good evening, Professor Van Halestrom. I trust now that *you* are here everything is under control?" He threw me a disparaging stare.

"Ah. Herr Renner. Good evening to you, sir. Yes, of course, everything is in order. And I trust you are well?"

He squinted over his glasses. "Well? I have been better."

"Good, good. And tell me, your lovely wife, I trust she is well also?"

Renner seemed bewildered and eyed Van Halestrom with inctredulity before answering, "Yes... She is well *also*." He looked between us and shook his head then climbed the stairs.

Van Halestrom waited until he had closed his door then sighed, "They have kidnapped his wife to stop him from accusing Zwack. Luckily, as you saw, he does not seem to know."

"Damn it!" I spat, "Why is nothing ever simple? What are we to do?"

"You will have to do your best to stop him from finding out until we can free his wife."

"Free his wife? But..."

"Until then you must delay him from testifying or else they will kill her."

"Stop him from testifying? Kill her? I am no lawyer, sir. I know nothing of the courts... their rules... their protocols. How will I achieve this miracle?"

"Bacon will help you."

"Bacon..? But how...?"

Completing my discombobulation the pompous old butler appeared from the shadows behind Van Halestrom and announced himself in his grindingly sarcastic tone, "Yes, sir, Bacon, sir. You might remember me well as, I believe, our paths have crossed before."

I could not help but spit under my breath, "Thunder and lightning." I already had three old coots to look after. The last thing I needed was another one.

The Professor gave his most resolute smile. "Bacon will aid you here while I try to locate Renner's wife. I'm sure you could do with a little help." He looked between us, "Now, Gentlemen, I'm afraid that I must leave you. Bacon, I will take the coach and hopefully return with our charge. Good luck, my friends. I hope to see you soon in happier circumstances."

With this he shook my hand, nodded at his old friend and disappeared into the shadows as quickly as he had come. Damn the unpredictable old goat.

Bacon offered, "We should go to your room, sir. There is much to deliberate." He nodded upstairs and, after permitting myself a most lengthy sigh, I led him up to my room.

And so it was. I stayed up with Bacon half the night hatching a plan. He assured me that the men outside were of no concern as they must be aware of the kidnapping and, therefore, under the impression that we were already silenced. Because of this it was pointless to move to other lodgings as they had found us so easily before they would, no doubt, be able to do it again. What was more important was to keep Renner away from the court for as long as possible whilst ensuring that he remained unaware of his wife's plight. This may sound easy but we had no idea how he might find out. Would someone come and tell him: a brother, a father, or some other relative? Did other people even know? We decided to make sure that all three men spoke to no one and Bacon set about writing a letter to the court explaining that we could not attend as the professors were ill with fever and that we did not want to infect the other members of the hearings

To my great relief and surprise this simple plan worked and we were excused from the proceedings for three days. However, this meant that the five of us became virtual prisoners in the tavern and remained locked inside at all times. Although Bacon and I took shifts to relieve one another I thought that I might go mad with the stress and the cramped conditions.

This is to say nothing of the professors who complained incessantly about their forced incarceration even though it was endlessly explained to them that it was for their own good. Once or twice I sensed that they were becoming suspicious but we succeeded in keeping the truth from them, though I knew it was a deceit we could not keep up for long.

After Bacon wrote the court another letter extending our absence for a further two days I was nearly at the end of my tether and considered anything to relieve the deadlock. In my darkest moments, lying on my bed in my stuffy room staring at the ceiling, I considered telling Renner the truth and demanding that he go through with his testimony. I even contemplated the possibility that the Illuminati would kill his wife forcing him to accuse Zwack in a fit of suicidal revenge.

Alone with the bickering professors, Bacon's constant facetiousness, Zwack's thugs mounting their permanent vigil and no word from Van Halestrom, I was not sure how much longer I could last. I was truly at my wit's end. With these stresses bearing heavily on my mind, to say nothing of the extra time that I was missing from university, the days continued to add up since we had attended court. Until, by the end of the week, after ignoring several notes delivered to the tavern asking when we would be returning, a court official eventually paid us a visit. We had to meet his demands, in part, and Bacon agreed to escort Cossendy and Grünberger to the court the next day. We assured the official that Renner would also return soon but this was still impossible as he was the one most affected by our recent illness. So we managed to get a further breathing space. Or so I hoped.

Chapter 20

Wit's End

"How could you lie to me?" blubbed Renner, glaring up at me from the edge of his bed with tears streaming down his cheeks.

"We were trying to protect you, sir. We meant you no harm."

I glanced at the others crowded into the tiny bedroom as the distraught man put his head in his hands and wept, "Oh my Isabella. My sweet Isabella. What will become of you?"

My eyes fell on Grünberger sitting on the stool in the corner and he turned away crossing his arms. The idiot had told Renner the news after one of Zwack's henchmen had muttered it to him in the courtroom privy.

I could not be with them at all times, sir," murmured Bacon from beside me and raised an eyebrow at Grünberger.

I clenched my teeth and tensed, "I understand, Bacon. It's not your fault."

Cossendy moved to the foot of the bed and sniped, "No, it's *your* fault, boy. It's *all* your fault. If you have lied about this outrage then what else are you hiding from us? My God. My own family might be hostages of these monsters. What will become of us? What will become of us now?"

"Please calm yourself, sir. Panicking will help no one," I said with as much conviction as I could muster but it was getting hard. I looked past Renner through the crack in the curtains and could see Zwack's men in the street outside. Damn them!

The young court officer shuffled in the doorway. He had been standing there playing with his hat since returning with the others and I noticed him peep at me under his eyebrows. I challenged him, "Why can the court do nothing about this intimidation? It is obvious this man is being threatened by the accused. It is a travesty of justice."

"The court has no proof, sir, only the word of your friend here which I heard first but a moment ago. As you know Herr Zwack is held in the highest regard by the court and commands much authority with the magistrates. I am sure these allegations will be investigated in due course but the law moves slowly in matters such as these." He cleared his throat before going on, "I'm afraid the court can delay its business no longer, Gentlemen. Now that I find you recovered from your recent illnesses," he looked suspiciously between us, "We must proceed with all haste. All the other witnesses have given their evidence, only Professor Renner's testimony remains."

Bacon pondered briefly and suggested, "Pardon, sir, I know that it is not your place to air such an opinion but, would you say enough evidence has already been collected to make charges?"

The young man lowered his eyes and played with his hat.

"I see," noted Bacon with a frown.

We stood in silence listening to Renner's moping until the officer put his hat on, saying, "Professor Renner must attend the court next week on Monday the 10th of October. I have a magistrate's warrant here ordering his presence on that date." He passed Bacon a piece of paper and bowed to him. "If he is not there, Gentlemen, I fear there will be repercussions for you all."

"Why is this happening to me?" sobbed Renner, shaking his head in his hands, "My poor Isabella. My poor Isabella."

Bacon put the warrant inside his coat and showed the officer out. Cossendy glared at me before following them and Grünberger got up from the stool but stopped as he passed and started, "It is only right that he knows. I..."

"I think it best if you leave now, sir," I rumbled, staring him down and he scowled at me before leaving. When he had gone I shut the door behind him and drew the curtains before kneeling at Renner's feet.

"Sir?" I whispered, tapping his knee to get his attention, "Before I leave I have a secret of great importance to share." He stopped snivelling and I carried on, "Professor Van Halestrom searches for your wife as I speak and, if any man can find her, then I'm sure that he can. If he found her, sir, would you... could you... still tell the truth in court?"

He raised his bleary face and sniffed, "If he finds my Isabella, young man, I would claim the world is flat."

I smiled sympathetically and asked, "One more thing, sir, do you still have Zwack's letter?"

He reached inside his coat and pulled out a piece of paper that had obviously been folded many times. He ran his fingers over it muttering through his tears, "It never leaves me."

I patted his arm and rose then opened the door to leave.

"Young man?"

I turned in the doorway as he hung his head once more and mumbled into his chest, "If Van Halestrom does not find her then you also know what I must do?"

I solemnly bowed and closed the door whispering under my breath, "Come on Van Halestrom."

That weekend passed as fast as a lame donkey dragging an over laden cart with a broken wheel. We did our best to calm the professors whilst preparing ourselves for Monday's ordeal though this was hard in itself as we had no idea what to expect. In the end I selected a pair of stiletto knives in a secretive leather chest holster which Bacon had brought along and which I could hide under my coat in case Renner changed his mind and we had to fight our way out of court.

On Sunday night I lay in my bed with my mind a turmoil of morbid confusion and angst: kidnappings, threats, miles away from home, loveless and with my own life in mortal danger once again. What a life. I had thought exams daunting up until now.

How ridiculous. I tried to go to sleep but with the sound of Renner sobbing down the hallway and a howling wind gathering outside it was impossible. Before I knew it I awoke with a start on my bed in the chilly morning light and set about gathering our party. Once Grünberger and Cossendy were ready along with Bacon at the foot of the stairs I patted down my coat making sure my knives were concealed before going to knock on Renner's door. I had been leaving him till last.

"I am ready," came his cold response and I opened his door to find him sitting on his bed staring blankly at the wall. He did not look well and I guessed that he had not slept since finding out about his wife. I held open the door and he stood up and walked past me without catching my eye. I was about to follow him when I spotted his folded letter on the bed and I picked it up.

"Sir, I think you have forgotten something," I said, catching him up on the landing and passing him the note. He took it off me and mumbled, "It looks as though I won't be needing it, young man."

"Please, sir," I urged, "Don't give up hope."

His shoulders slumped and he placed it back inside his pocket before slowly plodding down the stairs.

The five of us boarded the coach outside in total silence and set off for the courts. To make matters even worse Zwack's horsemen appeared from around the corner and followed behind us. Renner sat between me and Bacon staring into space whilst Grünberger and Cossendy fretted in their seats constantly eyeing the men through the rear window. My spirits fell another notch when we pulled up outside the courtrooms and I spotted Zwack arrogantly alighting from his carriage on the other side of the street. He fell in with the rest of his men who were loitering under the trees lining the street and they greeted each other while, from time to time, sneering loutishly over at us. Hell's bells.

We dismounted ourselves and made our way inside whereupon Zwack and his entire entourage followed right in our footsteps.

"Capital," I whispered through my grinding teeth.

"Don't let them frighten you, sir," murmured Bacon, "They would not be so brave if they were alone."

We filed into the courtroom and I showed the professors to their seats as Zwack and his men helped themselves to a whole row at the back. While they mockingly removed their hats and dusted down the seats I remembered Zwack's face from the table in Louisenlund and my fists clenched with anger. The courtroom steadily filled with lawyers, clerks and all manner of legal staff until every bench and even the standing room was taken. The three magistrates entered from their own door and found their places behind the raised bench at the head of the overflowing hall and finally the proceedings began.

After the usual legal ceremonies were completed, at last, Renner was summoned to take the stand. He slowly rose from his pew and squeezed to the front to where he was followed by Bacon who whispered something in a clerk's ear. While Bacon came to sit back down the clerk approached one of the magistrates and the two of them exchanged hushed words before the clerk turned round and announced, "It has been brought to our attention that some of the gentlemen present are carrying arms. This is strictly forbidden by the court so I must ask them to immediately surrender their weapons to the sheriff's men."

I peeped at Zwack and saw him scowling at us before angrily motioning his men to do as they had been ordered.

"Ha. Well done, Bacon," I whispered.

He murmured in my ear, "While it makes me feel slightly safer, sir, I fear it may not waste enough time for the Professor to get here."

"Get here!" I hissed, "Surely he has left it too late?"

"Did I not hear you tell Herr Renner that he should not give up hope, sir?"

Fiddle sticks. The old rascal was right but before I could think of a clever answer he whispered, "I must leave you now, sir. But I shall return."

"Leave?" I blustered, noticing him fondling a couple of apples, "Where the blazes are you going? A blasted picnic?"

But he slipped away out of the room past Zwack's men who were busy removing their numerous scabbards, daggers and flintlocks. The whole process lasted a good ten minutes before the sheriff's men were satisfied that they had collected everything. One of the deputies came over to inspect me but I shook my head and showed him my empty belt so he went away and I thanked God that I had hidden the knives under my jacket.

At last the rigmarole was over and to my relief Bacon returned and sat back down as the magistrates began their questioning. Renner mumbled his way through his testimony, recounting his story in between frequently glancing at Zwack and his guffawing friends. Our humiliation at the hands of these louts was the last straw that morning and I wished that there was something we could do to turn the tables on them.

Once or twice I heard the courtroom door bang open and could not help but peep over my shoulder hoping beyond hope to see Van Halestrom heroically striding up the aisle with Renner's wife on his arm. But, of course, on both occasions it was merely another clerk coming in carrying a pile of papers.

After an hour, Renner was nearing the end of his testimony and the chief magistrate took over. "Now, Herr Professor, we must turn to an alleged letter sent to you by Herr Zwack containing an invitation to join the Illuminati. So far you have given a verbal testimony but without any written proof, it is impossible for us to evaluate the authenticity of your charges.

Obviously, if you can prove this attempted initiation it would indicate the accused's involvement. With this in mind you must understand the importance of this letter?"

Renner stared at the floor and sighed, "I do, sir."

"Then, Professor Renner I must ask, do you have the letter in question?"

Renner looked up at me, his despairing eyes welling with tears. He opened his mouth to speak but broke down and shook his head. By this point I had totally given up the ghost. So when the door at the back banged again I did not even look and kept my eyes firmly on Renner as he tried to speak. He glanced up again but this time his expression changed to one of pure astonishment. There was a stilted gasp from behind and the sound of hurrying footsteps but I still dared not look. The tension was unbearable and for a second I closed my eyes but when the sound of shouting voices filled the air and Bacon stood up next to me clapping his nands and calling out, "Bravo, sir. Bravo!" I had to open them and turn around.

Chapter 21

Race to the Grave

I have been extremely pleased to see Van Halestrom on several occasions in my life but watching him stride up the aisle of the packed courtroom with Renner's startled wife by his side that day was one of the best. A wave of excited gossiping swept through the hall and the bemused woman ran to join her husband at the stand. Renner threw his arms around her and they enjoyed a moment of tender embrace.

The Professor joined us looking a little less blasé than usual and panted, "So sorry I'm late, Gentlemen."

"Believe me, sir, your timekeeping could not be better," I could not help but exclaim as Bacon nodded in approval and pandemonium took hold round the room.

"Order! Order!" called the senior magistrate, "We will have order in the courtroom!" He cast a stern eye around the hall and slowly a hush fell over the crowd before he went on, "Professor Renner, I trust you are ready to continue. I'm sure I don't have to remind you that we had reached a rather important point in the proceedings?"

Renner nodded and let go of his wife who came and sat down by us. Zwack and his men anxiously muttered at the back as the magistrate continued, "Professor Renner, I believe I had just asked you if you had a certain letter?"

Renner hastily dug around inside his coat and brought out the folded note which a clerk relayed to the senior magistrate. There were stifled cries from behind and much whispering as the magistrates opened it out and frowned at one another.

While they deliberated the Professor nudged me in the ribs and murmured, "Are you ready, Sebastian?"

"Ready for what?" I asked but there was no time for him to answer as the magistrate banged his hammer again trying to control the growing chatter in the hall. "Order! Order! The court demands silence to pronounce its ruling."

"Ruling?" noted Bacon, "That was quick."

The magistrate managed to bring order to the room and straightened the neck of his robes before gravely beginning, "After inspecting this new evidence we have decided to mount an immediate investigation into charges of treason and unpatriotic membership of the Illuminati secret society and grant all necessary warrants for seizures, fines and arrests..."

There was a flurry of shouting and the magistrate had to bang his hammer several times to bring the crowd under control. He glowered round the hall before finishing, "So by the power vested in me by this court I hereby formally bring these proceedings to a conclusion..." There were more outraged shouts which almost drowned him out and he had to raise his voice over the furore, "Professor Renner, you are free to go!"

Renner crumpled with relief and had to grip the sides of the stand to prevent himself from toppling over.

"Ah ha, I expected as much," said the Professor, "The letter is cast-iron proof of Zwack's Illuminati membership and his efforts to initiate Renner. I have seen it for myself. That's why I asked Sebastian if he was ready." He nodded expectantly at me.

"For what?" I answered, shaking my head in confusion.

"To leave."

"Leave..? When..?"

The magistrate had to shout to be heard over the commotion and summoned, "Herr Zwack! We would like to see you in our privy chambers please. Now!"

"Now," nodded the Professor as another huge outburst of angry shouting erupted from Zwack's men.

I searched his eyes. Damn it! Why was there never time to argue? He took my arm and led me down the aisle, whispering in my ear, "Transport awaits us outside. It is imperative that we beat Zwack back to his house for he plans to destroy vital evidence hidden there incriminating the Order."

"Now?" I implored as we approached Zwack's snarling men bunching round the door.

"Yes, Sebastian. Now," repeated the Professor pushing me through them and out into the corridor.

We marched towards the exit as they piled from the courtroom behind us and I cursed under my breath, "Horse piss!" I had thought it was all over and that we were going home for a celebratory drink and a slap up meal. When would I get a rest? We strode out of the main doors seconds before our pursuers caught up and as the Professor led me up the street, I struggled for something to say and ended up blurting, "But why us, Professor? Is there no one else who can help?"

He stopped at my shoulder, answering breathlessly, "No. Not today, Sebastian. We're going to have to sort this out ourselves."

Zwack's men were almost upon us and came striding up. Thunder and lightning! I was sick of these bullies following us about everywhere and we were not in the courtroom any more.

"Stand back, pig dogs!" I roared, shoving my hands inside my jacket and grabbing the handles of my knives. The Professor also stuck his hand under his cloak and the first man hesitated as he reached us. The dandies behind him swore and committed oaths encouraging the idiot to take a step closer. That was far enough and I braced myself for action. Seeing Bacon bundling the three professors and Frau Renner into the waiting coach, I whipped out my weapons and brandished them in the chancer's face. The fool went to find his own, but quickly remembering they were back inside, backed down and raised his lacy cuffs.

"I thought so you cowardly piece of shit!"

Without taking my eyes off him and, making sure none of his friends were foolhardy enough to rush us, I called out, "Where's this transport you promised, Professor? We need it! Now!"

"Do not fear, Sebastian. Here it comes!"

Lo and behold, the unmistakeable clatter of hooves and wagon wheels rattled up behind us and I inched backwards. Hearing Van Halestrom clamber onboard, I glimpsed the footboard out of the corner of my eye, snarled once more at my foes, flourished my knives, turned about and leapt aboard the waiting cart.

"Go!" I yelled as the reins cracked and I heard a familiar woman's voice holler, "Yah! No stop till Berlin you bastards!"

I was thrown back in my seat half by surprise, half by the jolt and in a perfect position to see Zwack's men running after us. They quickly gave up with some kicking the cobbles and bellowing curses whilst a few ran back to their waiting carriages.

"No matter, Sebastian," mentioned Van Halestrom, catching his breath, "I think Bacon has drugged their horses. Apples I think he said."

I muttered a few confounded oaths of my own then slid my knives back into their holsters and peered around him to check the identity of our driver.

"You!" I hissed, seeing Francesca Nicola Kropotkin sitting on the other end of the seat furiously whipping the horses and flashing me an imperious stare.

"I might say the same thing, Herr *Blunder*kind!" she retorted and stuck out her tongue.

"What is *she* doing here, Professor?"

"*She* drives the cart, Sebastian," he laughed and slapped me on the back, "Beautiful Francesca has been helping me rescue Renner's wife. Now we must complete the next part of our mission. My dear, did you have time to find anything out?"

"Yes! We need an amulet or a ring or something else bearing the mark to get into Zwack's house. There will be guards but because so many come and go, they will not think it odd if a stranger seeks entry who shows the sign!"

I looked between them trying to keep up with the day's hectic events and harangued, "The sign? The mark? What... what is this now?"

"Remember the amulet, Sebastian: The serpent entwining the cross? It's the mark members of the Order use to gain entry into other initiates' houses. We need one to break into Zwack's house in Landshut before news of the court's ruling reaches there."

My mind raced for an answer to the conundrum. "Damn it man. You gave the one we had to Barruel."

"It is true, Sebastian, but think again. Didn't you tell me you had seen another somewhere else?"

I struggled to remember where when I suddenly recalled, "Of course! How could I forget? The chase from the rickety house. The man we killed that night on Francesca's *ridiculous* coach," I shot her a glare. "One of them wore a ring which bore the sign. But that was nearly a year ago. Francesca blew his head off and I paid some old hag to bury him. Surely he is gone?"

"It is the only chance we have, Sebastian. Now, how fast can you dig a grave?"

"A grave?" I cried, wondering if it would be my own.

"We may have to dig up your friend to take a look at him."

"Friend! Dig a grave? Take a look at him? Rescue the papers from Zwack's house? By God! Whatever next? Whatever next?"

Francesca frowned at me and the Professor stirred an eyebrow. Some friends they were. Were friends not the people who you relied upon to make everything better, not worse?

But so it was. We raced on through the twisty country lanes to the village where we had given the body of the headless agent to the old hag. Though our journey took us over four hours we still found something about which to argue the whole way and the three of us despondently got down from the footboard as night time fell over the neglected chapel graveyard. Francesca pulled out a lantern from the back of the cart and the Professor lit it with his flint box.

"But what if we can't find him?" I moaned, pulling up my collars and gazing around our latest inhospitable surroundings.

"Instead of problems, Herr *Blunder*kind, how about some solutions?" Francesca lifted the lantern, lighting her peevish leer.

"Perhaps we can work out where he is buried?" suggested the Professor, sniffing out into the darkness like a bloodhound.

"Then what?" I hissed, following his stare over the rows and rows of crooked headstones.

"Then we shall dig him up," he answered. *[23]

"Dig him up?" I wailed, "I am no gravedigger. I'm a history student who has not eaten all day and should be at home studying his Latin."

"There'll be no digging anyone up while I'm in charge," wheezed the old hag, emerging from behind the cart. "Who you after?" she coughed and, before anyone could tell her, answered herself, "Him with no head ain't it? Thought I recognised you." Her eyes darted about, "Yes... Recognised you I did," and she waved at the graveyard, "He's over there. But pay me you must."

---

23. **Illuminati Hunter & Grave Robbing.** In the first book I considered making the tenuous claim that Professor Van Halestrom may have been the inspiration for the character Abraham Van Helsing in Bram Stoker's classic gothic vampire tale *Dracula* (1897). The intriguing synthesis of themes also resonates through Mary Shelley's famous *Frankenstein* (1818) which features an oddly similar graverobbing scene and is set in Ingolstadt University. These strange coincidental paralells seem to provoke the question that the author's exploits were of such infamy that they entered local folklore and, as such, were used at a later date as a background for the fictional works noted.

She rested for breath giving the Professor the chance to prompt, "He wore a ring. It is important to us."

Her eyes narrowed and she slowly wiped her nose with the back of her hand. "... I see ... " she slyly croaked, "Then pay me *more* you must. Yes, yes. Pay me *much* more." She glanced between us and circled a finger over her head, urging, "Then follow me you must. Yes, yes. Follow me you must."

She shuffled off as we shared looks of happy surprise before trailing her over to a dank hovel which we had to stoop inside one by one. The three of us crowded round a smokey fire as the hag pulled down a box from a shelf and, after scratching about with her back to us, she replaced it then turned around holding out something. We all leaned in closer trying to get a better view amongst the dimness and there, on her filthy palm, was the ring. I could just about make out the bronze serpent winding round the cross and went to touch it but she yanked it away, wheezing, "So you want it do you?"

I went to remind the crone that we had already explained this but the Professor put a hand on my arm and asked, "Tell me, old woman, why did you take it off?"

She glared at him and spat, "'Tis mine to take it off. I've done nothing wrong. Nothing! 'Tis mine."

He gave her a beguiling smile and mentioned, "But you know what the symbol means? Do you not?"

He looked her right in the eye and she cowered back under her shelf, clasping the ring to her ragged clothes and gasping, "Everyone knows His mark. What of it? The beast has many marks. This mark - That mark. In the end they all mean the same: Evil. Yes, that's what they mean." Her eyes flashed about as though she expected Satan to leap out from the shadows. "Anyways, I don't want it here. 'Tis bad luck to have it. So take it you will." She came back into the light, holding it out and insisting, "But buy it you must."

The Professor nodded and went to take it.

"But pay me you *must*," she wheezed, clutching it back to her rags with both hands.

"How much?" he asked.

"Twenty thalers."

"Yes of course," he replied, patting his pockets until, eventually, his eyes fell on me, whereupon he said, "Sebastian."

"What? Me again? Twenty thalers?"

"Yes, Sebastian. Pay the woman."

She thrust out her hand and squeezed the ring to her bosom with the other. Struth. I rummaged around in my pockets and found my purse before counting out the coinage into her grasping fingers. When the last piece of silver had crossed her palm she gave Van Halestrom the ring and he left the hovel with a contented hum.

Francesca winked at me and impersonated, in a low voice, "*Yes, Sebastian. Pay the woman.*"

She tittered to herself and followed him outside. Beautiful but infuriating. Moments later we were back onboard the cart hurtling through the black countryside while she lashed the reins and the Professor examined the ring.

"Will it work, Professor?" I asked.

"It has to Sebastian. And there's only one way to find out. So we will know soon." He looked down the road and shouted out, "Landshut is only an hour away!"

"Right then!" I called back with facetious bravado, "Landshut it is then!"

Oh dear. We were definitely back on the road again but as far as I was concerned, travelling in exactly the wrong direction. For now we were heading straight to the heart of the beast: The house of Xavier Zwack.

Chapter 22

A Knock at the Door

It must have been five o'clock in the morning when we reached the town of Landshut. At last the weather had broken so we had spent much of the journey in the pouring rain. By now I had been awake almost twenty four hours but still felt no need for sleep. This was chiefly due to the troubling conversation that we had been having all the way there about breaking into Zwack's house. While Francesca had argued that it should be her, as a woman would be 'less threatening,' and the Professor that he should do it, as he would 'know what to look for,' I had spent the whole time dreading that they would change their minds and choose to send me into the home of an Illuminati leader to rifle through his belongings, knowing that the master of the house might return at any moment. Mercifully, in the end, it was decided that I was to wait outside with Francesca while the Professor committed the burglary. Van Halestrom estimated that we still had time before Zwack got back but we would have to hurry. He would certainly return today and it would soon be dawn.

Already knowing the house's location the Professor led us straight there and we pulled up in the growing twilight under a row of sheltering trees at the foot of a steep hill. As promised, at the end of the deserted street which climbed all the way to the brow of the hill, two men stood guarding an austere three-storey town house.

"Herr Zwack's residence," muttered Van Halestrom and pulled on the ring. He whispered, "This shouldn't take long. I'll see you in a bit," and dismounted.

I grabbed his hand on the side of the footboard and queried, "*A bit*, Professor? What shall we do if you do not return?"

He smiled and winked, "Trust me, Sebastian. Have I ever let you down before?"

With this he nodded reassuringly before walking off while Francesca gave me a belittling stare. I gave her one back and we both watched Van Halestrom confidently stroll up the hill. I hunched on the seat biting my nails as he approached the men and greeted them. They were too far away for us to hear what they were saying but I still leaned forward trying to catch a word amongst the gusting wind and rain. The Professor showed them the ring and one of them laughed and slapped him round the back.

"Go on, Professor," I whispered, certain that the deception was working.

The other guard knocked on the door and, while the three of them chatted away, it opened and an ugly-faced man poked his head out. Somehow I thought that I recognised his pugnacious features from somewhere but before I could remember he called over his shoulder and another man joined him. Shit! This one was Kolmer and he barked something at the guards who quickly grabbed Van Halestrom and bundled him inside the house. Damn it! The first man stuck his head back out and glanced up and down the street before slamming the door. Now I recognised him. It was the rat-faced little devil with the musket from the crossroads. I punched my fist into my hand.

"Thunder and lightning!"

"What are we going to do now?" hissed Francesca.

"I'm not sure if you recall, *Mademoiselle*, but I had already tried to ascertain that from the Professor before he left."

"Your famous sarcasm is useless little boy. We need answers not foolery."

"Then perhaps we should do what you suggested and send you in next as you will be *less threatening*?"

She reared up like a cat preparing to swipe a dog but before she could lash out we both heard the door slam again and ducked down in our seats. The rat-faced cur scurried around the side of the building, pulling up his collar against the foul weather and looking extremely suspicious.

She seethed under her breath, "Whatever we are going to do we need to do it fast. The Professor's in mortal danger. It's a matter of life and death."

"Is it, fair maiden? I had not noticed for I had been asleep," I jibed and we sat there smouldering at each other.

What could we do? We could not storm the door. There were only two of us and God knows how many reinforcements inside. I had but two daggers and my lady nothing more than a riding whip and an old lantern. I had also noticed, some time ago, that underneath her velvet cloak she was dressed in a dainty evening gown with more petticoats than Marie Antoinette's ladies-in-waiting and, as such, thoroughly overdressed for any type of street fighting, clambering over rooftops or sneaking through blasted windows. Curses! With all hope fading fast I tried to think where we could get help and thought out loud, "The police! Zwack is now a criminal. Surely we can find the local sheriff and demand that he raid the house."

She scowled at me before her expression slowly lifted, along with a painted eyebrow and she declared, "Mon Dieu. You're actually right."

I muttered something ungentlemanlike as she flicked the reins to quickly turn the cart about and we headed towards the centre of town. Before too long we found an old man in the street who told us where the local constable lived and five minutes later we were urgently banging on his door. The sleepy man appeared in his nightshirt rubbing his head and waved us inside. Being half asleep it took us an age to explain to him what was going on and, though he was thoroughly displeased to be woken so early, he eventually sent a young lad to fetch the sheriff. The suspense was maddening and I paced around his quarters praying that the Professor was safe while we waited and listened to the rain beating on the windows. Two nerve-wracking hours later the boy returned with the sheriff who waddled into the room shaking his tunic dry.

"Thank God you have come, sir," I fretted, "We must act with great haste to prevent a murder and catch an Illuminati agent red-handed."

He lumbered over to the table and lowered his sizeable rump into a chair then rubbed his chin. "The Illuminati eh?" he raised an eyebrow at the constable, "You don't get many of them round here."

"Oh, but you do, sir. Xavier Zwack is a wanted criminal known for his involvement with the Illuminati. You must mount a raid on his house at once. Our friend is held prisoner there and in terrible danger."

"Herr Zwack eh? He's a very respected gentlemen in this town. You want to be careful who you go around accusing of being a criminal."

"But he was in court yesterday in Munich and the magistrates found him..." I realised that I could not remember the exact details of the court's ruling.

"Yes, sir?" prompted the sheriff and grinned at the constable.

There was an impatient sigh from behind and Francesca sauntered past wearing her cloak about her naked shoulders to reveal the top of her frilly gown. She had also done something with her hair but before I could work out what it was, she was at the sheriff's side toying with his braided epaulette and purring, "Herr Sheriff, I'm sure that you and your constables are very busy men but you really should listen to my young companion here." She wiggled a finger at me and smiled down upon him,

"Although he is excitable and foolish he does know of what he speaks. Our friend is currently locked in Herr Zwack's house and needs you to set her free. And I should tell you, sir," she stroked her neck and carried on, "Our friend is a lot like me and will be very, very grateful for this favour." She ran her finger down her breast bone and leaned over him whispering something in his ear while her bosom heaved not two inches from his flustered face.

After a moment she pulled herself away and winked at him while he blabbered, "Right, constable, better get Michael, Eric and Herr Kroll, Thomas and little Peter too. Tell them to meet us in the town square."

I coughed and tapped my foot to remind her that we were in a hurry and she pouted, "Oh, Sheriff, as quickly as possible."

"As quickly as possible!" he spluttered and hauled himself from the chair pushing the constable out of the door with his stomach.

She clapped her hands and smiled triumphantly, "That's how you get help, Herr *Unter*kind," before following after them with a naughty grin. I gasped with exasperation and chased after her trying not to imagine what she had said.

Within five minutes the small brigade was lined up in the rainy square and the sheriff busied himself shouting at his men in between throwing Francesca amorous looks. When he was satisfied that his company was ready he marched them off and we boarded the cart and followed behind them back to the bottom of the hill.

The sheriff brought his men to a halt in the shelter of the trees and announced, "Now, men! Gather round. All we're here to do is extricate this lovely lady's friend from Herr Zwack's house." He winked hopefully at Francesca and finished his address, "Nothing more, so try to be polite lads. Remember, Herr Zwack's a very important man."

The men marched off and I quietly grumbled at Francesca, "What's going to happen when they find out our lady friend is a blasted man?"

"By that time we will be inside and it will be too late," she whispered but I noticed that her fingers were crossed behind her back. Damn it. She was as nervous as me. I had already noticed that the men were hardly armed at all, possessing only truncheons, night sticks and a few pairs of shackles and I worried that this feeble armoury would not be enough to overcome any stern resistance that we met at the door. At least there were five of them including the sheriff so I felt that we had strength in numbers and, as we trundled up the hill behind them I saw that, promisingly the guards were no longer there.

The sheriff reached the door and gave it a knock then waited patiently for a reply. Before too long Rat-face edged it open and looked out from the crack.

I clenched my fists as he called out, "What do you want?"

"We seek entry, sir," greeted the sheriff, "This young lady informs me that her dear friend is currently inside."

"Polite is right," I wittered from the side of my mouth, "This will never get us anywhere."

Predictably, Rat-face jeered, "You cannot come in without a warrant. As the sheriff you should know that."

The sheriff looked a little embarrassed but carried on undeterred, "Now see here, young man. We only want a quick look around to calm everyone's nerves then we will leave you in peace."

"My master says no one is to enter."

"Then we will talk to him. Now stand aside." At last he pulled himself closer to the door.

Rat-face nervously looked behind him and turned back, warning, "No! No one is to enter."

"Now, now, young man," continued the sheriff, "There's no need to be like that. That is, *if* you have nothing to hide?"

My eyes widened upon seeing the sheriff stick the end of his boot against the doorframe. Now we were getting somewhere. I jumped down from the cart and came up to the back of the constables gathered around the door. Francesca joined me and we stood on our toes watching the confrontation.

"I say again, sir, let us in or we shall use force."

"No!" shouted Rat-face, trying to shut the door but the sheriff wedged his boot in and barged his shoulder against it to keep it open. The rest of his men quickly joined in and after a brief struggle they managed to force their way inside.

"C'mon!" yelled Francesca, picking up her petticoats and leaping over the threshold where one of the constables had fallen over in the tussle. I jumped over him too and chased after the others into the house.

We raced down the central hallway and quickly came to a reception area lined with several doors. Rat-face fled down a stairwell at the far end and the sheriff ordered one of his men to go after him. The rest of us looked around the doors and the sheriff shrugged but Francesca did not ask what to do next. She stepped up to the nearest and flung it open but finding nothing there, opened the next where, to our surprise, we found two men sitting at a table playing cards as though nothing was out of the ordinary. Something was not right and I stepped into the room demanding, "Where is he?"

The men looked at one another and innocently shrugged their shoulders but I recognised them as the guards from outside and saw a couple of fresh droplets of blood on the floor leading to a large cupboard at the side of the room. Looking closer I noticed that one of the men had a black eye and bruises on his knuckles. They suddenly jumped from their chairs as the others piled in and I yelled, "The cupboard! Quick!"

The sheriff and his men quickly overpowered them and I pushed through the melee to the cupboard and flung open the door to find the Professor hunched up inside. He was gagged and tied and his face looked as though he had been badly beaten. Francesca came over and we dragged him out and sat him against the wall where I loosened the gag as she worked on the knots in the rope.

"You promised that you'd come back, Professor."

"Believe me, lad, I was just on my way," he gasped, shaking the ropes loose from his arms and shouting, "Downstairs! Kolmer is in the cellar with Zwack destroying the evidence!"

I did not need telling twice and bolted out the door then down the stairs which Rat-face had used to escape. It was pitch black at the bottom and I squinted around the gloom pulling out my knives. Despite my heavy breathing I could hear someone moaning and, as my eyes adjusted to the dark, I saw the silhouette of the constable sent down earlier lying in the light flickering from underneath a door. I rushed over and placed an arm across his back as he croaked, "They're in there," He motioned at the door before falling on his face with a gasp and I gave the handle a twist but it was locked. I was not going to be stopped now and, as the others came down behind me, I brought back my shoulder and threw my full weight into the door. I smashed into the room trying my damnedest not to fall over or drop my knives and slid to a halt finding Zwack and Kolmer throwing some papers onto a huge roaring fireplace.

"You!" snorted the man in black.

"That's right you bastard! I've come to pay you another visit!" I took a step towards him and wheeled my knives.

He chucked his handful of papers into the flames and unsheathed his sword. The others burst in with Francesca bravely leading the charge and fearlessly throwing herself at Zwack.

The cad smashed her to the floor and drew a large dagger preparing to engage the others. Kolmer was obviously startled and took a step back shouting, "Where's the box?"

Zwack parried a swipe from the sheriff's truncheon but managed to nod to the fireplace. I followed his eyes and there, next to the hearth, it was the box. Before I could move Kolmer swept it up and hissed at me, "If you want to catch me, boy, then you will have to die!"

With this intrigue he covered himself with his cloak then, to my utter astonishment, jumped straight into the flames. Holy Mother of God! Surely he was dead? All I could do was gaze at the roaring fire while the others overwhelmed Zwack in the corner. I glanced over to see them wrestling him to the floor and Francesca punching him in the face while the Professor helped the sheriff and his men put him in shackles.

"After him, lad!" yelled the Professor.

I took a step towards the flames but the heat drove me back.

"Trust me, Sebastian!" He ordered and grappled with Zwack, shouting, "After him, lad! Now!"

Damn it! I leaned forward and put my arm over my face, muttering, "C'mon Seb. You can do this." Before I had time to convince myself that maybe I could not, I took a deep breath, closed my eyes and jumped into the fire.

*24

---

24. **The 'Illegal' Raid On Xavier Zwack's House.** On the 11th October
1786 an illegal raid took place at the house of high-ranking Illuminati member Xavier Zwack (codename Cato) at Landshut in Bavaria. The reason for
its illegality has always been difficult to ascertain, so the author's account
gives us fresh insight into an event which has long been contested by historians. There is no doubt that the police raided the house and that arrests and
confiscations took place including the seizure of secret documents, codes,
plans, letters, depositions, membership lists, seals, amulets, special exploding
strongboxes and other evidence, Xavier Zwack was later freed and subsequently escaped from the authorities when they again tried to press charges
and fled to Gutenberg in neighbouring Austria. One way or another the raid
stands out as an critical turning point in the authorities' fight against the Bavarian Illuminati which, by this time, was considered a 'national emergency'
and, because of Zwack's high-profile as a government lawyer, it was a huge
blow against the Order and the pressure upon them to retire underground or
leave the country altogether reached a climax.

Chapter 23

The Caves of Landshut

I landed in a cave bathed in the dappling light of the flames
roaring behind me. Good God! I was still alive. Having not
thought what I would do had I survived, I stood there glancing
around momentarily before moving away from the heat on
my back. Kolmer was not dead. It was an escape route. There
were two rows of burning torches set along the glistening walls
running to a hole at the far end of the cave. I gripped the handles
of my knives and gasped, "After the bastard you idiot!"

I pelted down the cave and through the hole but ten strides into
the darkness, realised that I would have to go back to get a torch.
"C'mon Seb. He's getting away. He's getting away," I fretted
and dashed back into the cave, noticing that the holder nearest
the exit was empty. Of course! Kolmer had taken it. I grabbed the
next torch along, stashed one of the knives in my jacket and shot
back through the hole. I found myself barrelling down a narrow,
winding tunnel carved through the rock. Fortunately, it was large
enough for me to run along and, as the bottom was reasonably
flat, I could keep up a blinding rate. But after sprinting a hundred
yards I started to wonder how long it was and, more importantly,
where it would lead? *[25]

Even though I was tearing along there was still no sign of
anyone, so I upped my pace. I was young and fit back then so I
fairly bolted through the shadowy tunnel, leaping over the small
rocks with my knife at the ready and my torch showing the way.
Although I was as nervous as a startled rabbit, I was as hungry
as a wolf for revenge and much bolstered by the fact that the evil
bastard had run away from me.

25. **Xavier Zwack's Illuminati Hideout Landshut.** Landshut is a medium
sized town in southern Bavaria lying amongst the foothills of the Alps. The
town is built around the river Izar but there are several sizable buildings on
a large promontory. If S. Drechsler's recollections are correct one can only
assume that the action described took place somewhere under this hill.

"C'mon Seb! Let's catch the fiend," I grunted and sprinted off into the dark.

After a couple of minutes I cursed my luck when I came to a junction and had to stop to catch my breath and work out which path to choose. I held my torch into the mouth of the adjacent catacomb, seeing that it led upwards. Surely Kolmer would be going upwards: Upwards to an exit. "Yes. That's right Seb."

I hesitated, pointing the torch back down the other way and cursing my indecision, "C'mon Seb. You're wasting time. You're wasting time."

In between my panting I became aware of the faint sound of trickling water and, in the torchlight round my feet saw a tiny glimmering stream winding its way in the same direction that I had been going. A voice whispered in my head, 'Down. Kolmer travels down,' and I pelted off down the tunnel.

I blundered deeper into the twisting catacombs for what seemed like an age and, though, it was probably more like ten minutes, I began to have doubts about following my instincts. So certain had I been that the voice in my head was right, I had not thought what I might do if it were wrong. My concentration slipped and I banged my foot into a rock, annoyingly twisting my ankle. Blast! I had to slow down and I hopped along cussing myself. As I did I was distraught to find the entrance of yet another tunnel. Shit. I peered round the darkness like Theseus chasing the Minotaur in the labyrinth, but with no Ariadne to give me the life-saving twine, if I came across any more junctions I might have trouble finding my way back out again.

My torch flickered dangerously low. Thunder and lightning! That was if I did find my way back out again.

"C'mon Seb. Purpose," I muttered and, seeing that the tiny trickle had become a small stream, I once again chose the downward path. I held up my spluttering torch and splashed off doing my best to avoid the puddles. I did not like getting my feet wet but I was determined to follow my instincts. A little further on, with my torch frighteningly low, I thought that I could hear the sound of fast moving water and, after another hundred feet,

I was certain that I could make out a huge river roaring up ahead.

What was this? I took a few more steps but when I saw the reflection of another torch on the tunnel wall round the next bend, I dived behind a rock trying to hide the glow from my own. I stared out into the dark and after a couple of seconds I saw the light again but, this time, I also heard voices. It had to be Kolmer, and by the sounds of it he now had company. I tiptoed back up the tunnel and leant my torch behind a boulder not wanting to put it out but realising that I would need it if I came back. I gulped and tried to control my beating heart which was pounding like the water over my shoulder.

"Do it for Karl," I murmured and returned to my hiding place trying to make out what the voices were saying but it was impossible because of the noise. I slipped down the tunnel hugging the shadows and feeling my fingers start to sweat round the handle of the knife. Along with the roaring the light steadily grew until I realised that the voices were shouting at each other and I edged up to a large rock and peeped over the top. Ten steps ahead of me the tunnel opened out into a vast cavern filled by a churning pool and, leaning over it with his foot on a pile of boxes, Rat-face held out an immense lantern with a lamp stick. On the far bank Kolmer was bullying his men to load more boxes into a pair of wheelbarrows and, high above us all, a mighty cascade blasted out from a jagged fissure in the side of the cave and thundered down onto the water below.

"Come on you swine!" shouted Kolmer above the din, "If you're not quick the rainwater will fill the pool and you will all drown!"

"But not me, master, eh?" squeaked Rat-face.

"No. Not *you*, Hermann," smirked Kolmer, "We need you to lure the children into the coach with your good looks."

Damn them! This was it. I inched forward keeping my head down so they could not see me from the far side and got ready to deal with Rat-face first. I skulked up behind him with my knife at the ready but as I approached a face appeared at the bank between his feet and gasped, "Behind you!"

Curses! There was another man in the water passing the boxes to the other side. Rat-face spun round blinding me with the lantern and whipped out a dagger from his belt. I feigned a thrust at him but instead kicked his friend in the chin and sent him flailing over the edge. Rat-face took his chance and lunged at me but as he stepped in I swept his ankles away with my leg, flipping him onto his back and making him spill the lantern. Before he could get up I stamped on his wrist, forcing him to let go of the knife then I fell on him, driving my knee into his neck. My anger exploded and I half choked the rodent to death then turned him over and pulled him up by his hair to face his *master* one last time. I made sure Kolmer was looking before slitting the vermin's throat with one decisive swipe. Rat-face gasped with deathly surprise and I threw his head down then stood up pointing the knife at Kolmer and bellowing at the top of my voice, "You're next pig dog! I'm taking you with me to Hell!"

Without looking I jumped into the pool and smacked awkwardly against the unconscious man who was floating face up in the gloom. I went up to my chin but, as the bottom was higher than I had expected, my foot painfully jammed between two boulders and I could instantly tell that I was trapped. No! I tried to shift it but it was useless. Damnation! I was stuck fast.

Kolmer saw my predicament and cackled down from above, "Then it seems you're going there on your own, my friend! Ha, ha, ha! Oh yes. All on your own. No, wait! You can give Herman our regards. Ha, ha, ha!"

"Damn you!" I yelled, struggling to drag myself to the bank behind and, in my efforts, dropped the knife in the churning waves.

His eyes sprang open and he yelled at one of his men, "Go in and get him!"

The older man glanced at the thundering cascade, procrastinating, "But, Master Kolmer, like you said, the water is rising so fast... surely he will die."

"Get in fool!" ordered the man in black and raised his whip above his head.

The man watched me helplessly splashing around and quibbled, "Then I will take off my boots first, sir."

He proceeded to take off his shoes before arranging them neatly on the bank then bit his knife and hesitantly lowered himself into the ripples. I yanked at my foot, almost tearing it off with the effort. The pain was excruciating but I knew that I must get away or die. He pushed himself from the rocks and, as he slowly swam towards me spitting out water past his blade, I scrabbled for the other stiletto inside my jacket and slid it out. The coot had no idea that I was armed and foolishly carried on until he was two feet away then wafted his hands about to steady himself. I looked coldly at him and as he went to grab his knife I stabbed him underneath the splattering waves. For some reason murdering this old chump like this made me feel sick and I let go of the handle as the knife tumbled from his mouth and he slowly slipped below.

"Devils' eyes! Where can I find a decent servant?" seethed Kolmer, kicking one of his men up the arse and shouting down at me, "You might be well-trained, boy, but it won't save you!" He glared at the waterfall pounding a dozen yards from my face and gloated, "Nothing will save you now!"

He slapped one of his lackeys around the head and roared, "Hurry, oaf, or I'll throw you in too! I don't want to keep the coach waiting. You can leave the rest here."

I flung my body around desperately trying to free myself as the unconscious man drifted into my face and I had to push his body away. It was becoming impossible to keep my chin above the waves and I spat out a mouthful of water and wrenched at my leg but it was no good. My shoe was rammed in tight. Why had God sent me here to die like this? I glimpsed one of Kolmer's men pushing his wheelbarrow away and the others filling the last one with the remaining boxes. "No!" I yelped.

Kolmer herded his men towards the mouth of a tunnel at the back of the cavern but had time to grin at me floundering in the shadows. I caught his eye and spat out another mouthful of freezing water, coughing, "Tell me!"

He stopped and stared at me unsure of what I meant.

"...If I am to die I want to know why!" I stuck out my chin, trying to stay afloat and spluttered, "Tell me!"

His wolfish eyes lit up and he came back to the pool's edge, snorting, "Don't you see, boy? Dearie, dearie, me! Even when your fate is - how do you Bavarians say - so ironic?"

"What... do you mean?" I gasped through the waves, "...Tell me!"

He put his foot on the bank, conceitedly resting his arm on his knee. "Why, boy, it is obvious! Have you not worked it out yet? Just like you drowning here we are going to drown the world. But we are going to drown it in money. Ha, ha, ha! *Our* money boy! *Our* paper money: the money that bears *His* mark!" He clenched his fist and even through the darkness I could see his ring bearing the devilish serpent wrapped round the cross. He called out over the crashing deluge, "Don't you see, boy? Then no one will be able to keep their heads above the water! Ha, ha! As above so below, my friend! As above so below! He turned to go and I saw him check the mysterious box under his coat.

"The stone," I gurgled, swallowing another mouthful.

His laugh reverberated around the cavern, "Ha, ha! *That* part of the puzzle you will have to work out for yourself! But you'd best be quick, *brother*. Oh yes! Very quick indeed. Ah, ha, ha, ha! Goodbye, my friend! Goodbye!"

He grabbed the last torch from the top of a boulder before disappearing through the mouth of the tunnel and plunging me into darkness.

I tried to shout, "I'm not your blasted friend, pig dog!" but my mouth filled up again and I choked and coughed as the blackness surrounded me and the water relentlessly pummelled down next to my head. I thrashed my arms about one final time and tried with all my fading strength to jerk my foot out, pitifully wrenching it from side to side but to no avail. I was sure that the pool was rising even faster and that the thundering cascade was pounding ever harder.

All of a sudden my limbs flooded with fatigue and freezing cold poured into the core of my being. I felt myself give up as another wave washed over me. I choked and spluttered trying to gasp what I was certain would be my last breath, for I knew that I was going under. I could not hold my head up any longer and, after helplessly flailing about one last time, I sunk beneath the waves. It was no use. I was going to drown. *[26]

---

26. **Illuminati & Debt.** Conspiracy theorists have long held that a secretive cabal controls the supply of major world currencies and, by this means, exercises power over global economic activity and the distribution of wealth. S. Drechsler's reminiscences seem eerily in line with such conspiratorial ideas concerning the purposeful over-production of money to induce debt.

Chapter 24

Dead Man's Shoes

My head plunged beneath the waves and I was cocooned in a throbbing silence. All I could hear was the muffled sound of the water crashing above me and my blood pounding in my ears. I searched my freezing body for any remaining strength and in desperation thrust my head down even further. Reaching below me I felt the top of my shoe and grasped around amongst the rocks until, somehow, I felt my hand brush across the henchman's knife. There was nothing else for it. I picked it up and stabbed it under my shoe's buckle. I screamed through a stream of bubbles as the blade sliced agonisingly into my foot and I tried to slit the tongue apart. With my last remaining effort I managed to tear a tiny split in the leather and, one second before I passed out, the blade ripped past the buckle. Even though I was half unconscious I knew that I had gained the necessary inches to wriggle out and, with my last thimbleful of life, I pushed down on my other foot and pulled myself free.

I bobbed above the water's surface gasping the air as if it was my first breath and blindly thrust out a hand in the darkness searching for the bank. I floated across the splattering waves and, just as I started to sink, finally felt the reassuring face of a boulder in my hand.

"God wants me... to live," I coughed and pulled myself to safety. I violently retched up a belly full of water and clung to the boulders trying to get my breath. Then, as soon as I was able, I yanked myself onto the bank and crashed down on my stomach where I felt something uncomfortably wedging underneath me. I quickly realised that it was the dead man's shoes and lay there for a moment panting and staring about the pitch black until, feeling a mighty rage flooding my depths, I sat up, stuffed the knife inside my jacket, wriggled off my other shoe then grabbed the dry ones beside me and pulled them on. I took one more trembling breath before lifting myself up and staggering off. I was going to kill that son of a bitch even if I had to go to Hell to do it and, at least, when I got there I was going to have dry feet.

I fumbled around in the darkness but soon found the exit and, a short way along this next tunnel, stumbled to a halt when I saw daylight shining on the walls ahead. Where was I now? I crept forward until I was sure that the coast was clear then sped off again. Twenty yards further on, I paused once more upon seeing the bottom of a misty, wooded valley outside the mouth of the cave. It had stopped raining and, unable to hear anything beyond the shadows, I cautiously moved off again until, at last, I stepped out into the light.

"Thank you for saving me God," I breathed and darted off between the dripping trees. I barely had time to get used to the fact that I was still alive when the next awful part of my story began. For, as I crept through the forest I caught sight of Kolmer's black coach in a small clearing up ahead and his remaining men lifting the last boxes onto a wagon. My attention was drawn to the wagon when I noticed that, aside from the other packages bulging underneath its canvas, I could make out the tell-tale shape of an obelisk. My God! Kolmer must have retrieved it from Louisenlund. The Professor was right. They were going to hold another ritual.

The man in black pulled himself up on the lamp next to the coach's doorway, growling, "We're late you dogs! If we do not reach our destination by nightfall I'll thrash the lot of you!" He slammed the door shouting, "Quick! Quick!" and his driver cracked his whip, guiding the team of six black horses up a shale road leading from the clearing. Watching the coach rattle away I had to hug a tree to stop myself from falling over when I heard a boy's voice squeal from inside, "Help! Please!"

"Oh no, not again," I gasped as the three men hurriedly loaded the last of the cargo onboard the wagon before abandoning their wheelbarrows and clambering on the footboard. With a loud cry they raised the four white horses and followed after their master.

"Now I cannot fail," I grimaced, pushing myself from the tree and, keeping my head down amongst the bracken and bushes, ran up behind the wagon. Seeing that the men were concentrating on the road, I sprinted up to the back and lifted the canvas then dragged myself aboard.

I shuffled around in the dark keeping as quiet as possible but realised that my face was pressed against the disgusting stone penis and pushed myself away so fast that I knocked over a stack of books, causing a large casket to crash down next to my face. Terrified that I would be discovered I lay as stiff as a plank and held my breath. While my eyes shot around in the dark I noticed that the casket had fallen open and inside was a powder charge wrapped in greased paper. Good God! It was an exploding strongbox of the kind that I had seen in my training. *[27]

After a moment I figured that I had not been heard so I grabbed the charge and stuffed it in my jacket pocket. I patted myself down then found the knife and got it out. There were three of them and one of me. I had to strike now before we caught up with Kolmer. I pushed myself off my chest but the wagon bumped through a pothole sending me slapping back to the floor. When I felt someone lift up the canvas ahead I coiled up in the shadows pressing my face against the cursed stone. Damn it!

27. **Illuminati & The Exploding Strongbox.** In the official records several exploding strongboxes of the variety seen by the author were reportedly confiscated in the raid at Xavier Zwack's house. S. Drechsler's account details the charge contained within the box's mechanism and this would seem to be borne out by existing histories. The charge would have been big enough to destroy the contents of the box whilst also maiming the person who tried to open it. (See footnote 24.)

I thought of the boy trapped in the coach and clenched the handle of the knife. It was time for action.

Right on cue, the wagon banged over one last set of potholes before quickly gathering speed and soon we were briskly rattling along. I figured that we had come to the top of a hill and had started down the other side. Sure enough, I heard the driver holler at the horses and felt him lean on the brake. I pulled myself to the side of the wagon and peeped out from under the canvas. The three men were all sat up front facing forward and, as I poked my head a little higher, I saw that we were bearing down a steep road cut into the side of a valley and,, sweeping through the bends up ahead, was Kolmer's black coach.

This was my chance. I had to be merciless. These bastards knew that the boy was in the coach. They knew what was going to happen to him. They were as good as dead right then. I climbed out from under the canvas and crept up behind them, edging along the side of the devilish stone with the knife in my hand. When I got two feet away I steadied myself as we bounced over some more bumps and almost screamed when the nearest man turned to watch something go by. That was close enough. Remembering that I must be decisive and deadly, I pulled back the knife then rammed it into the side of his neck. He quivered horribly in his seat but I concentrated on my task and whipped the blade out fast enough to do exactly the same to the pig in the middle. The driver realised what was going on and glared round at me amidst the stunted screams of his confederates. But it was already too late for him and I slayed him in exactly the same brutal fashion, skewering his neck as I had been taught. He hopelessly clutched his spraying throat with his freehand and I recognised his contorting face from the crossroads.

"Die scum!" I hissed, grabbing the reins from his other hand and elbowing his twitching carcass into the road.

I pulled myself into his empty place and viciously kicked the other two off their seats, having to stamp on the last one's hands to get him to fall away. The back wheel banged over his corpse as I released the brake and cracked the reins pushing the horses to a gallop. Damn them all!

The wagon lurched forward, rapidly picking up speed and I was soon hurtling down the road. I stuffed the knife back inside my jacket as we thundered on and, obsessed by the thought of catching Kolmer, I pushed the team round the next corner so hard that the wagon's wheels began to vibrate with the strain. I heard the obelisk slide across the back and smack into the side but relentlessly lashed at the reins to bring my lead horses up to the rear of his coach. At last the driver noticed me and yelled out, "Herr Kolmer!"

The fiend instantly appeared at the window and saw me. "You again!" he bellowed as his eyes filled with fury and the child screamed from inside.

"Yes me, pig dog! I'm back to take you to Hell!"

He roared to the driver, "What are you waiting for, fool?" and the startled man lashed his horses pushing the team to a gallop. But I still had the momentum and, seeing the road opening ahead, I stood up on the footboard hollering at mine for more speed. The brutes surged on once again giving me all they had and steadily pulled us level. I glanced inside the black coach as I passed and saw Kolmer clutching the sobbing child to his waist and holding a sword across his throat. Blast! Now the next terrifying prospect: We flew neck and neck into a series of tortuous bends and, before I knew it, I was being forced to the outside of the road with the steep banks of the gorge flashing by hundreds of feet below. I tried to keep us from going over but Kolmer's coach swerved into me, pushing the wagon precariously close to the edge.

The driver sneered at me and I heard Kolmer scream, "Careful man!" but he purposefully barged the coach into the wagon and drove my front wheel off the road. By now I was virtually leaning against the coach and when the bend sharply tightened I hoisted myself up on the lamp next to the door as the wagon tipped and, in one terrifying moment, fell over the edge and plummeted into the gorge. I hung onto the lamp for dear life and watched in awe as the wagon and the team of screaming horses tumbled into the ravine horribly tearing themselves apart. Then, with one almighty crash, the obelisk flew into the air and smashed into a million pieces on a huge boulder.

"Satan's eyes!" roared Kolmer leaning from the window and staring in disbelief. He shot a glare past me at the driver and bellowed, "You'll pay for that dog! Slow down!"

The driver went to pull on the brake but I managed to kick it out of his hand and haul myself up onto the seat. I pulled out my knife but he elbowed me in the guts, knocking the wind out of me and making me drop the blade. My knees buckled and I went down on all fours as the knife fell off the footboard. I looked up to see his boot kick me in the face and I crashed on to my back with my head hanging perilously next to the wheel. He flicked the reins and raised his boot to finish me off. This was it. Surely I was going to die.

Chapter 25

The Whip Cracks

The driver snarled at me as he raised his heel to kick me off the footboard and kill me for sure. But before I had time to scream there was an ear-splitting crack and Kolmer's whip wrapped three times round his neck. The terrified man clutched at his throat as Kolmer braced himself in the coach's open doorway, incredibly holding the child by the hair in one hand and tugging his whip with the other. With a huge yank he dragged the driver from his seat and launched him screaming headfirst into the rocky gorge. After snorting at his devilish work, in one horrid movement, he hauled the child over his head and threw him on the roof then swarmed along the side of the coach like a huge black spider before jumping into the driver's seat and grabbing the reins. It all happened so fast that I was only pulling myself up on my elbows as he glared down on me.

"You don't know what you are up against, boy!" He reached behind him and dragged the wailing child across the roof then manhandled the waif under his arm. "I have a covenant with the one true celestial master," he snorted, sticking out his chin with incredible arrogance, "I have delivered Him so many souls that He will only let one who is prepared to give his own take mine. So you will have to die to kill me! That's right, boy. You'll have to go to Hell!"

He cleverly pulled on the brake with his heel then clutched the boy to him and sniffed his hair with disgusting relish. But the child bit his ear and forced him to let go then clambered back onto the roof. Seizing my opportunity I kicked off the brake and, as we jolted forward, pulled myself to my knees and fiercely head butted the bastard in the balls. His eyes crossed as he reeled backwards and I managed to grab his legs and drag him down.

We wrestled on the footboard as the coach plummeted down the hill and he bit my cheek goading me into such fury that I broke loose and repeatedly smashed him in the face then wrenched him up to finish him off. But as I pulled my fist back in front of his blooded nose, I heard a scream and turned to see the boy about to fall off the side of the coach as we swerved uncontrollably around another bend.

"No!" I yelled, frantically hauling myself onto the seat then throwing my body along the roof with my hand out as the coach careered round the corner so fast that it almost toppled over. I watched in desperation as he lost his grip and flew off the roof but, at the last moment, I flung out my fingers to grab his hand and pulled him back from the brink. I swept him to my chest and braced my feet against the luggage rack only to see Kolmer kick out the pin connecting the horses to the hitch. He flashed me a wicked grin before dragging himself over the backside of the closest animal and driving his heels into its flanks. Damn it!

To my horror the team of horses galloped away leaving us dangerously swerving about in their wake. It was no good. We were obviously going to crash and the coach veered inevitably towards the side of the road. There was no time to think and I clutched the boy to my chest then hurled myself off the back of the coach. I flew through the air and tried to land on my feet but it was impossible and my legs crumpled beneath me the moment I smashed down onto the road. I slid along tearing myself to shreds but with the child cradled in my arms and, hearing an almighty crash, scarcely had time to glimpse the coach smash through a low wall at the side of the road before it disappeared into the gorge in an explosion of masonry.

I ground to a halt inches from the side of the precipice and lay there in some agony until, suddenly remembering the child on my chest, yanked myself onto my elbows to see his bewildered face gawping back at mine. Thank Christ! He was still alive!

I sprang onto my skinned knees and held him out before me. Was he all there? Yes! He seemed to be; ten fingers, two ears, two arms, two legs and two wild blue eyes staring back at me in absolute terror. I struggled to my feet and turned to see Kolmer thundering down the valley pushing his team of black horses on with a barrage of blasphemies and curses. God knows where he was going? But wherever it was I knew that I had to stop him. Snapping from my stupour I knelt back down in front of the child and grabbed his shoulders, looked him right in the eyes and demanded, "Can you understand me?" He nodded nervously. "Go home now!" I shouted, "Run! Go back to Landshut and find the constable's house. Tell him what has happened."

He gazed vacantly at me with tears filling his eyes so I shook him trying to get him to understand.

"Go now!" I urged and pointed behind him but much to my surprise he threw his arms around my neck and hugged me for all he was worth. I hesitated for a second before tightly hugging him back. After a moment I held him away by his shoulders and repeated, "Go now! Don't look back! Do you understand?"

He put a finger to his lip then nodded and slowly turned to go. I watched him uncertainly meander away then blurted, "Stay in the shadows boy!" That did the trick and he peeked at me before pelting off. I waited till he had disappeared round a bend before throwing a hand down to steady myself and gasped from my deepest depths, "Thank you God for protecting us."

I looked myself over. My jacket was ripped to pieces and there was skin hanging off my elbow weeping blood. I wobbled to my feet seeing that my left hip was also torn to shreds and, when I wiped my forehead, saw more blood on my hand and big red stains all over my tattered clothes. Heavens above. I looked like a soldier returning from war. I guessed that I was. But I was not home yet. So I tentatively brushed myself off before turning the other way and hobbling down the road.

An hour or so later a cart rolled past travelling in the same direction. After taking pity on me the driver, a farmer off to market, offered to give me a lift. Being so overcome by the heat of battle I idiotically refused him at first but quickly realising how fortunate this coincidence was, I soon saw sense and joined him on the front seat.

Looking back now I am sure that this lucky meeting might have actually saved my life. For by then on that extraordinary day, I had been awake for forty eight hours and not eaten for as long, I was badly injured and I had been through the most tumultuous events of my life. I was utterly exhausted and, with all these contributing factors weighing heavily on me, I now believe that I would have suffered badly, even died had I fallen asleep by the roadside and not met with that charitable traveller when I did. I was so consumed by rage and my determination to keep up the the pursuit that I did not consider my own frailty but, in truth, I had to rest and once aboard I soon fell asleep as the cart lazily bumped down the road.

I was broken from my slumber by the farmer shaking my shoulder and I rubbed my eyes. Where was I now? Night had fallen while I had been asleep which meant that I had done so for nearly a whole day and I looked around to discover that we had arrived outside the walls of, what I estimated to be, a sizeable city. We were slowly rolling between two lines of covered wagons and their occupants who were preparing to set up camp on a small field. I rubbed my eyes again trying to wake myself up as the terrifying memories from the past two days returned to haunt me in a storm of harrowing recollections. Good God. How was I even here? I refocused and shook my head, murmuring, "Where are we?"

"Passau, my sleepy friend," replied the farmer, "The farmer's market where we can get shelter and something to eat."

We soon pulled up and dismounted and the generous man busied himself introducing me to his friends and relatives then saw to it that I was fed and bandaged. Fortunately, these decent folk were of such kindly disposition that they did not enquire about the circumstances which had brought me to be stranded on the road looking like I had been to hell and back. Though I could tell they were curious they seemed to understand that, whatever it was, it was obviously of some gravitas and did not pry. So, luckily I did not have to tire myself out any further having to explain. God knows what they would have done if I had? Probably dropped down dead or turned me over to the city's watchmen simply because of the number of men that I had so brutally slain. I was now a murderer of some magnitude and, as I sat with the farmers' families watching them innocently chat and play instruments round the campfire, I self-consciously glanced about thanking God that they could not read my mind. I shuddered at the thoughts myself but remembering the heinous crimes of my victims, I felt they had got exactly what they deserved and tried to dispel any natural feelings of remorse.

Feeling a little better after my rest and something to eat, I went to relieve myself behind some bushes and stood there gazing out amongst the fires, wagons and resting animals. Good Lord, I had done well to find myself in the company of such helpful and decent folk. I was about to thank God yet again for looking over me and guiding me to this haven of tranquillity when I almost soiled myself upon hearing Kolmer's spiteful voice growl from somewhere behind me, "So, if I win you will tend my horses?"

I stood as rigid as a fence post and turned to see him crouching next to a fire not ten yards away preparing to throw a horseshoe at a spike in the ground. He sneered at one of the men watching nearby, "That is the wager, my simple friend. Don't dare to breach it as I have had a long day already and am extremely vexed."

The man grunted in agreement before Kolmer confidently threw the horseshoe round the spike where it clattered down on top of the others.

"Then tend my horses you shall, fool," smirked the bastard and nodded at his team of black glistening horses which I now saw standing some distance away.

Shit! I squatted down in the shadows feverishly stuffing my manhood back inside my trousers. This time he was alone and I was surrounded by people who might actually help me fight him. More importantly, I had the element of surprise. But what was I to do? Then I remembered the explosive charge in my pocket and fumbled it out. Kolmer was stood with his back to me warming his hands by the fire and I spotted a small axe on a chopping block a few yards behind him. That would do. I took a few steps and leaned forward aiming the charge at the fire. It was a tricky shot from where I was, maybe twelve feet, but something told me that I could do it.

"C'mon Sebastian," I whispered and bit my lip as I chucked the package through the air. I held my breath as it missed Kolmer's leg by two inches before landing in the flames but the villain saw it and spun on his heel. I dashed over to the axe and grabbed the handle only to hear a terrifying crack as his whip lashed tightly round my wrist. Searing pain burned down my arm and I looked up to see the man in black glower at me like the devil incarnate as the charge exploded in the fire behind him, sending an enormous burst of burning orange sparks into the air. Curses! He did not even blink but dragged me towards him, reeling me in like a fish.

"Damn you, you dog!" I swore, furiously wriggling my arm around but it was useless. I lost my balance on the damp grass and took two faltering steps closer, waggling the axe like a fool.

"Ha, ha!" He jeered, "Now you are mine, boy!"

Chapter 26

Tug of War

Kolmer's wolfish eyes shone in the firelight as he dragged me towards him with the whip and flashed his grinning teeth, "Come to Papa, boy!"

Holy Mother of God! What could I do? Fight! That was what I could do. "I'm no boy!" I roared and grabbed the axe with my other hand then frantically sawed it across the leather and managed to cut it in two.

"Curse you!" he roared as the whip dropped limply to the floor and he gathered it in. I fell onto one knee as it released but forced myself back up as he got ready to strike again. I took a defiant step towards him but with one hair-raising 'snap!' he twirled the whip twice round my neck. I almost passed out with the pain but dug my heels in and grabbed the beastly thing then sawed at it again before quickly going through.

"Satan's eyes!" he roared, retrieving it once more and nervously glancing about. The men crowding round us were holding back but I sensed that they might intervene at any moment. I unwound the length from my neck while Kolmer circled me before savagely lashing me round the face. This time I caught the whip and held it taught between us as the blood streamed from my cheek. His eyes narrowed at this and I dropped to the floor, pinning it under my knees and raging, "I won't give up you bastard!" then chopped it in half with a proper cut. 'Smack!' He dragged back what was left but seeing that it was practically useless, scowled at it before throwing it away and unsheathing his sword.

Finally one of the bigger men stepped in, peacefully holding up his palms but the man in black snorted and heartlessly ran him through. The wounded man fell on his side and while Kolmer flashed the sword at the others to hold them at bay, he hissed at me, "See you in Hell, boy!" before running to a nearby grazing horse and skilfully jumping into the saddle then galloping off.

In the commotion someone came over and threw an arm around me but I was so consumed by the red mist that I shook him off, stuffed the axe in my belt and unsteadily got to my feet before staggering off towards Kolmer's horses, wiping the blood from my face and preparing to carry on the chase. Keen to see their friend avenged the farmers gathered around to help me mount up and pick out the best three horses from the six. We calculated that this would be enough for me to alternate without taking too many to handle and, though the animals were tired, there was no alternative. So, within minutes, I was cantering the small team of horses away from the camp with the farmers' shouts of encouragement fading into the night.

The men had told me that Kolmer had ominously claimed that he was travelling to the 'Ends of the Earth' and his journey would take him east. He had also bragged that he carried 'A great treasure.' Blabbering idiot. Now I was certain that he had the stone. Though at that moment it was irrelevant and it would not have mattered if he was delivering his whore some flowers. I wanted him dead and nothing could have stopped me from going after him so I chased off into the night with the lights of the city and potential safety disappearing behind me.

Looking back now I choke in horror at the very thought of these impetuous decisions. But such was my state of mind that I did not understand how possessed by rage I had become. For, I was drunk with rage. Yes. It was like being drunk. I constantly found myself mumbling furious obscenities while I pounded along and repeatedly imagined killing the fiend in a thousand different ways each one more blood-thirsty than the last. Such were the depths of my obsession that I did not realise how intoxicated I was. All I knew was that I had lost him before and I was not going to lose him again. Also, I knew that I had stood up to him more than once and survived, so I could carry on forever if I had to. I prayed that God would protect me long enough to kill the bastard and galloped on up the road.

I rode all night regularly swapping the horses when they got tired and must have travelled two score miles into the dawn which filled the sky with a dramatic blood-red splash of crimson. When I started to worry that I had lost him again I came across an abandoned, horseless dogcart by the side of the road next to an empty rolling field. Looking around I noticed Kolmer's stolen horse grazing in a distant pasture and I swiftly checked the horizon making sure that he was not lurking nearby. So where was he? I slowly walked my horses over to the cart and tensed when I saw a greyish hand poking out from the side.

As I came closer I discovered a man slumped on the seat but there was no need to check to see if he was still alive. He had a blood-splattered gaping gash right across his neck. Kolmer! It must have been him. I guessed that he had killed this lonely traveller to steal his horses but, of course, there had been no need for this unnecessary slaughter. I looked towards the red rising sun and muttered to myself, "C'mon Seb. We have to kill this bastard before he murders half of Bavaria." I touched the corpse's hand. Christ! It was still warm. My heart started to trot again. Damn it! He must be close.

I roared at the horses and galloped off recalling Kolmer's cryptic words about his contract with his '*Celestial master*' and how no man could take his soul without dying. Blasted Illuminati devils from hell! I pictured the look on his face while I repeatedly stabbed him in his black heart and I bellowed at my horses, "C'mon there! Come on! Yah!"

A hour later I came to a stop at the crest of a small hill as I had spied a convenient spring by the side of the road and I let the horses drink. Much as I wanted to carry on I knew that I must tend to the animals or they would be ruined. They were not going to last much longer anyway, especially without something to eat and I would soon have to rest them properly.

However, when I squinted into the distance through the dull morning light and saw a solitary black rider with two horses slowly making his way along not half a mile away, I instantly dropped the rope round the other animals and dug my heels into my stallion causing him to rear up and gallop off.

I knew it was Kolmer. I could have smelled the swine from a hundred miles away. I leaned down over my horse's mane and pulled the axe from my belt as we thundered down the hill. At the bottom the road was flat and the going good and within minutes I came around a bend to see my nemesis slowly swaying along not four hundred yards ahead.

Of course, he had no idea that I was bearing down on him. I could tell by the trees that the wind was blowing in my face so I knew that he would not hear me coming up from behind. Now I had him in my sights again I was determined not to let him get away. Though my steed was nearly exhausted I pushed him on ever faster and, when I got within a hundred yards, such was my speed I knew that I would catch my prey. I raised the axe above my head and waited for the devil to hear me and, as I had anticipated, with only yards to spare, he turned his head but it was too late. I flung the axe and sent it spinning into his back.

'Crunch!'

"Yes! Take that pig dog!" I roared as the weapon lodged into his shoulder and he arched forward in the saddle. Somehow he managed to hold onto the horse's neck as he fell forward and to force his spurs into its flanks. As I had predicted my momentum took me past him but his horse reared up and was soon galloping alongside. Having no other weapons I haplessly tried to kick him off as he came past but as I did, my horse faltered and almost buckled beneath me.

Kolmer saw this and gritted his teeth, grimly wincing, "Seems we're... not in Hell yet... boy." He spurred his horse again as mine stumbled and nearly fell on its face.

"Not now! Not now!" I roared, thrashing my bridle but it was no good, Kolmer's fresher horses soon pulled out a couple of lengths and as he bounced up the road, to my despair, the axe fell away from his back.

"Why do you punish me like this God?" I fumed and kicked and urged the horse again and again but it was useless the poor animal was spent. It stumbled once more before, with one final wheeze, falling flat on its knees and we both ploughed through the mud and stones and puddles into a shallow ditch. Luckily, I was thrown away from the heavy beast and, though I was thoroughly shaken and disorientated, I instantly leapt up and staggered back to the animal, shouting, "Get up you useless nag! Get up! Come on! Get up!"

I kicked the beast in the belly before coming to my senses. Good God Seb. What's wrong with you? You sound like the man in black. I knelt down and stroked the creature's sweating neck as it gasped for breath. Poor thing. I cast an eye up the road but of course Kolmer had disappeared. Shit! I had been so close. It would take me an age to go back and get the other horses by which time he could have travelled miles. I stroked the beleaguered animal once more before pulling myself to my feet and running back to retrieve the others.

This was extremely difficult as it was a lot further back than I had remembered and, by the time I had got there the stupid animals had decided to wander off in search of something to eat. Altogether these diversions must have taken at least an hour before I returned to the fallen horse to see how he was faring. But as I trotted up I realised that something was wrong and when I got closer I saw that it was dead by the side of the ditch.

Oh Lord. I had killed the poor thing. I crossed my chest trying not to look down and quickly rode on by, not wanting to spook the others. How many more innocent creatures would die before I killed this fiend?

I rode on for the entire day following Kolmer's tracks but by nightfall when there was still no sign of him, I found an old barn and spent an uncomfortable night trying to sleep in the damp straw. The next morning my spirits fell even further when the weather turned and a biting easterly wind began to blow in my face. Now I was hungry, aching, sore and cold, not to mention the state of my saddleless horses and, as I surveyed the barren landscape surrounding me on that chilly autumn morning, I also unhappily concluded, rather lost too. This was true. Though I had been travelling east on pretty much the same rolling road since the chase began I had only a rough idea of where I was. There was no one around to ask and I had not seen a signpost for two days.

Later that afternoon I came across a small nameless town on a windswept plain and, after establishing that the locals had not seen a suspicious rider in black I went straight to the blacksmith where I sold my weakest horse for a song in order to buy some essential provisions. These were more than essential as I had not eaten for some time and worried that I might die if I did not put something inside my belly. But before I had chance to eat I had spent nearly all my pittance on a tattered old saddle, a stout coat to protect me from the wintry conditions and a rusty old flintlock simply to protect me. Another purchase that I made, which may seem slightly trivial but, at the time, I felt of some importance, was a pair of old boots and once I had them on I threw the dead man's shoes in the river. Though they had fitted me well, for some reason, they had been making me feel rather uncomfortable for a while.

After pigging myself at the tavern in the town square I loaded my meagre provisions onto my remaining horse and trotted out of the place, heading east on the only road Upon seeing a lone traveller leading a donkey towards me I stopped to ask for directions and to enquire about the conditions on the road ahead. He told me that I was only two days' ride from Prague, of all places, and that the road ahead was fair so, on the off chance, I asked him, "And tell me, sir, have you seen an injured man in black travelling with two brown fillies?"

The contents of my bladder turned to ice when he replied, "Oh yes. He rode past me less than an hour ago. Must have stopped here too. Didn't like the look of him though. Nasty fellow that."

Shit! The blasted locals had told me that they had not seen him. I would have to be more careful in the future. I had spent the last two hours calmly ambling around the town doing some shopping and stuffing my face when I should have been permanently on guard with my weapons at hand in case the evil devil sprang out from the butchers. I waved farewell to the traveller and flew off up the road.

All the planets! The chase was on again. But a little further on, I pulled up at the first junction that I had seen in days and hurriedly scanned the tracks in the mud. I wished that the Professor was there to help me but I tried as best as I could to work out which ones might belong to Kolmer. Within the criss-crossing markings I thought that I could make out a fresh pair of horses' tracks leading east. It was all that I had. So I flicked my horse's reins and galloped off as the overwhelming purpose of revenge filled my soul once more. I had to find him. I had to find him or I would die.

Chapter 27

The End of the Road

Three days later, after riding non-stop day and night through the icy wind and beating rain, every moment searching the horizon and the faces of those I passed, I stood on the banks of the mighty river Oder certain that I had come to the end of the road. I did not even know what day it was, I had the longest beard that I had ever grown, I smelled like a Prussian sausage factory, I was penniless and I ached as only a man who has ridden hundreds of miles in a week can ache. I tentatively touched the sores on my backside and reflected that it *had* actually been that long. Also, how I yearned for the company of my distant friends; the reassuring words of the Professor, the beguiling smile of my lover and even the monotony of Bacon's constant abjurations. That was to say nothing of my university career which, as far as I knew, lay in shreds. What had I done?

I tried to buck myself up and followed the river north for a few miles until I came across a dilapidated old church. Uplifted by this fortuitous discovery, I dismounted and went inside hoping that it might even be Sunday. Alas, whatever day it was, the ruin looked as though no living soul had been there for years. I respectfully knelt in the aisle before dragging myself up to a pew and flopping my aching body down. Resting my elbows on the splintered wood in front of me, I put my hands together in quiet contemplation and, after settling my inner self and my sore backside, tried to talk to God.

"Why have you sent me to this place Lord?" I mumbled, "For what reason have you led me here?" I thought that I heard some rustling but when I looked behind me there was nothing but shadows and I presumed that it must have been some vermin scurrying about amongst the fallen beams.

I shivered in the draught coming from the doorway and pulled up my collar. Through the broken windows I could see that the weather was worsening. I let out a weary sigh and stared back to the empty space where the altar should have been. Seeing that God was obviously not in residence, or interested in answering any of my questions, I pulled myself up, crossed my chest, bowed humbly and traipsed back outside.

I hauled myself into my saddle and took a look around the darkening sky. Not only was it becoming heavily overcast but a few light snowflakes were falling over the trees on the far side of the river. This change in the weather was serious. I would need to find shelter soon as there were only a few hours of daylight left. I turned away from the church and walked my horse a little further along the path, where I was most encouraged to see a thin taper of smoke rising over some nearby trees and, as I came around a bend, I discovered a ramshackle old cottage with a barn. "You *were* listening God," I praised, "Somewhere proper to sit down." I trotted up to the humble abode, jumped down from my saddle and peeked in through the window.

"Hello! Is anybody there?" I called but there was no answer only the nagging whine of the east wind. Though the place was a little shabby it certainly looked habitated. I rubbed my hands together and muttered to myself, "If they don't come back soon maybe I can break in?"

"Get away from there, idiot!" rasped a voice from behind me and I turned to see an old woman dressed from head to toe in furs wobbling through the tall grass.

"Hello there," I welcomed, as gracefully as I could muster in my hour of need and went to meet her halfway, pulling my tired horse behind me.

"Are you deaf as well as stupid, idiot? Get away!"

I decided to assert myself a little whilst, of course, retaining my modest charm, "Ha, ha, yes, very good, old lady, very good.

Though I'm no idiot but merely a weary traveller stranded upon the lonely road."

"You are an idiot," she grouched and rudely shambled past me without stopping, "And don't call me old."

Determined not to have to find another suitable place where I could put down my head, and further motivated by the sweet aroma of rabbit stew wafting from the cottage, I tried to flatter her whilst following in her footsteps, "Please... Madam, I assure you that I am no idiot. I simply saw your ...beautiful home here in this ...picturesque spot and was going to ask if I may take shelter therein?"

She turned to face me, stopping me in my tracks. "You are an idiot and I can prove it."

I stooped condescendingly low to hear her better and, with the smell of rabbit stew going up my nose, conjured a smile, "Please carry on, Madam, I'm sure that will be of great interest to me."

She frowned with considerable doubt before beginning, "You're on the road in the winter without a proper hat," she pointed at her own and shook her head, "You're obviously lost so you don't have a map." She glanced at my hairy face, "Or food," then at my filthy clothes, "Or money, and you're in the habit of sitting in empty churches asking God ridiculous questions when you should know yourself."

I went to butt in at this point but she droned on like a wasp stuck in a wine bottle, "And now you're relying on an old lady that you met in a field who didn't like the look of you in the first place, who thinks you're only being nice to her because you smelt her rabbit stew." She raised a fuzzy eyebrow and finished, "I wouldn't put it past you to have been considering breaking in. Eh?" She watched my smile falter all too noticeably and poked me in the chest, grunting, "You see. I proved it. You're an idiot," With this she hobbled off towards her cottage wittering to herself.

Lord, give me strength. Why did I always have to meet the most obnoxious, foul-mouthed, old women in the world? Where were all the nice ones who would give you a lovely piece of pie as soon as look at you?

"But, Madam," I persisted, glancing up at the darkening clouds and catching her up as she stepped onto the porch, "Would you not give shelter to a lonely traveller who was prepared to pay?"

"You have no money as we have already established." She opened her door and gave me one more withering look, before grumbling, "Idiot," then slamming it in my face.

Jesus wept! If this woman was the reason that God had sent me here He certainly had a sense of humour. Feeling a fresh snowflake on my nose and seeing a couple bluster over my shivering horse I decided that it was not funny at all.

I bit my lip and turned back to the door, calling out, "Pray tell, Madam, what do you want from me?"

I could hear her banging pots around and talking to herself before her face reappeared at the door and she rasped, "I will take the horse. No more - No less. For this I will give you enough money to get back from where you came. So, not very much at all."

"That is ridiculous! I ..."

"No more - No less," she interrupted, "Now I have said all I want to on the matter. So I must kindly ask you to leave me in peace while I eat a most pleasing meal on my own."

She slammed the door. Curse this woman's insolence. I peered round the gathering gloom and shook my head. Was this really how it was to end? Surely not. I had come through such great odds and overcome so many daunting challenges. Surely I could not be defeated by this one single obstreperous old witch.

"No more - No less!" she shouted from inside and I gasped with frustration and frowned at my exhausted horse.

Two minutes later I was joining her at the table inside the cluttered cottage and eagerly devouring a steaming bowl of rabbit stew. I could not believe that, after everything I had been through to lead me to that faraway place, it was a bowl of broth and the promise of a warm blanket for the night that had finally brought my epic quest to an end. But that was the way it seemed. A wave of relief swept over me as I greedily ate my fill and it dawned on me that I had, as the English say, 'Let myself off the hook,' or, more accurately, as the Prussians say, 'Out of the hangman's noose.'

It was over. I simply could not go on without a horse. At least I had chased the bastard half-to-death and survived to tell the tale when so many others had fallen by the way. A mighty task in itself, I reflected with some pride. The ritual was ruined. The obelisk smashed. Kolmer was routed and, gratefully I believed, my companions were still alive. I had done it. Thank the Lord. I even relaxed then about my university work. If I was ten years behind in my studies it would be as nothing compared to this awesome journey and I considered, with much earnest introspection, how much I had learnt about myself, and indeed the world, while on my daring escapade. In my youthful ignorance I found it impossible not to consider that I was now a man and felt the challenge of university a mere inconvenience in comparison to the wild adventures which I had survived.

Whatever illusions I was suffering at that time, I knew, above all else, that the Professor would be able to sort everything out when I eventually found him and, of course, the delectable one herself. I prayed that they were safe as I suspected and tucked into my meal while the old woman discussed the terms of our deal. It was late. I did not argue. She had me over a barrel.

After eating I was soon fast asleep in a chair with a blanket over me and, for once, had an amazingly positive dream.

In this vision I saw again the same light that I had seen so many times before, radiating ahead of me as I travelled through my life. But this time its dazzling beams were lighting the back of a curved horizon and somehow, in one transcendant moment, I realised that I was looking back at the Earth ablaze in the light of the sun.

I awoke with a start to find the old woman stoking the fire in the dark. She saw me stirring under my blanket and grouched, "You won't be going anywhere today, idiot. Now your horse is useless."

What was she talking about? Intrigued, I hoisted myself up with my blanket wrapped around me and went to take a look outside. The windowpanes were so dirty that I had to wipe them with the blanket before sticking my nose against the chilly glass. Good Lord! The old woman was right. Thick blustering clouds of snow were lashing down from a leaden sky and the surrounding grassland had become a bleak wintry wilderness. I gazed out amongst the windswept drifts that had seemingly come from nowhere realising that my travel plans were ruined and forlornly mumbled to myself, "What are you going to do now then, eh Seb?"

"You will tend my horse in the barn and stop asking stupid questions while I stoke the fire."

"Strewth. But... when do you think it will stop snowing?" I asked over my shoulder, bewildered about how I was going to get home.

She facetiously licked a finger then held it up pretending that it would help her find out and nagged, "One day, two days, three: Forever? How do I know idiot? Tend the horse and shut up."

Curse all the blasted saints. This woman would have confounded the Professor whilst probably forcing Bacon to commit suicide and also, I reckoned as I watched her wobble over to the woodpile muttering insults to herself, even given the tongue-lashing Francesca a run for her money. The prospect of being trapped inside this tiny cottage with her while she repeatedly called me an idiot was maddening, but it appeared that there was no alternative. I was stuck again. Another swirl of flakes licked across the windowpanes and I wondered when it would end.

Well it certainly did not that day and on the second, if anything, the weather deteriorated. By the third I felt like the Prisoner in the Iron Mask and convinced myself that I would go mad without a feasible plan of escape. But as that day dragged on a powerful storm enveloped the house plunging us into near total darkness though it was the middle of the day. A fierce wind rattled the window panes and shook the doors against their frames and howled up the chimney sending the fire into wild spits and spats. It was a good job that I had found shelter when I did. Surely I would have died had I been stranded out on the open road.

We huddled under our blankets in front of the fire listening to the almighty storm pass overhead while the jumping flames threw eerie patterns around the room. I pulled my blanket tight and nestled down in my chair praying that the roof would not be torn off by the raging wind outside. Up to then I had been tight-lipped about what I was doing so far away from home in such strange circumstances and the old woman had not seemed to care about the reasons which had brought me to her door.

But as the hours dragged on and the flames thrashed about in the hearth and the storm tried to take the house with it wherever it was going, it was impossible not to talk and, perhaps unsurprisingly, I could not help but steer the discussions toward topics which were playing deeply on my mind. The conversation inevitably turned to matters of a spiritual nature and I was trying to find out whether my host believed in God or not and, perhaps, more appropriately, the Devil.

But surely, Madame, if you believe in God then you must believe in the Devil?"

"Of course I believe in them alright. Sometimes I think they are the same thing."

"The *same thing*? How can this be?"

"Not everything can be split in half, idiot."

I frowned deeply at her, most perplexed to have been called an idiot for the hundredth time that hour. She noticed me scowling and scorned, "The world is not cut in two halves is it? Men call the ends the North and South or East and West but they always end up back in the same place they started, right over the middle. Ha. Men: Idiots. Man is one thing, but he still can be both good and bad. That's why I think that God and the Devil are the same thing because they are like a man." She threw me a sideways glance and croaked, "But I still dream of the Devil."

"Oh yes, Madame? And what is the Devil like?"

"When I dream of the Devil he comes to me in my bed and sticks his claws into my hand. So I go to pray to God but He does not listen." She shook her wrinkled head in the firelight and tossed a twig into the flames. "But then I tell him to fuck off and he goes away."

I chuckled to myself and pulled my blanket round my shoulders preparing for another night in the chair.

When I woke the next morning I was surprised to find her squinting out of the window with bright sunlight catching her ancient face and I stupidly asked, "What's the weather like now?"

She held up another licked finger and rasped, "Better."

Requiring a little more information, I pulled myself from the chair and joined her to see that the sun had indeed come out.

"Good Lord," I whispered under my breath. Though the cottage was completely snowbound, with deep, rutted drifts running from the furthest horizon all the way up to and over the window ledge, it was a gloriously sunny day with not a cloud in the sky.

She grimaced and said, "You must go now or the snow won't let you leave. Remember, idiot, go straight home and follow the map I gave you. Whatever you do don't stray from the path. There are marshlands around the river that will catch you out." She pushed her nose against the glass and sniffed, "Many get caught on the road. Bad things happen to those who get caught."

Of all the people in the world who did not need to be reminded about the dangers faced by a lonely traveller it was me and, with still so many hundreds of miles lying between myself and home, I knew that she was right because my fluttering heart told me so.

Ten minutes later, after quickly packing my things into a bag including; a spare shirt, a fur hat, some socks and a map which she had *sold* me, I trudged away from the little cottage through the snow waving goodbye. I may have been without a horse but I had a proper hat, warm feet, a belly full of rabbit stew, enough money for my journey and, for once, I knew which way I was going. Praise the Lord. I was going home.

The old woman had reckoned that it would take me two weeks to get back to Bavaria depending on the weather and how far I had to travel before the roads were clear enough for stagecoaches. But I was sceptical about this and thought three weeks more likely, maybe even a month if the weather changed again.

Still, as it was a crisp winter's day, after I had found the path crossing the top of the rolling plains which was only lightly dusted with snow, I strode along cheerfully humming Awake the Voice is Calling Us and set course for my first port of call, a village called Olawa some twenty miles south along the banks of the winding river.

After several hours I came to a lonely frozen signpost and had to wipe the ice from the bent old wood to reveal the words 'Olawa 11 miles.' "Excellent," I cheered myself. I was already halfway there and, judging by the sun's position, it was not yet midday. I would still have to keep up a good pace to reach my destination by nightfall, so I walked off again up a steady incline keeping the river to my left a couple of miles away.

Ascending to the top of this hill I gazed all around me from my impressive vantage point. As far as the eye could see, from past the frozen river in the east to the desolate horizon on the west, the countryside was one white endless wasteland in every direction. Every tree, bush and blade of grass was completely buried in snow and there was not one sign of life anywhere. There were not even any birds in the pale blue sky and, since I had set off not long after daybreak, I had not come across another living creature along my way. Not one. It seemed that nothing, neither man nor beast, was stupid enough to come out on this freezing cold day – except for me. As I looked around the silent icy scenery tapering off to all points of the compass, I wondered out loud, "Who would ever want to come to this place? How would they survive?"

Well, 'General Winter' has defeated many a worthy opponent in its time, not least Napoleon, but still there were others who were even harder to stop than the French tyrant.

For as I reached the top of the hill I put my hand across my forehead and strained my eyes towards the river. Somehow I thought that I had seen a solitary black speck standing out in the distance. Sure enough, as I panned back round to the east, there it was. Like a tiny piece of coal in the middle of the otherwise pristine whiteness, lying perhaps a mile from the glimmering river. I watched it through my clouding breath for a while and, as I narrowed my eyes, I was certain that I saw the piece of coal move.

I took a step closer keeping my eyes fixed on the dot but now I was sure that it was stationary. I scratched my nose and stood waiting for something to happen but, after another minute or so when nothing did, I guessed that it was a bird or maybe an old rag or something blowing in the wind. 'That's right,' I thought: 'Something blowing in the wind.'

I was about to carry on my way when I definitely saw it move again and now, as I focused harder, I was sure that there were, in fact, two specks instead of one.

"What is it?" I murmured to myself. I was baffled. What kind of lunatic would be out on a day like this? There was something strange about the specks that I could not quite put my finger on. Like an itch that I could not scratch. I looked above me once more and calculated that I had enough time to make a small detour from the path to take a closer look. How could it hurt? I would not need to go far down the hill to be able to see what it was and that would put my mind at rest. No problem at all. Not for a man like me.

I strode down the hill all the time staring into the distance trying to make out what it was. But upon reaching the bottom I entered a shallow dip which I had not seen from the top and, because of the lie of the land, I could no longer see whatever I was looking at, which I now estimated, was about half a mile away. I pushed on through the dip toward a gentle rise and felt the ground become squishy under my boots, even though the rest of the countryside was frozen solid.

"Don't want to get your feet wet Seb," I muttered, suspecting that it was part of the marshland about which the old lady had warned me. When I came to the top of the rise my interest only deepened as the specks came back into view. Though they were much closer now and not specks at all but clearly two black objects lying in the snowy field up ahead. What could they be?

For some reason I started running towards them until, taking one more crunching stride, I froze like an icicle when one of the objects shifted and I was sure that I could see a white face sticking out amidst the black. Focusing harder I was also sure that I could see a pair of wolfish eyes gleaming back at me. It was as though I had disturbed an animal eating its dinner. Surely not? I blinked and rubbed my eyes to check that they were not deceiving me but, when I opened them again, there he was, as clear as day. I was positive. My God! I took a faltering step backwards - It was the devil himself - The man in black!

Chapter 28

Black as Coal

"What in Hell's name is he doing here?" I panted as Kolmer got to his feet not four hundred yards away and stood staring right at me. After chasing him halfway round the world and a week after seeing him ride away half dead, the demon who had a contract with the Devil was back. Maybe he had been slowed by his injuries or stranded by the weather and I had overtaken him? Whatever mysteries had surrounded him during the past seven days, they had contrived to bring him here. What was I going to do? One way or another I would have to decide quickly because he was already striding towards me and unsheathing his sword.

Come on Sebastian. Think! Not being equipped with the barrels of fury that had previously propelled me after the fiend, I was thoroughly unprepared to come out with all guns blazing. Though, judging by the way that he was fiercely marching toward me, he was as ready for a fight to the death as always. Then I remembered the old flintlock. Yes! I had packed it in the bag. My mind returned to the old woman's cottage where I had hastily collected my things as she repeatedly called me an idiot.

"Shit!" *Had* I packed the flintlock? I threw down the bag, dropped onto my knees and quickly began throwing everything out. I glanced up to see that Kolmer was now sprinting so fast that he had to hold on to his hat.

"Come on! Come on!" I hissed, flinging my shirt and spare socks on the snow. But the ground opened up beneath me when I reached the bottom and found that the bag was empty. Empty! God damn it! I threw my hand around inside once more but it was not there. I had forgotten to pack the gun. Idiot! The stupid old woman was right. Then I felt it bulging in the bag's front pocket and yanked it out.

"Thank sweet Jesus Christ for that," I gasped and hurriedly checked the mechanism. Though I had never fired the rusty old thing I had been assured that it was loaded. I prayed to God that it was. The powder seemed dry and, by the looks of it, there was still enough inside the sealed pan. So I pulled out the ramrod, stuffed the wadding and shot, cocked the hammer and stood up defiantly pointing it at him as he ran towards me with snow flying up from his boots. He promptly slid to a halt when he recognised my face and saw that I was armed.

"That's right, pig dog. It's me again," I muttered under my breath, "God has brought you back to me." I squeezed the handle and snarled back at him.

He might have been an evil, vicious, devil-worshipping bastard but he was not stupid. He obviously did not fancy his chances against me now that I had a gun and stood there catching his breath and looking about not knowing what to do. I took a step forward and noticed something dark on his lips. Holy Mother of God! Even from this distance I could tell that it was blood. Damn it! I had seen it before. Where was this demon from? I cursed his devilry and charged at him roaring at the top of my voice. "I'm going to kill you, you filthy son of a bitch!"

That made up his mind for him and he turned round and ran back the way he had come. Incredibly the chase was on again and I tore after him pleading, "Please God let me finish the quest you have sent me to remove this thorn from your side once and for all."

I felt like an avenging angel sent to do God's work. How else could I explain this miraculous turn of fate?

"Come on Sebastian after him!" I yelled and sprinted off through the snow. But he was fast. Even though I had always been the swiftest runner back in my village and never beaten in any race, I was disconsolate when I saw that he was getting away from me.

"Come on!" I wheezed as my lungs burned with the effort and I undid my coat buttons to help me breathe. Two hundred yards ahead I saw him run past the other black speck and wondered what it could be? But as I came closer I started to feel sick when I realised that it was a horse and its steaming guts were spilled out over the snow. My God! He had been eating the thing – raw! He *was* a devil. I clutched the flintlock against my brow as I swept past and dug deeper.

For a second I lost sight of him when he disappeared over a small hillock. "Not now. Not now." I puffed, having to shade my eyes from the sunlight reflecting off the snow. But a hundred yards further on I spotted him again, though now he seemed to be lying down. Sensing an opportunity, I pushed my body to its very limits and, with my heart pounding in my chest and my legs beginning to cramp, my boot suddenly went through the snow and the horrid feeling of cold water engulfed my foot. In my eagerness to throw out a steadying pair of hands I nearly dropped the gun.

"I told you not to get your feet wet you fool!" I fumed, dragging my soaking boot from the snow. I shuddered and as I pulled myself up it dawned on me that Kolmer had fallen through too. I looked into the distance with my hand across my eyes and was amazed to see him wading up to his waist through a pool of slush, holding up his sword in one hand and something else in the other. God's dinner! It was the box.

"The stone," I murmured and took another step but hesitated upon seeing more wet patches seeping through the ground. I edged forward avoiding the puddles as best I could but realised that I would have to speed up or he would get away. He had already reached the far bank and was about to pull himself ashore. Blast! I was still too far away to get off an accurate shot. I splashed over to where he had gone in as he hauled himself onto the ice and, seeing me half-heartedly training the gun on him, he shouted, "Ha, ha! Not from there, boy! Seems like you've come up short again! Someone obviously has plans for me!"

He pulled himself to his feet before quickly getting his bearings and running off towards a snowy hedgerow in the direction of the river.

I looked out across the pond and cussed, "Damn it Lord! Could you not tell me what it is you want me to do instead of constantly leaving me to make up my own mind?"

I gulped and stared down at my soaking boots then took a deep breath, held the gun above my head and hesitantly stepped forward. Even though I was extremely careful I immediately slipped through the ice and went in up to my waist. I had expected it to be cold but nothing could have prepared me for the shock and the icy rush crushed my body like a vice. I almost passed out and had to fight to stay conscious as I awkwardly waded along with my arms out by my sides. The pain was unimaginable but, knowing that there was no going back now, I pushed onto the far bank.

At last I came up to the place Kolmer's tracks started on the other side and heaved myself out. I slithered onto the ice shivering in pain with my freezing britches clinging to my legs and, after taking some juddering breaths, checked the flintlock. Thank God. At least the powder was still dry.

I pulled myself up and set off again, wrapping my trembling arms round me to try to regain some warmth. 'Onwards,' whispered the voice in my head and I staggered off following Kolmer's footprints. I did not have to go much further when I saw him pulling himself from the frozen hedgerow and jumping a ditch on the other side. He turned back to check my progress and even from a hundred yards away, I could hear him contemptuously snort before he ran off towards the river.

"Where is he going?" I chattered as I crunched after him. We were getting very close to the riverbank now and, though the ground was frozen in many places, as I had already discovered it was treacherously soft in others and we would soon be right on top of the river. I sprinted up to the brambles and pushed myself through, having to tear myself to pieces to get out of the other side, from where I jumped the narrow ditch and landed on the far slope. I clambered to the top and could see Kolmer running off ahead so I set off once again as fast as my frozen legs would carry me.

I took the opportunity to check the gun's powder pan but when I next looked up I saw that Kolmer had practically come to a halt and was cautiously inching along with his foot out in front of him. 'What's this now?' I thought only to hear a loud crack from below me and, as my next sttep hit the ground, I heard the same spine-chilling noise again. Shit! The ice was breaking and I slid to a halt as another ominous creak rippled from below. Then, in one awful moment, I distinctly felt the ground move under my feet. No! Kolmer was heading straight across the middle of the river and ahead of him I was sure that I could see the ice floe moving. If we went in the water again we would die for certain. What was he thinking? Did he want to die? I heard the ice snap again and anxiously inched forward holding my breath.

He was only fifty feet away now but still too far to shoot accurately. So, seeing that we were nearing the middle of the river where the ice was perilously shifting, I bit my lip, half closed my eyes and gently tiptoed a handful of steps nearer. He saw me closing in on him and nervously inched forward still clutching the box to his chest. Now he was only a few feet from being in range. If I could make up that much ground again I could get a shot off. I had to guarantee that I hit him and where it hurt. If I missed I would be helpless against his sword. I had one chance. I had to kill him or surely he would do the same to me.

I surveyed the ice in front of me trying to judge if it was strong enough to bear my weight before crossing my chest, closing one eye and tiptoeing another dozen feet. Now I was definitely in range but it would still be a tricky shot. He glared at me realising that I would soon be close enough and, as he did, he stumbled and went down on one knee. Yes! He had gone through again. This was my chance. With him seemingly stuck, I held up my gun and bounded toward him excitedly yodelling, "I'm going to get you pig dog!" and instantly plunged into the water, but this time there was no bottom and I painfully smacked down on my elbows and chin. I threw out my hands in my desperation to cling on to something and dropped the gun, sending it spinning out over the ice.

"No!" I roared and slid deeper into the hole. The cold was like fire burning my body and the shock made it almost impossible to breathe. Then my heart began to pound like the guns of a firing squad when I saw Kolmer gingerly edging towards me. Damnation! He had freed himself and his surprised expression turned to a dastardly grin as he realised my fate.

"Please God! Not now! Not now! Am I not your servant?" I whimpered, trying in vain to grip the ice and drag myself out. I threw out a hand at the flintlock but it was inches out of reach and my elbows slipped as I struggled to keep myself afloat. I heard his cackle and glanced up to see him almost on top of me.

"Ha, ha. Dearie, dearie me. You have the most unfortunate habit of becoming stuck don't you, boy? And always in the worst places." He wiped the blood from his mouth with his sleeve and clutched his precious box to his chest as I frantically tried to haul myself out, knowing that I only had seconds left before the cold killed me or he did. I flung my freezing fingertips out one final time but could only brush the flintlock's handle and push it even further away before sliding back into the hole with a gasp.

"P'ah, ha ha. Pathetic!" he scoffed, "Sometimes trying is not enough, is it, boy? In this world you need friends in high places, or perhaps low ones, eh?" He checked the ice in front of him before edging forward, "That's when we have to give in to our fate like your poor little friend. And it seems that your fate is nigh."

He was almost standing on top of me by now and I could see right up his snorting nose as he glared down on me and gloated, "I couldn't decide whether to let you drown or kill you, but I have decided on the latter. Yes. That's right," he beamed, "Maybe another drink will do me good eh?"

His eyes opened wide and he came in wiping his sword on his black coat and flashing his white teeth. Good God! Surely this was the end.

Chapter 29

Cold as Ice

"No!" I roared. It was now or never. With one last monumental effort I yanked myself over the ice and grabbed the flintlock then dragged it back, pointing it up at him. He hesitated for a second, hovering six feet away with his breath condensing in the air, until his eyes filled with wolfish pride and he jeered, "I don't think so, boy. You just don't have the right connections."

He took a step nearer. That was close enough. From this range I could not miss the arrogant bastard and I pulled the trigger. 'Boom!' The explosion blasted from the old barrel but his reactions were as fast as lightning. He whipped up his elbow to protect himself and the ball bounced off the box's banding then shot through the ice at his feet throwing up a blast of slush. He regained his balance and we exchanged startled glances as it dawned on us what had happened.

"I don't damn-well believe it!" I gasped, throwing the gun away and frantically trying to scramble from the hole. No! No! No! Why did I have such bad luck with guns? His nostrils flared and, confident that I was now for the taking, he took a bold step towards me, laughing, "Ha, ha. Like I told you, boy, *He* protects me well."

"No!" This was definitely the end.

We both heard the crack and his eyes sprang open wide as he suddenly disappeared with a crunch and a splash. Good God! The bullet *had* done its work. I watched in astonishment as he floundered about in a hole, coughing up water and scrabbling the sword and the box around on the ice fighting to stay afloat.

"Now Sebastian!" I hollered and summoning every remaining ounce of strength, pulled myself out but only by an inch. "Come on!" I raged. Seeing Kolmer's terrified face wheezing and spluttering not six feet away gave me the tiny fragment of energy that I needed and I hauled my knee onto the lip. Knowing that I would die if I did not succeed I wrenched myself up and, with one last gargantuan effort, finally flopped onto the ice with an almighty gasp. I glanced up to see him choking and going under but pulling the box with him.

"No!" I clambered over on my hands and knees but stopped when I heard another worrying creak from below. I dropped onto my stomach while he used his sword to get a purchase and I could only lie there and watch as he managed to get his knee onto the ice then begin to pull himself out. Damnation! He was going to make it. I slid towards him on my belly, gasping, "Not now you dog!" and kicked his knee back into the water. His face splashed under the waves and he dragged the box with him but I grabbed it inches from the edge.

"Damn you!" I cursed, wrapping my arm around the casket and fighting to tear it from his clutches.

His pale face resurfaced and as he fought for breath he gasped, "Curse... your eyes! It belongs... to my master!"

I punched him in the mouth with my free hand and yelled, "*That* part of the mystery... you'll have to work out yourself... you bastard! And I think you'd better be quick!"

He waggled his sword but I viciously gouged his eyes and pushed his face under, leaving his hat floating on the waves. He splashed around and sliced the sword but I raked my ankle over the hilt whilst keeping one arm round the box and driving my other palm down on his scalp. He desperately tried to force himself up but I could feel his strength ebbing away.

"Die you bastard!" I screamed, thrusting down with all my might and seeing a plume of bubbles come to the surface as he shouted out something, but I drove my hand down even harder. Finally, he let go of the sword and, after one last flaying lunge across the ice, his right hand splashed under the water. But his left continued to cling onto the box with extraordinary resolve. Christ! He was strong. I thrust down on his thrashing head keeping it under the surface until, one by one, his fingers lost their grip and, at last, he let go and his palm slapped onto the ice.

"Yes!" I bellowed ripping the casket free.

His head shook around limply once more but when I put my full weight on it, this time, he sank a whole foot. I instinctively pulled myself back from the freezing water, and his bony hand which still clutched the air searching for the box. I clasped it to my chest and waved his fingers away then, with a single deathly jerk, his outstretched hand finally dragged under. As his fingers slipped below I saw the sinister ring one last time and reached out to grab it but I was too late and it disappeared beneath the ripples with a plop.

I quivered convulsively and stared at the pool for a few seconds until gathering enough breath to howl, "Go to Hell and stay there you bastard!"

Overcome with rage and the horror and the fatigue and the shock of it all, I burst into tears and collapsed in a wailing heap. Unable to hear anything but my blubbering or feel anything other than the awful cold tearing through my body, the awesome recognition swept over me. Was it really over? Had I actually killed him? I wiped my eyes to see his hat gently bobbing in the hole and his sword lying next to the edge. Holy Mother of God! I had done it. The evil shit was dead. I squeezed the box to my heaving chest and realised that I was more than halfway there myself. At least I had killed the wretch before I went to meet my own maker and, as the shock sank in I rolled over, resting my cheek on the ice and panting with the exertion.

"Do you want me to carry on Lord, or have I done enough?" I exhailed and, just for a second, I closed my eyes. I was so cold.

How could I go on? Had I not achieved what I had set out to? Perhaps I should just lay there and die? A lonely, mournful moment passed as I listened to the wind whining across the ice floe and I opened my eyes to see Kolmer's ghostly face lunge up at me.

"No!" I choked, oggling at the apparition. He was back! Back from hell! I sprang to my knees as his grey forehead tapped under the ice and I realised that it was his corpse floating in the current. I shook my head in wonder as his face faded back into the murk. Holy smoke! He was dead all right. But I was still alive. I looked back towards the riverbank. What would any of my efforts matter if I did not return the stone to the Professor and prove that I had done it? Or see my family again? Or lie down with Francesca with her naked arms around me next to a warm fire? 'Come on Sebastian,' I told myself, 'You're not dead yet.'

Fighting the crippling pain wracking my body I trembled to my feet and sloshed back the way I had come. I knew that I must get warm or die so moving around fast was essential but it was impossible due to the weakness of the ice. I had to be so careful, doddering on like a pathetic old man with my hand wobbling in front of me and the box under my arm, that I became colder with every step. The pain was intolerable and, though I made it off the shifting, creaking ice, when I eventually crawled back onto the river's bank some twenty minutes later I was so bitterly cold that I found it almost impossible to walk.

Somehow I managed to limp along and retrace my steps until I reached the ditch that I had jumped before. Now, as I surveyed the dimensions the leap looked far more daunting but it was the only way back to the path and, before that, hopefully my bag. The dry clothes there might even save my life. 'That's right Seb.' I said to myself, sliding down the slope in my squelching boots, 'You can make it if you have warm feet.' I squatted at the bottom to make sure that I did not fall in and managed to jump to the other side but when I reached the row of icy brambles at

218

the top I had a tortuous time getting through. I was so stiff and exhausted that when I finally dragged myself out the other side I was even wetter and twice as cold.

Intensifying my ordeal I had to hobble at least a mile out of my way to circumnavigate the slush pool and, by the time I had found my tracks on the other side, I was in utter agony and deliriously chattering to myself. When I came to the horse's carcass I knew that I had reached my limit and that I had to stop for a while. Not too long though. I knelt down in terrible discomfort but knew that if I closed my eyes I might become unconscious and then there was a chance I could die. I had heard rumours of stormbound travellers lost on high mountain passes, believing that it would be better to rest, never to wake up again. But I would not go to sleep. Anyway, it was impossible. I was in far too much pain.

I scanned the near horizon searching for the bag but there was no sign of it. After a moment I got back to my soaking feet and managed to drag myself to the exact place where I had scattered my clothes, even recognising the marks in the snow but strangely they were nowhere to be seen. This was extremely confusing. I was sure that I had come far enough. I looked about again and strained my eyes into the distance noticing that my vision was starting to blur. Blast! I was losing my bearings. I told myself that I would be all right after a rest. Yes. That was right.

I knelt down once more trying to catch my breath and balanced the box on my knee. But I was so stiff with the cold that it was hard to fill my lungs, so I slouched down further taking a series of shallow breaths. Feeling the box press into my guts I realised that I had not even looked inside the battered old thing. Such were the nature of the day's events that I had not thought to. I ran my hand across the curved lid and shivered in agony. If I was going to die I wanted to know why. So I undid the latch with my trembling fingers and opened the lid only to hear myself chatter,

"What… on God's… Earth?"

Having expected to find a mighty jewel sent from the very heavens above I was disconsolate to discover a dullish green gem sitting on a threadbare, velvet cushion. What was *this*? It looked as though it had come from a beggar's pocket rather than 'The Burning Star.' I picked it up and held it out, gibbering, "Of all the… stupid… wastes of time… in the world. All this… for that? … Ri… dic… ulous."

I shook my head and, just for a second, I thought that I saw a greenish glow shimmering inside the dusty old stone but as soon as I concentrated on the flickering hue, it disappeared. I presumed that it must have been a trick of the light but when I checked overhead the sun was now covered by a thick line of clouds. Maybe I was starting to hallucinate? I edged the gem back onto its cushion and closed the box. Taking a look up ahead and had to fight the urge to burst out weeping from the pain.

I pulled myself back to my feet determined to make some headway and generate some heat but it was no good. My clothes were still completely sodden and the weather was not warm enough to dry them out. If anything it was getting colder: a lot colder. The easterly wind bit into my flesh making my whole body quiver and soon I could not stop shaking. I managed to get another half a mile or so but had to come to a halt climbing the hill back to the path and squatted down once more. I would only do this for a moment then move off again. That was right, only a short rest. I went down on one knee and leant against a snowdrift trying to stop myself from shivering and feverishly chattering through my teeth, "That's… right. You're… not… going to die. You're… going… to… make… it. Just… like… before."

I closed my eyes for a second and put down my hand but was surprised when the snow was no longer cold. 'That's odd,' I thought, patting my fingers about. I checked my back and noticed that it was also warming up as were my toes and, as I contemplated this sensation, I realised that even my legs were drying out. I put down my other knee and softly encouraged, "That's... better. Don't give up... hope... You're not... going to die. You're... gong... to...live..." and rested the box on the snow.

Maybe at that moment I heard the voice inside my head again. Maybe it whispered something in my ear or maybe the voices were from elsewhere. I do not know, but when I try and recall what happened next I distinctly remember that it was as if I was looking down on myself. Perhaps somewhere in my distant memory I remember lying down and rolling on my back because I recall staring up into the sullen sky before closing my eyes. Perhaps I did this. Perhaps I did not. Though that part is vague what happened next is certainly not. For what I remember then was like nothing that I have ever experienced before or since.

At first I became aware of a geometric pattern hypnotically swirling before me and, this time, I definitely heard the voice inside my head. I know this because I distinctly remember it whisper, "Let go." Strangely, the voice called me by another name other than my own but it was so calm and inviting that I was compelled to do what I had been asked.

Then in one magical instant I awoke to find myself soaring above what, in my wondrous state, I took to be the world. Far below me, enveloping the aura of the globe, shone the dazzling light that I had seen before in my dreams but this time, it was so bright that it permeated my soul. Before I knew it I was inside the sea of light, knowing that, at its very essence, dwelt everything in the universe and that it was both limitlessly benign and divinely sentient: All of it as one. When I realised this I was instantaneously everywhere at once, omnipresent throughout the galaxy, encompassing the moon and planets and stars and then, in one profound flash of light, propelled beyond them all. When I looked back in wonder from the end of the universe I was amazed to see that everything was, in fact, one cosmic man and that all the energy was trapped inside this single celestial body in a colossal rainbow of vibrating light which formed an endless figure of eight - flowing from his outstretched hands then crossing at his navel and returning through his widespread feet. While I gazed in awe I saw that, in the place where his head should be, a separate world existed radiating like a sun. Concentrating on its beams of light, I discovered, within its shimmering halo, another Being with flowing locks beating an anvil with a hammer and I remember thinking, 'But how is he connected to the infinite rings of energy?'

Before I could understand, the extraordinary vision took another form and I was thrown into an alternate trance where I fell forever inside myself. I realised that my body was, in effect, the same as the cosmic body containing the universe and, as such, the microcosm and the macrocosm were the same.

For, at the end of my journey through this infinitely small place I came, once again, to the same endless shore running along the same endless sea of energy and, yielding to its original call, slipped effortlessly into its eternal waves feeling my soul, at last, return to the place from where it had first come. I was home. *28

---

28. **Illuminati & Illumination.** It is sometimes difficult to remember, with all the illicit goings on, sinister plans and conspiracies surrounding the Illuminati, that the secret societal movement in the Age of Reason to which the Bavarian Order pays homage - with its arcane hermetic and other mystic traditions - was, in fact, based upon the adepts' aspiration to attain, be that spiritual or intellectual, illumination. S. Drechsler's transcendental journey, mirroring perhaps that of a near-death experience, can, therefore, I believe, be seen compellingly and rather fittingly as the crowning pinnacle of this process and the Hermetic student's astral arch to move from one state to the next: As above, so below. Much information and theory exists regarding these altered states on the internet, as one may well imagine, and I have sifted through these to choose one of the most enlightening for E Book readers to view while considering the author's Gnostic adventures. Enjoy.

Chapter 30

Angels and Demons

I do not know what happened next. The phrase everything went black certainly seems most appropriate and if anyone were to ask me how the following hours felt then that would be the only way I could have described them. Was I dead? I honestly did not know. Of course, it will come as no surprise to discover that I was not. But then perhaps the manner in which I found out might. Because when I did open my eyes I truly thought that I had died and gone to Heaven. For, in one fabulous moment a glorious angel appeared before me in a radiant aura of brilliant white with flashing eyes and glowing skin. She reached out to touch me and I was surprised when I felt her warm hand on my cheek and a manly thought crossed my mind. I clearly remember thinking that I had not expected Heaven to be warm or to be allowed such carnal thoughts when I had arrived. But as I pressed my head against the angel's hand I felt the earth move and her warmth flow into my frozen cheek and the same feeling penetrating the rest of my body. I tried to focus my bleary eyes and heard myself breathe, "Am I... dead?"

"No. You're not dead," spoke the angel, "You're just very cold. Here, let me warm you up." The feminine spirit leant over me and kissed my lips and I felt her rejuvenating power flood the very depths of my soul. I must have passed out at this moment because my mind went blank once more. Though, it seemed the very next instant, I awoke in a bed next to a gently crackling fire.

Where on earth was I now? My eyes roamed around a pleasant room. One thing was certain. I was not in Hell. It was far too homely. I raised my head from the pillow as it slowly dawned on me that - My God - I must be alive. Straining my ears, I tried to hear any other signs of life beyond the door but could only hear the flames flickering on the hearth and the window softly rattling in the draught. I rubbed my forehead and realised that my hand was bandaged. The vision of the angel slipped back into my mind. Where had she gone? Looking around the hospitable room, I had the feeling that she was no angel at all but real flesh and blood.

Still hearing nothing outside, I swung my legs out from under the covers but almost went down on my knees when I went to stand. I put my hands down to keep myself up and to my great surprise saw that, beneath my nightshirt, I was wearing embroidered stockings. What was going on? I tottered over to the window, having to support myself on the ledge to pull back the curtain. In the courtyard below some servants were leading a couple of horses into the stables of a fine coaching house and over the nearby trees the sun was sinking as evening drew in. Or was it morning? I did not know. I scratched my bristles mumbling to myself, "What day is it?"

At that moment the door opened and I turned to find a startled maid throwing up her hands and exclaiming, "He's awake!"

"How do you do," I absentmindedly welcomed, somewhat taken aback to see this stranger at the door. I went to bow but straightened up on hearing a familiar voice squeal from behind her, "Wunderkind!" and had not the time nor chance to move before Francesca burst into the room. I was so shocked to see her excited face crash into mine that I keeled over onto the bed as she covered me in a flurry of passionate kisses.

"You!" I croaked but she did not stop and kept nuzzling me like an excited puppy.

"You will have to think of another way of greeting me, sir. That one may soon start to bore me."

I was still so utterly stunned to see her on top of me, lavishing me with affection, that I had not yet embraced her.

"I thought you said he was romantic?" tittered the maid from the doorway. Francesca stopped for a moment and inspected me with her beautiful brown eyes, sulking, "He used to be."

Her expression returned to a happy smile and she went to kiss me again but I grabbed her arms and begged, "But... how? I thought that... I was dead."

"You're not dead, sir. Now why don't you prove it to me?"

"But..?" I protested, doing my best to hold her at bay.

At last, she arrested her affections and rolled her eyes before starting, "We were following Kolmer too. The Professor went one way with some of the sheriff's men and I came the other way with the rest. We did not give up. But he got away." She shook her head laughing, "It wasn't my fault."

"But...?"

She pushed a finger onto my lips, chuckling, "We kept going and I told everyone that he would get stuck in the snow by the river but they did not listen."

"But..?"

She pushed down harder carrying on, "So I made them listen. Finally they did what they were told and I showed them the right way and we found Kolmer's dead horse, then we found the tracks, then we found the bag. Ha, ha. With your socks and shirt all over the ground," she beamed her beautiful smile and laughed, "Which I picked up. Then we walked in circles for a while following your tracks then... we found you." She tweaked my nose and giggled, "Idiot."

Great God above us all! It was a miracle of such extraordinary proportions that even God's own angels could not have performed it. That was why I could not find my blasted bag. I knew that I had been looking in the right place. I held her at arm's length as she described how she had discovered me collapsed in the snow and got the sheriff's men to carry me back to her coach where she had removed my wet clothes and dressed me, even giving me her stockings, at which point I had briefly regained consciousness before passing out again while travelling to this place where I had been asleep for two days until, eventually, waking up now.

I gaped open-mouthed as the entirety of the wonderful truth sank in and it eventually dawned on me that at long last it was over - truly over. Thanking God for putting this wonderful woman upon the Earth I pulled her to me with joyous rapture and, with my heart bursting with unadulterated gratitude and joy, shut her up once and for all by burying my lips into hers and kissing her deeply. She had saved me from the very jaws of death and finally we were together again.

"Wait!" I tried to shout past her wriggling mouth as the last question sprang to mind. But she, being one step ahead of me as usual, pointed to a dresser at the far end of the room where I saw the box sitting safe and sound. She breathed between kisses, "I knew you'd kill the bastard, darling."

She was a good girl and I prepared to show her how much I thought so. After a night of incredible pleasure the details of which, though I constantly recall them myself - especially now in my older years - I cannot share for reasons of common decency, personal reputation, natural law and probably religious edict too, our celebrations carried on. For the very next morning my love informed me that I was to have the pleasure of meeting her father, the Grand Duke - of all people - especially when I had thought this so impossible only a few months before. Had I not come a long way? Apparently, he would be meeting us at another coaching house down the road and we were to travel there that day to see him. I was even more surprised when Francesca informed me that there was something of great importance about which he wished to talk with me. Me, of all people. I had *indeed* come a long way.

So later that day, after wearing out the bed in our room, we boarded Francesca's coach and journeyed to our rendezvous where we met her father the imposing Grand Duke Nicholas Alexi Kropotkin III. Though, in truth, he was not imposing, well, not in a bad way, he was a very stout, cheerful man who, having barely arrived himself, welcomed us warmly in the doorway of the inn. Sporting a huge fur coat and hat and an even bigger beard he energetically shook my hand. "Ah, yes. Herr Drechsler you look very Bavarian indeed. I have heard much about you and look forward to hearing much more. Hello, hello, hello."

"Forgive my father for the way he speaks, Sebastian. He is only a Russian."

"Ho, ho. Stupid woman. Just like her mad mother eh!" he roared, slapping me hard enough on the back to loosen my teeth. "You must forgive my daughter young Bavarian. After all, she is only the *daughter* of a Russian." He winked and elbowed me in the guts, jollying, "Now let us eat. There is much I wish to talk about. Quick. Quick. While I can afford manners, I wouldn't know what to do with them."

At the table he certainly did not mince his words and we had not even started our first course before he was questioning me about Kolmer. After I had described the destruction of the obelisk, the freeing of the child, my journey into the wilderness then subsequent final battle with the fiend and the recovery of the stone, he nodded solemnly, "You have done well young Bavarian. The Order is everywhere in these dark times. The demons hide in the shadows of all the great countries and also the not so great. Oh yes, my boy: Old Mother Russia too. Everywhere they go it is the same; if the people are like this, then they are like that, but if the people are like that, then they are like this. Everywhere it is the same. That is the trick of their revolution." He pulled an exasperated face and I could see from where Francesca got her mannerisms, though perhaps not her dainty waistline.

She twisted her nose and said, "What my father is trying to say is the idea of revolutionary change created through the catalyst of diametrically opposed political ideologies is greatly effective." She popped a piece of bread into her beautiful mouth and searched my eyes to check that I knew what she meant. *[29]

".. I see," I said, attempting to seem wise but failing dismally.

She went to explain but her father interrupted, "For millennia the best way to cause revolution has been the same: divide and rule. Divide and rule young Bavarian. The Illuminati know this well and aim to use it in my homeland. Sometime soon I fear. I don't know how and I don't know when, but I know they plan it. Oh yes. I know it because I feel it in my Russian blood." *[30]

29. **Hegelian Dialectic & The Illuminati.** Hegel was a German philosopher (1770-1831) and is widely renowned for first understanding that the dialectic between conflicting ideas can be used to bring about desired change: Thesis – Antithesis – Synthesis. The technique has many given names including the more modern, and perhaps more well-known, 'Problem – Reaction – Solution.' 'Divide and Rule' - the Roman equivalent - explains the theory in another way; the 'division' coming from two opposing ideas, Thesis and Antithesis, bringing about the product or 'Synthesis' which, in turn becomes the new thesis. Conspiracy theorists argue that this technique is used to bring about control on a geopolitical level whilst, interestingly, psychologists contend that it is equally effective on a personal basis.

30. **The Illuminati & The Russian Revolution.** Conspiracy theorists, and even some mainstream historians, have long claimed that the roots of The Russian Revolution were not entirely organic and that the epochal political events which swept the nation in 1917 were fomented by outside influences. In terms of world power the USSR, as it came to be, or opposing atheist communist state can be seen as the counterbalance to the US, setting up a classic left-right paradigm (thesis - antithesis) often associated with Illuminati global goals. A great deal of evidence exists backing up this claim. Notable inclusions to this long list are Prof Antony C. Sutton's *Wall Street and the Bolshevik Revolution* (1992) and Prof Carroll Quigley's *Tragedy and Hope* (1963) which provide excellent source material for those wishing to explore an alternative view of international politics.

He puffed out his chest and thumped it with his fist while Francescagave him a frown. He sniffed at her as his demeanour darkened and he leaned closer, probing, "And what of the stone young Bavarian?"

"What of it? It's in the carriage. I can go and get it if you want?"

"Oh, no, no, no" he waved a hand and crossed his chest with the other, "I would rather not thank you, my boy. But I feel that I should tell you," he glanced at Francesca, "We think it should be taken back."

"Taken back?" I coughed. "Did you not hear me tell you how hard it was getting it *here*?"

"Back to where it belongs," said Francesca, squeezing my arm and assuring, "Then the Order cannot use it."

"Use it?" I gawked. "Surely you don't believe the stone has some sort of *mystical power* that they can use against us? You - of all people?"

"It is an important relic, Sebastian. It can be used as a political tool: to bribe, to compromise, to control." She crooked an eyebrow. "You obviously thought it important enough to go after."

"But I must take it back to the Professor. That is my mission."

Her father tapped his knife on his plate to break the deadlock. "If that is your wish, young Bavarian, then we cannot stop you." There was a pause before he looked between us and laughed, "Anyway, enough of such talk. With so many of Satan's whores sent back to Hell where they will burn for eternity in their own excrement we should be merry. So let us be merry!"

Stone me. He was like Francesca. And so the banquet continued and we were merry. Very merry indeed. After that moment we did not speak of the Order, or the stone again but only of matters of a frivolous, or sporting, or laughable, or purely outrageous nature and laughed and drank and feasted deep into the night. In the very early hours, on the very best of terms and very much the worse for wear, we eventually parted company with the amiable Duke before turning in ourselves. I saw him once more the following afternoon before he had to leave on important business that would take him back east. And so, after several hearty farewells and much shaking of hands and painful back-slapping, he left us on our own. Hurrah!

Over the next two days, snuggled up in the coaching house with my true love by my side, even the thought of my journeys and my failing university career did not trouble me in the slightest and I wanted for nothing more. And why should I? For once I truly had everything in my grasp. Truly. So, on the afternoon of the third day, I was almost unsurprised when, upon returning from a stroll, my lady casually informed me that she had to leave again.

Confound it! I should have known. Apparently her sudden change of plan was due to the fact that she had neglected to share something of 'great importance' with her father. Such was my fractious mood upon hearing this news that I forgot to mention my surprise on finding her driver sneaking about with a basket full of pigeons and during the ensuing argument, I said many cruel things to her, which in retrospect, were probably unnecessary. But she, not being without the ability to respond in the most hurtful manner herself, did not help matters by provoking me further with several outrageous allegations regarding my carnal abilities and, as such, we did not reconcile our love that evening. So, before we both knew it the very next morning, we departed from a coaching house but, once again, in opposite directions with her travelling east to meet her father and me west returning directly to Ingolstadt. Good God! When would I get some proper time with this woman?

Adding to my woes the journey home was anything but easy. For when I say returning 'directly' to Ingolstadt, in reality, it was nothing of the sort and over the next two weeks I was sent hither and thither through the countless principalities of Bohemia and became lost on several occasions amidst a miasma of over-complicated stagecoach timetables. Constantly being at the whim of this foreign and most unreliable transportation system did nothing to improve my ailing spirits and the long journey home only intensified my sad and lonely feelings for Francesca.

"Damn it!" I cursed, leaning against a dozen misty coach windows, "Why did she have to leave?" I was so downhearted that my spirits did not even lift when I eventually saw the familiar road sign proclaiming, '*Ingolstadt 10 miles.*'

My subsequent homecoming which I had imagined to be quite some affair with crowds of well-wishers lining the streets elated to see the slayer of the dreaded Illuminati, at last, safely returning was, of course, nothing of the sort and I dismounted from the stagecoach into the thick of a foggy winter's night before wearily trudging back to my lonely lodgings. I was further depleted upon coming through my door to be greeted by a pile of bills and letters. Importantly, and I read them with growing dread, much correspondence from the university regarding my unexplained absence. When would my living nightmares end?

Not yet was the answer. Because, the very next morning being a Monday, I meekly returned to the university, not forgetting to bring the all-important stone in its precious box. Upon my arrival I made my way straight to the Professor's study, bursting with anticipation and an overwhelming urge to explain everything that had happened. Though this happy prospect was finely balanced with dire apprehension because of the drubbing I was inevitably about to receive as soon as someone in authority found me.

My heart sank when the Professor did not answer and, after

trying again, I moved to the clerk's door but before I could knock the slight young man peeped around it. He stared at me as if he had seen a ghost before glimpsing the box under my arm and nervously beckoning me inside, whispering, "The Professor has not returned since he went to the trial many weeks ago." His eyes shot from side to side and he flustered, "I am worried for his life. I am always worried for his life."

This was certainly not the welcome of which I had dreamt. Good Lord. Where was the mad Professor now? Of course, it was impossible to know and one might as well have placed a finger on a spinning globe and looked there as anywhere else. I rechecked the gloomy corridor and sighed, "Then, sir, we shall pray for his safe return."

With this I scurried off to my first lecture but no sooner had I reached the stairs that I heard Herr Lipstad's voice ominously call, "Herr Drechsler. Can you come with me please?"

Dreading what was to come I dragged myself back up the corridor with my head hung low. Over the following two hours I received the worst dressing down of my student life. I suppose the faculty had every right to have their misgivings. Including the time that I had spent at the trial I had been away for a grand total of ten weeks without any explanation whatsoever. Herr Lipstad was beside himself with anger as was, according to him, the entire History department not to mention the rest of the university and, as far as I can remember, the townspeople of Ingolstadt and greater Bavaria too. To my horror I found out that a letter was to be sent to my parents informing them of my absence and I shook my head in my hands as the entirety of the faculty's punishments, recriminations and sanctions, including an appearance in front of Principal Vacchieri, were read out to me. Hell's bells. I cursed my long adventure and sat there fidgeting with the troublesome box not knowing what was to become of me.

The telling-off lasted so long that it was pointless going to my first lecture and now, wanting to see the Professor more than ever, I returned to his study. After checking the corridor was empty, I knocked again but was further deflated to receive no answer. I was about to try once more when the clerk reappeared at his door and excitedly gestured me inside. I slipped into his room to find that his demeanour had significantly brightened and that he was clutching a note in his hand.

"You have good news, sir?" I begged with hopeful anticipation.

"Yes indeed, Master Drechsler, the Professor returns this very afternoon. I have received word from his most trusted servant within the hour telling me that a message was delivered by horseman last night."

I clasped his arm upon hearing the good news and asked, "At what hour?"

"Three," he said, eyeing the box and suggesting, "Perhaps you should leave that with me, sir... if it's for the Professor and he returns so soon?"

Nobody else seemed to want the blasted thing and I did not blame them. Battered old casket that it was.

"Why not?" I smiled, jubilant to hear of Van Halestrom's imminent return.

The clerk took it from me and reminded, "Three then."

"One thing," I mentioned, feeling a whiff of caution, "May I see the note?"

He passed it to me and sure enough it was from Bacon. There, written in the old butler's unmistakable handwriting, it clearly said, '*The Professor returns to the University for a chess match at three o'clock.*' It could not be clearer. There was even a black oblong drawn below denoting the clerk's door. I passed it back and excused myself, "Thank you. We must all be careful in these troubled times, eh?"

He showed me out and I strolled jauntily down the corridor as happy as Ludwig. Goodness gracious me. I almost broke into a chorus of Hallelujah but thought better of it in case Herr Lipstad caught me celebrating. The Professor was the last piece of the puzzle that had remained out of place and now that he was returning he would sort everything out. Yes. That was right. We would exchange our stories whilst hatching a plan to protect me from Herr Vacchieri and all would be well with the world. I put my hands in my pockets and even enjoyed a little whistle as I came outside into the university courtyard. I had barely left the gates when the bells of St Maria's rang out through the streets and Van Halestrom's voice echoed in my mind, "I swear we will never use a horseman again to deliver our messages."

"Good God!" I spurted, engulfed by a sudden wave of intuition, "The clerk's the traitor!"

I pelted back through the gates, crashed through the doors, raced along the corridors then up the stairs and flew round the corner to the Professor's study. But my heart dropped out of my backside when I saw the clerk's door sanding open. No! He's gone! I shot past glancing inside but of course it was empty.

"The eastern entrance!" I roared, bolting down the corridor and shouting at some students to get out of the way. I dashed past a window overlooking the street and nearly screamed when I spotted the clerk at the front gates beckoning a suspicious looking rider towards him. Damn it! He must have followed me outside.

I slid to a halt at the top of the stairs, almost bumping into Herr Lipstad, mumbled apologetically and ran back the other way. This time when I passed the window I was sure that the horseman was Kolmer's man from the cavern who I had kicked into the pool.

"Shit! He's still alive!"

I flung myself down the stairs bellowing at the students round the door to move and tore outside. I held my tongue as I raced across the courtyard hoping to catch the clerk by surprise. But as I sprinted up to the gates, bundling the students out of my way, he held up the box to the horseman.

"Traitor!" I roared and lunged at them but the clerk barged into my chest as the rider took the box and galloped away. "No!" I yelled into the clerk's face then looked down at my stomach feeling strangely tired. Damn it. He was holding the handle of a knife that was stabbed into my guts. Thunder and lightning. The bastard had killed me.

Chapter 31

The Box

I stared into the clerk's eyes as his hand slipped away from the knife. I had not even seen the blade before he had stabbed me but now there it was, sticking from my belly with blood beginning to seep into my jacket. I looked behind him at Kolmer's henchman riding off up the street with the precious box stuffed under his arm. Everything had been so well only a few seconds before.

"Pig dog!" I cursed and took a faltering step towards him. Well sometimes we are not in control of our actions and that moment in the street outside my university, facing that quivering traitor and watching the stone that I had risked my life for so many times, galloping away before my eyes was one such moment. I grasped the knife with both hands and, taking an anguished breath, pulled it out with one gut-wrenching heave.

"Son of a bitch!" I roared and punched the Judas in the mouth, sending him flying on his arse. Up the street Kolmer's henchman had become stuck behind a cart and I tried to run after him but a lightning bolt of pain shot through my guts stopping me in my tracks. I clasped my stomach and steadied myself then turned back to the clerk blubbering on the floor. He covered his face as I went to kick him but I was stopped by the sound of arriving hooves and Professor Van Halestrom protesting, "No, Sebastian! It's over!"

I was so surprised to see him jumping down from his horse with two mounted constables in tow that I hesitated and wobbled about on one leg. He took one look at my bloodstained knife and grabbed my shoulders repeating, "It's over, Sebastian."

Failing to notice my own injuries he left me in a daze and turned his attention to the clerk. I leant against his horse and, noticing it scraping its hoof on the cobbles, I stumbled along its flank and hauled myself up into the saddle. Kolmer's man pushed his way past the cart and I drove in my heels, roaring, "No! It's not over!" and thundered up the street lashing the reins across the horse's neck.

The rider veered around a turn up ahead and I clattered after him guessing that he must be headed for the Eastern gate. The bastard would certainly not be staying in The Eagle tonight! I came round the corner to find him at a junction trying to work out which way to go, but as I raced towards him he got his bearings and galloped off down Baker's Lane. We tore in between the gap in the buildings and he glanced behind to see me gaining on him holding out the bloody knife.

"Yes! You swine! I'm going to get you!" I raged as another torrent of pain tore through my guts. I began to feel light-headed and my vision started to dim as we galloped past the crowds of shocked onlookers. Ahead of me the rider jumped his horse over the hitch of a parked cart. Shit! I steadied myself and jumped my horse too but when I landed I was almost thrown off by jolt of searing pain.

"Hold on!" I gasped, desperately clutching the horse's neck as we hurtled on down the lane. My quarry's steed was much fresher than mine and, as he got into his stride, I realised that he was easing away.

No! We were tearing past the last few houses before the eastern gate with the river Danube beyond and a crowd of the city's watchmen standing lazily around. I tried to shout but had no breath to warn them to close the gate. Knowing that I would have to stop him myself, I held the knife above my head and took aim as but as I bounced along I bent double when another crippling spasm ripped through my guts.

"Purpose!" I grunted and pulled myself up then hurled the knife. It flew through the air catching the last faint rays of wintry sunlight before revolving once more and stabbing the rider right in the nape of his neck. Yes! He threw up his arms but sent the box flying through the air.

"The box!" I roared.

With no care for my own safety I threw myself from my horse and slid through the mud and shit and straw and somehow managed to catch the casket in my outstretched hands. I came to a grinding halt at the mouth of the gates covered in filth and rolled over in time to see the watchmen control the thief's horse while he slumped in his saddle.

"My God! I did it!" I gasped, spitting out the dirt and pulling myself up with the box under one arm and the other clutching my belly. One of the watchmen ran over to help me but I waved him away ordering, "Put that man over his saddle and bring him with me!"

My sense of urgency, and probably the fact that he had seen me perform such an act of heroic bravery, immediately convinced him that I was of some authority. He ran over to the thug's horse where the others helped to get the groaning villain down and stretched out over the saddle. I tried to pretend that I was not about to fall over whilst noticing that I had ruined yet another set of clothes and was conspicuously bleeding into my jacket. I limped unsteadily over to my horse where I was helped into the saddle, rather fortunately I think, by some charitable passers-by. Though barely able to hold myself up on my pommel I somehow managed to yell at the watchmen, "Follow me back to the university. Now!"

I clung onto my horse and led our small procession back through the lanes whilst every yard resolutely gripping the box for all I was worth. There was no way I was going to let the blasted thing out of my sight again. When we came up the street to the university I was surprised to see an excited crowd milling around the gates and, as we entered the courtyard there was a pleasing ripple of applause and even some cheering from those who had witnessed the affray. I proudly took a bow almost falling from the horse in the process. Yes sir! This was more like the welcome of which I had dreamt. I dismounted and faltered again while a group of students came over, with some of the more helpful ones keeping me on my feet. One of the constables pushed his way to the front and told me that he would look after the felon and that the Professor was inside interrogating the clerk before the sheriff arrived.

"I would interrogate the bastard," I fumed on hearing this news and instantly straightened up before barging my way through the crowd and stumbling off to the Professor's study. I staggered up to his door and without knocking - or damn-well looking to see who was watching first - burst inside to find Van Halestrom tending to the blasted clerk in the chair behind his desk. Damn it! The bastard had tried to kill me. I stormed over still clutching the box to my bleeding belly and, though the Professor turned to stop me, I managed to get my free hand round the traitor's throat as he languished in the chair.

"Stop! Sebastian!" yelled Van Halestrom, grabbing my arm, "It is over!"

"But the bastard stabbed me!" I roared as the clerk's eyeballs swelled in their sockets and he flapped around uselessly trying to get me to stop.

"They have his parents, Sebastian!"

I glared at Van Halestrom while he fixed me with his hawkish eyes and pulled at my arm, repeating, "It's over, lad" I squeezed my fist but he tightened his grip, urging me, "You're doing well, lad. Now let go. Let go." I eyed him with consternation before finally letting go and supporting myself on his desk as the two constables marched in through the open door. They lifted the clerk from the chair then escorted him out and I went to go after the louse again but collapsed against Van Halestrom.

"Damn it, Professor! He tried to steal the box!"

I held out the battered, banded, old casket and, at last, after hundreds of miles, countless deaths and numerous acts of incredible valour on my behalf, not to mention this last spectacular deed, I finally banged it down on his desk, gasping, "There!"

He sighed and shook his head before reaching over and opening the lid. My heart stopped dead when I saw a plain grey rock where the mystical green stone had been. No!

"Search him! I roared, lunging after the traitor once more but the Professor pulled me back by my tattered sleeve.

"Sebastian you are injured," he raised an eyebrow, "Though it seems not enough to stop you behaving normally." He helped me into the chair and began undoing my jacket and shirt.

"I assure you the biggest injury I have received, sir, is the slaying of my pride. The stone is gone. Gone! What shall we do? Whatever shall we do? Damn it! Damn it all!"

He threw me a sideways look and pulled a bottle of brandy from the desk's cupboard. "It has not been there for some time, my lad. Francesca stole it from you."

It was a good job that I was sitting down because I would have fallen over such was my shock upon hearing this. I went to speak but alas no words came out.

He wiped my wound with the alcohol and explained, "We decided that, should we find the stone, it must be returned to its rightful home; Shigatse in Nepal, or as it is Hermetically known, Shamballa. Hopefully to put it out of the Order's reach for good. I gave Francesca instructions to take it from you, had you found it but did not want to give it to her freely. Which I believe was the case?"

He squinted at me and I went to speak again but it was useless and I sat there with my mouth hanging open in stupefaction.

He took off his scarf and began wrapping it around me. "We used the empty box to lure the clerk out into the open as we were suspicious that he was the traitor and would try to steal the stone given the opportunity. Which, as you know, he did." He caught my eye and smiled, "Much has occurred in your absence, Sebastian. The authorities are going to print the documents confiscated from Zwack's house to show the Illuminati's plans to the countries of Europe. Also powerful new laws have been created enabling the police to arrest members of the Order. As you have seen they are fully prepared to use them and now it appears that, rather serendipitously, you have been the first to take advantage of these as you were part of this valiant effort to clear the den of vipers from the university." He winked and smiled, "Well done, Sebastian. You have excelled again. Ha, ha. Yes, my boy, you have excelled again."

I reeled in the chair as the momentous news settled in but was still sufficiently compos mentis to notice Herr Lipstad appear in the doorway.

He huffed discontentedly and went to speak but the Professor interrupted him without taking his attention from me, "Please do not even try to criticise this brave young man, my scholarly friend. He has just risked his life protecting this institution from a very real and grave threat and, instead of being told off, should be given a medal."

The agitated old duffer spluttered, "Principal Vacchieri will hear of this..."

Van Halestrom butted in, "I will personally speak to the Principal myself. Hopefully, before the authorities do as they will, no doubt, wish to discuss his Illuminati connections with him."

Old Lipstad's face turned as white as a ghost and he coughed into his handkerchief then left in a fluster.

"Right. That's that," smiled Van Halestrom, finishing bandaging my girth and giving me a wink.

"Thank you, sir," I gushed, "You are... a true friend."

"It is I who should be thanking you, Sebastian. You have taught me many lessons, not least in forgiveness eh? Perhaps a few years back *you* might have had to stop me from trying to knock out Old Lipstad's teeth?"

I shook my head in wonder but winced as he tied a knot in the scarf, "Is it... really over, sir?"

"Perhaps," he chuckled, "If you can forgive me for using you to catch the clerk?"

"Why, of course, sir."

"And tying this too tight?"

He yanked at the scarf almost causing me to squeal and I grimaced, "... Yes, sir."

"And for making you jump into the firepace at Zwack's house?"

I reflected how long it had been since I had seen him and laughed, "Yes, sir." My raging thoughts returned to my journey and I told him, in a more sombre tone, "I killed him, sir. I killed them all."

"I know, Sebastian," he flapped his hands like the wings of a bird, "Remember our feathered friends?"

Suddenly realising what Francesca's driver had been doing with a basketful of pigeons and that she had left me to give her father the stone, I moaned, "But, Professor, without my news and without the gem, I feel that I have brought nothing back from my adventures."

He pulled himself up and put his hands on his hips. "On the contrary, Sebastian, you have come back with the greatest prize of all: Knowledge." He lifted his finger going to recite one of his maxims, "And..."

This time I anticipated him and joined in, "Knowledge is power. Yes, Professor. Believe me, sir, I know. I know."

He laughed and slapped his tigh, beaming, "Well done, lad. Well done. We'll make a scholar of you yet and a funny one at that. Ha, ha. Yes, a funny one at that." *[31]

---

31. **The Publication of the Original Writings of The Illuminati.** As S. Drechsler describes the Original Writings of the Illuminati *Einige Originalschriften des Illuminaten Ordens* confiscated from Xavier Zwack's house in the illegal raid were published by the Bavarian authorities in late 1785. They were sent to the leaderships of all European countries in an effort to warn them about the Illuminati's revolutionary activities. The author is also correct in his assertion that new laws had been granted to the police at this time allowing them to arrest Illuminati members on the spot. The crime of membership was now a serious offence and those found guilty could face severe jail sentences.

Chapter 32

All's Well That Ends Well

Was it really the end? It seemed to be. The Professor was right, as usual, about my injuries. Though I had lost quite a lot of blood by extremely good fortune, the knife – to be fair an envelope knife - had missed anything inside me of importance. Good God. I had been lucky. There was not that much of me to go around. It was another shot in a million. After being tended by several doctors (finally being at the finest medical university in the world was useful) I was sent home to rest and did precisely that. Two days later I was once again at the Professor's desk but this time bathed, brushed, bandaged, combed, cleaned, sporting a new outfit and proudly standing to attention with my lucky hat under my arm. I took care to straighten my fringe as I had even indulged my yearly custom of having a haircut.

"You look better, my lad. A lot better," observed the Professor, nodding contently in his chair and puffing on his pipe. I smiled broadly from my deepest depths. Not only was I presentable, happy and alive but I had, only five minutes ago, received an official pardon from the university board and even an apology from a humbled Herr Lipstad himself. Adding to this I had also been most pleased to find that an article recording my exploits outside the university had been published in the local newssheet short, it would have to be said, of some of the more interesting details. More importantly, to my overwhelming delight, the communication to my parents had been tracked down and destroyed before it was sent. To top it all we had discovered that Herr Vacchieri had been ordered to take, what the university board had euphemistically described, 'a long sabbatical' while he was investigated for his Illuminati connections. Yes indeed. I was on top of the very world that sweet winter's day of 1786.

Such were my soaring spirits that I was finding it hard to stop myself from jumping around and hollering with delight.

The Professor noticed my exuberance and eyed me up and down wagging his finger. "Yes, yes, lad. No need to get ahead of yourself there." He opened his drawer and cocked an eyebrow, continuing, "You have obviously learnt a lot on your way but I sense," he looked me in the eye, "That there is more you want to tell me? Am I right?"

I nodded excitedly for, as usual, the mind-reading old bird was correct. Having had the opportunity to arrange my thoughts over the past days and reflect on my recent experiences I felt that I had developed a theory explaining the Order's plans regarding the Cintamani Stone and was chomping at the bit to share it. Obviously, the Professor was the perfect man to tell and, as I had hoped, he settled back into his chair, stroking his beard and urging me to explain with an expectant look.

This was my moment. I raised a finger for scholarly emphasis, cleared my throat, took a deep breath and announced, "It is my belief, sir, that Kolmer wanted to use the stone's alchemic powers to bless the Illuminati's undertaking - For the money they plan to create is the greatest alchemy of all: To turn paper into gold."

I proudly stood to attention and, expecting to be congratulated, was crestfallen when he stared back uncharacteristically blank-faced. So confident had I been about my theory that I had planned to tap my heels together before being lavished with deserved praise but now I began to doubt myself. An eternity seemed to pass before his expression lifted and he grinned, "You really are starting to understand aren't you, my lad?"

Annoying old bird. An enormous smile lit up my face as he began rummaging around in his drawer and throwing some bags of coins on the table. "I think you're right, Sebastian. Along with the phallic obelisk, I believe the stone was the symbolic egg and supplied the necessary female attributes of creational alchemy to the ritual. God knows what these lunatics will think of next to satisfy their deranged egos. But that's another matter. Now we must pay you some money. There are your clothes, your time, your rent, bills, Petrova..." *32

I laughed at his humorous manner and waved my hand chuckling, "I have more than enough money already, sir. I don't need any more."

---

32. **The Cintamani Stone & The Dollar Bill.** In support of S. Drechsler's theory the connections between this mysterious stone and the dollar bill are endless. Nicholas Roerich a Russian mystic and Henry Wallace US Secretary of Agriculture in 1933 (the politician most associated with the esoteriv design of the current dollar bill apart from President Roosevelt), were both deeply involved with the Cintamani Stone. Wallace sent Roerich on many missions to Tibet (Shamballa) in the 1930's to fetch and return the stone and intriguingly several of Roerich's famous paintings feature a mystical jewel being transported through a wasteland, some of which inexplicably resemble S. Drechsler's own experiences and begs the question that Kolmer may also have been attempting to return the relic. Roerich later fell from grace with the White House when he was suspected of being a Russian spy and Wallace's career, though not destroyed, was greatly undermined by rumours of unwarranted spiritualism when letters that he had sent to Roerich became public in which he called him his 'guru.' The Cintamani Stone's magical properties are still held in such high regard that it is easy to conclude those with occult objectives might seek to employ its supposed powers. Whether the stone's alchemic capabilities are real or not, it seems that the The Stone and the dollar's histories are so inexorably linked that there has to be something else behind the official story. The US Mint issued the first dollar in 1787 a year after S. Drechsler's account takes place and the '$' sign 'serpent entwining the cross' was incorporated shortly after in 1793. With this in mind is it too far-fetched to assume that what the author had accidentally discovered on his adventures was 'The Birth of The Dollar'? This frightening conclusion would mean that the world's reserve currency would be a creation of the Bavarian Illuminati but with no clarification, hopefully, this part of the mystery will be revealed in future instalments of the memoirs. A piece of The Cintamani Stone is now rumoured to be contained in the cornerstone of the 'Master Building' penthouse built for Roerich in New York on the corner of 53rd Street.

He stopped what he was doing so abruptly that I thought he might be unwell and was about to take a step to aid him when he asked, "How long have you worked for me, Sebastian?"

I did not know what to say nor had the time to answer before he carried on, "Two and a half years I think. Yes?"

I nodded, uncertain where this was leading.

"You have learnt quickly, which I like a lot, but today, Sebastian, you have truly surprised me."

For the first time since I had known him his eyes filled with a wistful, faraway look and he soulfully said, "All the planets, Sebastian. You really are starting to understand aren't you? I am very proud of you. Very, very proud indeed."

This unexpected and earnest praise from my master, the man I respected like no other, was extremely fulfilling and I wondered if I could be any happier. Of course, he gave me no time to rest on my laurels and leant back in his chair putting his fingertips together and puffing on his pipe. "So I presume you think that you know it all now, my lad? Eh? Am I right?"

This last remark from out of the blue totally blew me off course. What could he mean? I could not tell if he was joking or not and replied rather uncertainly but still with some bravado, "Well, I am proud of my accomplishments, sir.

He blew out a ring of smoke and smiled with inscrutable wisdom lighting his eyes, "Is not pride a sin, Herr Drechsler?"

He chuckled to himself whilst getting out of his chair and strolling over to the window. Before I could ask what he meant by this enigma he tapped his pipe on the glass and exclaimed, "Ah ha! There is perhaps one thing not even you would have been able to work out, my lad."

"What, sir? What is it?" A chill went up my spine as I wondered what could be next; more Illuminati servants, or even Kolmer back from his icy grave? Judging by the Professor's expression it was something far less threatening but I still got up cautiously to take a look. Well, if I had another lifetime to work it out I could not have guessed. My heart pumped like a steam whistle when I saw Francesca waiting at the university gates in her carriage with her miserable driver at the reins.

"My God," I gasped.

"Go to her, my lad. You've earned it," he said, slapping me on the back. I eyed him with some suspicion and he watched my eyes for a moment until reassuring, "A rest, my lad. You've earned a rest." He checked my eyes once more before asking, "Is all well with you?"

I sighed with much relief, "Yes, Professor," then bowed and loudly clicked my heels together as I had planned.

I rose from my bow to find him sticking out his hand and declaring, "Well done, Sebastian."

"Thank you, sir," I replied, sincerely returning the gesture and shaking his hand while we shared one last meaningful moment of friendship before, at last, I went to take my leave.

"Never forget, Sebastian," he called from behind.

I turned impatiently in the doorway and asked, "What now, Professor?"

"Stay in the shadows, my friend," he smiled and hurriedly gestured for me to go.

"Yes, Professor," I grinned and bolted off.

I dashed along the corridors bellowing at the other students to clear the way and flew down the stairs in unbridled ecstasy. Joy of joys! What a day. How could it be any better?

I bounded through the front doors and, seeing that my lady had drawn a crowd of admirers including a couple of the bullying third years, I attempted to make it even better. Ha, ha. Yes indeed. I remember that moment very well. After craftily returning to a stroll I crossed the courtyard with a confident air and, taking the opportunity to further impress my peers with my seemingly ever-growing swagger, casually walked up to the carriage where I took Francesca's hand and kissed it before hopping in beside her and winking at my salivating colleagues.

"Ah. My fine young Bavarian," she purred, playfully putting a finger to her chin and tapping the driver's back with her muff.

Yes! What a pretty picture we made. The returning hero rides into the sunset with the beautiful heroine. How could anything be better?

We rumbled away from the gates leaving the third year bullies in a spasm of jealousy and the other more reasonable chaps filled with much fraternal pride though, doubtless, a smaller degree of envy. Surely now I had rid myself once and for all of my father's stifling self-consciousness and was ready to assume the life of a gentlemen.

Well, life has a strange way of turning you on your head again and again. For, after my lady had asked me about my meeting with the Professor and I had explained my exciting theory regarding the mysterious stone, she chuckled, "I think there is one more thing that is perhaps a greater alchemy. Yes? To make something from seemingly *nothing*?"

"Pray tell, what is that, my lady?" I enquired with some confusion.

She watched my eyes for a moment before laughing, "Oh dear, so much for your rampant manly intuition."

What could she mean? Confound this blasted woman. I searched her eyes again but was still nonplussed.

She grinned from one rosy cheek to the other and laughed, "I am with child, idiot."

I coughed and spluttered and stuttered and speechlessly swooned like my own self-conscious father as we rattled down the road and she giggled and smiled and squeezed my knee.

That was how it could be better. What a night that was. Oh how we loved each other then. Yes indeed. What wonderful times we shared over the next few days and weeks but these are the beginnings of other stories of which I do not have the time to tell now because, as you may have guessed, this is the end of this particular chapter in my extraordinary tale. And what a pleasant end for me.

A pleasantness that only had to be interrupted once more before all would be well. At least, as well as all could be. A few days before Christmas - forgive my timing but it took me that long to pluck up the courage - I went to see Karl's father. Petrova certainly needed shoeing but, of course, this was not the real reason that I paid the blacksmith and old Thunder a visit. He calmly agreed to carry out the work before going about his business. When he had finished, with a heavy heart, I took the decent man to one side and told him the truth. He crumpled to his knees when I told him that I had killed those who had taken his boy away from him and gently helped him to his seat. I stayed with him as long as it took for him to pull himself together before going to take my leave. He thanked me and I gave him a bag of money telling him there was no need to count it. It was all that I could do. I wished him farewell and walked Petrova out into the snow that had started to fall.

Now it was really over.

There is only one part that I have left to tell. Though, that part, for me and my very particular future, was perhaps the most important part of all.

Chapter 33

The Man at the End of the Universe

It could have only been a week later when I next returned to the Castle Landfried eager to learn more about the riddles which I had experienced that the last piece of the story fell into place. On that afternoon Bacon was reading to me in his room and I was sitting in my usual seat trying, as hard as ever, to take it all in. Ah yes. Nearly seventy years later I still recall the day with great detail and I shall explain why. I had secretly been speculating about the vision that I had received after passing out in the snow when trying to hang onto my life and, of course, the mysterious stone. I say secretly because, for some reason, I had not told anyone about this experience, not even Van Halestrom, preferring to keep it to myself. In hindsight I believe this was because it was something that I wished to understand better before attempting to share. Also, perhaps more importantly, I did not want to sound like a romantic fool or deranged lunatic who perhaps thought that he had seen the secrets of the world revealed. Though, rather ominously, and even more secretivly, I was starting to believe that, in some way, I had. Either that or I had received an epiphany of enormous magnitude because, even in my immature mind, I could already recognise it deeply shaping my thoughts.

So, whilst Bacon read from his book '*Secrets of The Ancient Mystery School,*' my ears pricked up when he said, "Man's true spirit can be seen as a reflection of the universe. Whereas primordial man, Adam Kadmon, the 'original,' or 'above,' symbolises the universe itself, the first worldly man, Adam Harishon, the 'first' or 'below,' represents the universe within."

That was the sentence that did it. That was the sentence that changed my life. And I do not say that lightly. Oh no. Doubt it not.

For it was at that moment, as my own experiences melded with this ancient philosophy, that my entire being was transformed. I was no fool and I instantly realised that, of course, it was my vision; the man at the end of the universe, me, the universe within. All at once everything fell into place. Then, like a guillotine chopping down with a thump, I remembered Kolmer cackling, "Above as below, my friend! Above as below!" Thunder and lightning! It was all true.

I sat agog as Bacon went on, "Therefore, the quest of life is to transcend the worldly plane and to free oneself from the finite by submitting to the eternal thus moving to the Godhead to find the one who hammers out the new souls on The Anvil of Destiny."

Well, unsurprisingly, I was utterly stupefied. To have my spiritual experience which I had felt far too fanciful to mention to anyone even the village idiot without sounding like an escaped patient from the asylum, so perfectly described in this arcane text caused my mouth to fall open wide. It simply could not be a coincidence. My intuition rang like the bells of St Maria's on New Year's Day and my old notions were swept away by a wave of altered consciousness.

Bacon noticed my stupour and looked over the book, prompting, "Are you unwell, sir?" He added, in his usual excruciatingly condescending tone, "If I may venture, sir, you look as though you are going to die."

Such was my incredulity that I did not rise to his poor humour but murmured, "I saw it, Bacon. I saw it all: Adam Kadmon, the end of the universe, The Godhead, the Being hammering out the souls. I saw it all."

He watched me for a while and straightened up before contemplating with some seriousness, "Then maybe, sir, I wonder if you *did* die?" He peered knowingly in my eye and I threw him a sideways look as he insightfully pondered, "But somehow, someone brought you back?"

Good Lord! Of course! He was right. I had died in the snow
and *had* gone to meet my maker but Francesca brought me
back. Now it all made sense. My God! A shudder ran down my
spine as I remembered Kolmer taunting me about his contract
with his celestial master. The bastard was right too! I *did* have
to die to kill him. Damn him and his celestial master. I knew
who that was. Would the memories of the evil fiend ever leave
me? I doubted it. 'Lord save us all,' I prayed then realised that,
perhaps, He already had? Good Heavens. I was plunged into
a stupor as the amazing possibilities sank in, their profundities
shaping the very core of my soul. What an extraordinary world
in which I lived. My thoughts returned to my adventures and all
that I had been through.

Bacon closed the book and butted into my thoughts with a
cough, "I feel, sir, that that is enough for today. It appears there
is much for you to consider." *[33]

---

33. **Illuminati & The Kabballah.** (Adam Kadmon: The Man at the end of
the Universe). Historians and specialists in Hermetic philosophy will recognise aspects of Illuminati spiritualism within The Ancient Mystery School's
occult version of Kabballah. The Kabballah, a complex and little understood
religion/belief, the secrets of which are contained within coded layers and
originate from the dawn of time, is shrouded in mystery. Adam Kadmon,
as the author writes, is the supposed original celestial man at the end of the
universe containing the souls of mankind. While he represents 'Above' within the Hermetic tradition, Adam Harishon, the first man of Earth, assumes
the opposite symbolic and metaphysical role of 'Below' thus eloquently
completing the classical axiom: 'As above so below.' Another interpretation
could be found in the equally neat doctrine, 'The universe is a man and man
a universe,' describing man's position on the cusp between the macro and
microcosmic worlds, enabling him to perceive their respective infinite proportions and, in turn, realise that they are both, in essence, the same. The
Godhead, said to be beyond rational or mortal understanding seems to be, in
the author's depiction, the location where the soul arrives once freed from the
eternal cycle of death and rebirth and, as such, represents Heaven

Much was right. I left his rooms in a daze and led Petrova from the stables without even finding the Professor to say goodbye. Heavens above and little old me below. Good Lord. What mysteries surround us? What more would I discover on my amazing adventures? Where would life's incredible journey take me next? I paused at the castle gate and considered the religious heritage that my mother and father had bestowed upon me. There was no mention in the Bible of these things which I had experienced for myself but I could not deny their authenticity. How could I possibly balance these new ideas with my existing beliefs? I supposed that I would have to cross that bridge when I got there.

One thing was certain, I was now more of a man than I had ever been and ready to leap from one level of new understanding to the next, eager to find out more of this mystery. One way or another, I knew that this was not the end and that, whatever happened next or wherever I went, whether it was halfway round the world on my horse or to the end of the universe without taking a step, it would merely be the beginning of another journey. A journey that I was more than ready to take. I gazed into the glowing sunset beyond the distant misty mountains and pulled myself into Petrova's saddle, calling out, "C'mon, Girl! Let's fly tonight! Yeehaa! Take me home!

Again, as in the first book, we have ended up with 33 chapters bringing me to the conclusion that this simply cannot be a coincidence. It is impossible to know if S. Drechsler intended this number to feature in the book's original layout or if it was a decision made at a later date during further publishing. However, in keeping with these strange coincidences, I have decided to include 33 footnotes as well. It is important to note that the number thirty three is extremely significant within occult numerology and this one subject alone would take years of researching and much lengthy consideration to properly understand. All the best. Good luck searching on the web and, perhaps more importantly, in your own mind.

Special Thanks

I would like to take this opportunity to thank the thousands of readers from around the world who have given us their heart-warming compliments and much appreciated encouragement. There can be no better time to tell you all that the publication of these books would be a lot, lot more difficult without your support. Also, I would like to thank my researchers and editing staff, Robin and Carol, without whom, I am positive the books would never see the light of day. Thank you from the very bottom of my heart.

More information including forthcoming releases, reviews and other news of these paperbacks and groundbreaking 'Live' E Books can be found at the website: Illuminati Hunter.com & Illuminati Hunter II.com & @Facebook Illuminati Hunter Book

Footnote Appendix & Hypertext Addresses

1. **The Illuminati & Ingolstadt University.** Ingolstadt University was immersed in controversy throughout the end of the 18th century due to the activities of the Bavarian Illuminati. Adam Weishaupt, the founder of the Order in 1776, was Master of Canon Law at the university until March 1785 when he was sacked for his role in the infamous secret society which had, by then seen its ranks grow to over 3000 - see *Illuminati Hunter I.* Herr Vacchieri is not known to have been a member of the society though it is highly possible. He was definitely employed by the university during this period and is mentioned in a book called *Little Tools of Knowledge* (2001 University Michigan Press). The revolutionary zeitgeist associated with The Age of Reason which flourished throughout Europe's educational institutions during this period and prepared the ground for the American and French Revolutions, posed a threat to the authorities and this contributed to the university's closure in 1800. Interestingly, the campus also provides the backdrop for Mary Shelley's masterpiece *Frankenstein* (1812) set at the faculty in 1793 which is often seen as a metaphor for revolution; political, industrial, religious or otherwise. Though the author refers to Ingolstadt as a 'city' it remains a town to this day but during the late 18th century held such huge political influence, as many luminaries of the time were educated there, that this may explain S. Drechsler's exaggeration.

https://en.wikipedia.org/wiki/University_of_Ingolstadt

https://en.wikipedia.org/wiki/Illuminati

2. **Illuminati & The Central Banks.** Conspiracy theories concerning the Illuminati and the central banks have existed as long as the separate institutions themselves. As S. Drechsler states The Bank of England was established in 1694 and, since then, the pound has been devalued more than a hundred times giving his claims some weight. While it may be difficult to accept that the global financial institutions could ever be run in such a simple yet fraudulent manner, for some inexplicable reason, rumours of an over-arching centralised banking cartel controlled by remnants of the Bavarian Illuminati still persist to this day. To realise the true power of the world's financial institutions, then and now, perhaps consider the words of US state official H. Kissinger, 'Who controls money can control the world.'

https://odysee.com/@QuantumRhino:9/The-Capitalist-Conspiracy--G.-Edward-Griffin-(1969)--Documentary:d

3. **The Merchant Kolmer, Illuminati Mentor.** S. Drechsler's recollections of this illusive character, whose past is shrouded in mystery, is highly noteworthy as he is the only eye witness to have ever seen him. Though very little detail is known about the merchant Kolmer he is recorded to have spent much time in Alexandria where he gained a reputation as an expert in ancient artefacts. As S. Drechsler states he was reputed to have initiated Adam Weishaupt, the father of the Bavarian Illuminati, into the darker aspects of Egyptian occultism based on the Manichean teachings which focus on the conflict between good and evil.

http://www.illuminati-news.com/bavarian-illuminati.htm

https://en.wikipedia.org/wiki/Manichaeism

4. **Adam Weishaupt, Illuminati Leader & Professor of Canon Law at Ingolstadt University.** Adam Weishaupt founded the Bavarian Illuminati on May 1st 1776 (the same year of the US Declaration of Independence, the same date as the International Day for Communism, and also ancient pagan witch celebration). Throughout history there has rarely been another individual surrounded by more intrigue than the brilliant academic who could justifiably be known as 'The Godfather of Conspiracy' and has entered the popular cultural pantheon as one of the most profoundly influential thinkers of all time.

https://en.wikipedia.org/wiki/Adam_Weishaupt

5. **The Eagle Hotel (Hotel Adler) Ingolstadt Town.** This impressive hotel has been in the heart of the old city of Ingolstadt since the 15th century and will have hardly changed since S. Drechsler walked through the door over two hundred and fifty years ago.

6. **Illuminati & The Obelisk.** The obelisks in Washington DC, Vatican City and the City of London have always given rise to conspiratorial interpretations. For instance, the existence of a line from the Millennium Dome to the pinnacle of Canary Wharf (also an obelisk) which, in turn, runs exactly to the Bank of England. Use Google Earth if you don't believe me. In these cases it is claimed that the obelisks, or phalluses, are intentionally aligned over water (to represent birth water) with a dome representing the womb (for instance

the roof of the senate building) and, after that, the symbolic product of the union i.e. the child (Lincoln memorial) or, in London's case, the BOE.

https://www.ranker.com/list/secret-conspiracy-and-occult-symbols-in-washington-dc/amandasedlakhevener

https://www.illuminatiofficial.org/symbols/obelisk/

https://www.youtube.com/watch?v=-naYNqMx2XE

7. **Illuminati Beliefs & Egyptian Symbology.** The Illuminati's belief system allegedly centres on the Ancient Mystery School Religion which, in turn, draws heavily on a combination of Kabbalist spiritualism, Neo-Platonism, Luciferianism and Ancient Egyptian symbology. Main characters include: The Eye of Horus (All Seeing Eye of Providence) the pyramid, cap-less or otherwise, (featured on the previous $1 bill) and the obelisk, which can be seen inverted at the top of £5, £10 and £20 notes. The celestial triangle combining the three stars mentioned by S. Drechsler symbolises the eternal Egyptian triumvirate: Osiris (Betelgeuse) Horus (Procyon) and, as described, Isis (Sirius the Dog Star) which rises above the horizon in Egypt on the summer solstice signifying the start of the rainy season and the replenishment of the lands representing the Goddess's procreative power.

https://illuminatisymbols.info/

http://www.newkabbalah.com/plato.html

https://www.youtube.com/watch?v=dB-63aOF8sQ

8. **Illuminati World View.** The Illuminati's objectives were well-known even by this time: the destruction of all; religion, monarchy, family, nationality and property. Within contemporary historical context these objectives are most comparable to those of communism with the abolition of traditional social structures in favour of the state. Another political mode which fittingly describes this model is Malthusian collectivism, named after the philosopher Malthus, in which personal rights are given up in favour of the state; George Orwell's *1984* (1948) springs to mind.

https://www.youtube.com/watch?v=2piiBafkjVY

9. **St Paul's Church (Paulinerkirche) Leipzig 1785.** This impressive

church built in the city of Leipzig in the 13th century was destroyed in 1968 by the communist regime of Eastern Germany. When S. Drechsler visited the church it was part of the university and boasted a stellar list of organ masters within its long history including Johann Sebastian Bach. As the author rightly recalls it possessed an awe-inspiring steeple and belfry.

https://en.wikipedia.org/wiki/Paulinerkirche,_Leipzig

10. **Illuminati Creation & Control of Christianity.** Some conspiracy theorists have long-contended the existence of various Illuminati plots, both historical and modern, to shape Christianity, and indeed all other world religions, for their own ends. Certainly the Kabbalah, allegedly central to the Illuminati's Ancient Mystery School Religion, has very little in common with the New Testament and is, in the most part, diametrically opposed to the moral dogma taught within Christianity. Allegedly, the agenda, during Biblical times, was to 'turn things upside down' (See Isaiah 29:16) and, corrupt the real 'way' of Esu (Jesus). Through infiltration and scribal lies (see Jeremiah 8:8) these 'men who crept in unawares' (See Jude 1:4), 'creating a doctrine woven with lies.'

http://www.lovethetruth.com/false_religion/occult/all_big_religions.htm

11. **Illuminati Rituals & Louisenlund Holstein.** As S. Drechsler claims this grand 18th century mansion and its extensive grounds, owned by the Hesse Kassel family, was frequently used by the Bavarian Illuminati. The property survives to this day mostly unchanged and still contains from that period, amongst other anomalies, a mysterious pyramidal folly mentioned in the previous book pictures of which along with the impressive house can be viewed on the internet. Situated on the Baltic coast at Guby, Schleswig-Holstein in what used to be southern Denmark it is now a private school. Hermeticism is a religious, philosophical and esoteric tradition which deeply influenced its Western counterparts and was considered to be of great importance during both the Renaissance and the Reformation. The tradition claims descent from a doctrine affirming the existence of a single true ideology present in all religions given by God to man in antiquity.

https://en.wikipedia.org/wiki/Stiftung_Louisenlund

trianglebook.weebly.com/mystery-tower.html

https://en.wikipedia.org/wiki/Hermeticism

12. **Illuminati &The Comte de St Germaine.** S. Drechsler's hearing of this little-known but hugely intriguing historical character and his death, is inoteworthy. The Comte de St Germaine claimed to be immortal and was a member of several secret societies including the Bavarian Illuminati. He was an avid alchemist who was given a workshop at Louisenlund by his benefactor, Frederick II Hesse Kassel which is said to have been in a 'small stone tower' within the grounds. His death is recorded in February 1784 from pneumonia but if the author's claims are true then we now know better.

https://en.wikipedia.org/wiki/Count_of_St._Germain

13. **Illuminati Rituals & The Pentagram.** Illuminati rituals are commonly suspected to include a pentagram which is inverted when the practitioners wish to summon or trap negative of sacrificed spirits. The lure is an ancient horn either straight or curved the latter being the version seen by S. Drechsler. This curved version is designed to be carried when played and produces a distinct and threatening tone perhaps most associated with the Norse peoples; Vikings, Danes etc.

https://www.symboldictionary.net/?p=1893

14. **Illuminati & the Number 11.** It is an intriguing coincidence that the eleventh chapter of this book is called 'Judgement and Destruction' as the number 11, as well as other interpretations, also signifies that to the Illuminati. As S. Drechsler states these other interpretations include the 'Master' and 'Magician.' In the Kabbalah God is represented by the number 10 (male and female opposites) as there are ten sephirot (emanations) in the Tree of Life. Therefore, the number 11, being one *above*, is seen as an 'affront' to Him and the number nine, because it is one *below*, represents 'fallen.'

https://community.ebay.com/t5/Archive-The-Soapbox/The-Illuminati-and-the-Significance-of-the-Number-11/td-p/21958176

15. **Dora & Fitz Illuminati Surrogates**. S. Drechsler mentions hearing Dora's surname 'Jordan' and interestingly there was a famous actress from Dublin called Dora Jordan who fits this description and could well have been this character. This well-known celebrity was described as having 'the best

legs on the stage' and later went on to have twelve illegitimate children with William IV. The name (prefix) Fitz literally means 'royal bastard' persuading me to believe that the other individual might well have been a grandson of James II. Unfortunately as details of these children are scant, it is impossible to know for certain.

https://en.wikipedia.org/wiki/Dorothea_Jordan

https://en.wikipedia.org/wiki/Royal_bastard

16. **Illuminati & Monetary Occult Symbolism.** This famous coin would have been old when Drechsler saw it but certainly existed and as described. Interestingly 'Thaler,' Bavarian money of the period, is the word from which 'Dollar' is derived and also, tellingly, in the context of S. Drechsler's account, the serpent wrapping the cross is thought to be the symbol which inspired the dollar sign '$.' Though it is impossible to say whether the claims about this coin's design are true there can be little doubt that similar occult symbolism is contained within the current US $1 bill. There are hundreds of videos and texts available on the internet explaining the various interpretations of these coded messages. A wealth of information also exists suggesting many other denominations including; UK, Australia, EU and several other countries, not to mention other US bills, also contain hidden esoteric messages.

https://www.advanceloan.net/blog/hidden-symbols-and-messages-found-in-your-currency/

17. **Abbé Barruel (1741-1820) The Original Conspiracy Theorist.** This French Jesuit Priest and publicist could be genuinely described as the first conspiracy theorist. He fled to Moravia in Bohemia due to anti-Jesuit sentiment in France but returned in 1773 and went on to complete his magnum opus *Memoirs Illustrating the History of Jacobinism* (1797) expounding the theory that The French Revolution of 1789 was instigated by secret societies including the Jacobian Club and Philalèthes Brotherhoods which, in turn, were heavily influenced by the Bavarian Illuminati. This masterpiece is still highly regarded today and considered to make a convincing political argument.

https://en.wikipedia.org/wiki/Augustin_Barruel

https://www.conspiracyarchive.com/PROOFS_OF_A_CONSPIRACY_

John_Robison.pdf

18. **Illuminati Defectors; Professors Renner Cossendy & Grünberger.** As S. Drechsler claims official accounts record that these three professors were important witnesses at an inquiry set up to investigate the Illuminati in 1785. They had recently defected after not receiving 'special alchemic powers' promised to them by the secret society whilst also becoming disillusioned with its objectives and, as such, became targets for reprisals.

https://modernhistoryproject.org/mhp?Article=FinalWarning&C=1.2#Exposed

19. **The Cintamani Stone & The Illuminati.** This infamous relic, the precursor of The Sorcerer's Stone has a fascinating history. Pieces of it are rumoured to have been fashioned into the Holy Grail, as well as one of King Solomon's rings and, also, placed in the Kabba; the black cube residing in the Al-Masjid al-Haram mosque in Mecca, central to the Muslim faith. As S. Drechsler states it is also known as The Lucifer Stone and fabled to possess immense wish fulfilling powers. In regard to these memoirs, The Cintamani Stone has a remarkable connection with Nicholas Roerich, a Russian artist, diplomat and self-proclaimed mystic who, along with Henry Wallace, the then US Secretary for Agriculture, and President Roosevelt, oversaw the design of the one dollar bill in the 1930's. Wallace, who was deeply involved with the occult and later became US vice president, referred to Roerich as his 'Guru' and arranged for his 'master' to take several missions to the mystical Shamballa, said to be in Tibet and thought to be the home of the stone. It is revealing that its later history became so involved with a man who had such close proximity to The Great Seal, cap-less pyramid and All Seeing Eye used on the one dollar bill as this also seems to be its connection within this story. This is either an extraordinary coincidence or maybe there is another more telling interpretation to these events.

https://en.wikipedia.org/wiki/Cintamani#History

20. **Illuminati & The Blazing Star.** As S. Drechsler states Sirius or The Blazing Star - 'the sun behind the sun' is of utmost importance within the Ancient Mystery School Religion worshipped by the Illuminati. Within the Hermetic belief system the brightest star in the heavens is symbolised by

the pentagram. While the sun warms the physical world the blazing light of Sirius warms the spiritual plain and its radiant beams symbolise deity and omnipotence (The creator is everywhere) and of omniscience (The creator knows and sees all). Hence the 'All Seeing' Eye of Providence. The Blazing Star also holds unrivalled mystical prominence within Freemasonry which many historians and, conspiracy theorist alike, contest has a secret Illuminati connection. Sirius, situated at the bottom of the inverted pyramidal asterism called the Winter Triangle, is known in Egyptian mythology as Isis, the mother, with the other two stars Betelgeuse and Procyon, respectively being Osiris the father and Horus the son. The ancient family trinity can be viewed on the Star Tracker app.

illuminatihunter.com/vids/sirius.mp4

illuminatihunter.com/vids/sirius.mp4

https://en.wikipedia.org/wiki/Winter_Triangle

21. **Illuminati & 'As Above, So Below'.** This seemingly simplistic, yet subtly complex Hermetic maxim is, perhaps, the central pillar of the Ancient Mystery School Religion associated with the Illuminati and, without doubt, the most defining philosophy of the gnostic traditions. A compelling case could be made that, in its contemporary form, there is no place better to contemplate this mainstay of esoteric thought than Chaos Theory or fractals: the inner and outer worlds being in essence the same and only separated by matters of scale. As S. Drechsler's account mentions the same foundational overarching philosophy can also be found in The Lord's Prayer 'On earth as it is in Heaven.'

https://www.youtube.com/watch?v=JnzMqMnueEM

https://treeofknowledgecoven.com/2012/07/01/as-above-so-below-as-within-so-without-as-the-universe-so-the-soul/

22. **Illuminati Court Cases 1786.** Several similar court cases involving the Illuminati took place during this period. After discovering the Illuminati's intentions of usurping governments and destroying the aristocracy the authorities were determined to control the secret society, punishments for the membership of which had existed since their exposure the previous year. Though other details of this precise trial are nonexistent, amazingly, the professor's

testimonies are recorded in the publication ***Grosse Absichten des Ordens der Illuminaten, dem patriotischen Publikum vorgelegt von vier ehemaligen Mitglieder*** (*Great intentions of the Order of the Illuminati, presented to the patriotic public by four former members*) Joseph Lentner, 1786. (German speaking) E Book readers download available above for those who wish to verify the author's claims.

https://books.google.co.uk/books/about/Grosse_Absichten_des_Ordens_der_Illumina.html?id=bQdhAAAAcAAJ&redir_esc=y

23. **Illuminati Hunter & Grave Robbing.** In the first book I considered making the tenuous claim that Professor Van Halestrom may have been the inspiration for the character Abraham Van Helsing in Bram Stoker's classic gothic vampire tale ***Dracula*** (1897). The intriguing synthesis of themes also resonates through Mary Shelley's famous ***Frankenstein*** (1818) which features an oddly similar graverobbing scene and is set in Ingolstadt University. These strange coincidental paralells seem to provoke the question that the author's exploits were of such infamy that they entered local folklore and, as such, were used at a later date as a background for the fictional works noted.

https://www.youtube.com/watch?v=4pgRZY4gJLU

24. **The 'Illegal' Raid On Xavier Zwack'a House.** On the 11th October 1786 an illegal raid took place at the house of high-ranking Illuminati member Xavier Zwack (codename Cato) at Landshut in Bavaria. The reason for its illegality has always been difficult to ascertain, so the author's account gives us fresh insight into an event which has long been contested by historians. There is no doubt that the police raided the house and that arrests and confiscations took place including the seizure of secret documents, codes, plans, letters, depositions, membership lists, seals, amulets, special exploding strongboxes and other evidence. Xavier Zwack was later freed and subsequently escaped from the authorities when they again tried to press charges and fled to Gutenberg in neighbouring Austria. One way or another the raid stands out as an critical turning point in the authorities' fight against the Bavarian Illuminati which, by this time, was considered a 'national emergency' and, because of Zwack's high-profile as a government lawyer, it was a huge blow against the Order and the pressure upon them to retire

underground or leave the country altogether reached a climax.

https://second.wiki/wiki/franz_xavier_von_zwack

25. **Xavier Zwack's Illuminati Hideout Landshut.** Zwack's house was situated in Landshut, a medium sized town in southern Bavaria lying amongst the foothills of the Alps. The town spreads around the river Izar on mostly flat ground but there are several sizable buildings on a large promontory overlooking the city. If S. Drechsler's recollections are correct one can only assume that the action described took place somewhere under this hill.

https://en.wikipedia.org/wiki/Landshut

26. **Illumianti & Debt.** Conspiracy theorists have long held that a secretive cabal controls the supply of major world currencies and, by this means, exercises power over global economic activity and the distribution of wealth. S. Drechsler's reminiscences seem eerily in line with such conspiratorial ideas concerning the purposeful over-production of money to induce debt.

https://odysee.com/@Truth_will_set_You_Free:0/Money-as-Debt-III---Evolution-Beyond-Money-3-3:0

27. **Illuminati & The Exploding Strongbox.** In the official records several exploding strongboxes of the variety seen by the author were reportedly confiscated in the raid at Xavier Zwack's house. S. Drechsler's account details the charge contained within the box's mechanism and this would seem to be borne out by existing histories. The charge would have been big enough to destroy the contents of the box whilst also maiming the person who tried to open it. (See footnote 24.)

www.conspiracyarchive.com/2014/01/29/illuminati-conspiracy-part-one/

28. **Illuminati & Illumination.** It is sometimes difficult to remember, with all the illicit goings on, sinister plans and conspiracies surrounding the Illuminati, that the secret societal movement in the Age of Reason to which the Bavarian Order pays homage - with its arcane hermetic and other mystic traditions - was, in fact, based upon the adepts' aspiration to attain, be that spiritual or intellectual, illumination. S. Drechsler's transcendental journey, mirroring perhaps that of a near-death experience, can, therefore, I believe, be seen compellingly and rather fittingly as the crowning pinnacle of this

process and the Hermetic student's astral arch to move from one state to the next: As above, so below. Much information and theory exists regarding these altered states on the internet, as one may well imagine, and I have sifted through these to choose one of the most enlightening for E Book readers to view while considering the author's Gnostic adventures. Enjoy.

https://www.youtube.com/watch?v=2_YQcYnOtRl

29. **The Illuminati & The Russian Revolution.** Conspiracy theorists, and even some mainstream historians, have long claimed that the roots of The Russian Revolution were not entirely organic and that the epochal political events which swept the nation in 1917 were fomented by outside influences. In terms of world power the USSR, as it came to be, or opposing atheist communist state, can be seen as the counterbalance to the US, setting up a classic left-right paradigm (thesis - antithesis) often associated with Illuminati global goals. A great deal of evidence exists backing up this claim. Notable inclusions to this long list are Prof Antony C. Sutton's *Wall Street and the Bolshevik Revolution* (1992) and Prof Carroll Quigley's *Tragedy and Hope* (1963) which provide excellent source material for those wishing to explore an alternative view of international politics.

www.lovethetruth.com/books/pawns/08.htm

https://www.youtube.com/watch?v=RD_cJXOjYl8

https://en.wikipedia.org/wiki/Tragedy_and_Hope

30. **Hegelian Dialectic & The Illuminati.** Hegel was a German philosopher (1770-1831) and is widely renowned for first understanding that the dialectic between conflicting ideas can be used to bring about desired change: Thesis – Antithesis – Synthesis. The technique has many given names including the more modern, and perhaps more well-known, 'Problem – Reaction – Solution.' 'Divide and Rule' - the Roman equivalent - explains the theory in another way; the 'division' coming from two opposing ideas, Thesis and Antithesis, bringing about the product or 'Synthesis' which, in turn becomes the new thesis. Conspiracy theorists argue that this technique is used to bring about control on a geopolitical level whilst, interestingly, psychologists contend that it is equally effective on the personal level.

https://www.youtube.com/watch?v=v_F4WomLlq0

268

https://en.wikipedia.org/wiki/Georg_Wilhelm_Friedrich_Hegel

31. The Publication of The Original Writings of The Illuminati. As S. Drechsler describes the Original Writings of the Illuminati *Einige Originalschriften des Illuminaten Ordens* confiscated from Xavier Zwack's house in the illegal raid were published by the Bavarian authorities in late 1785. They were sent to the leaderships of all European countries in an effort to warn them about the Illuminati. The author is also correct in his assertion that new laws had been granted to the police at this time allowing them to arrest Illuminati members on the spot. The crime of membership was now a serious offence and those found guilty could face serious jail sentences.

https://archive.org/details/EinigeOriginalschriftenDesIlluminatenordens

32. The Cintamani Stone & The Dollar Bill. In support of S. Drechsler's theory the connections between this mysterious stone and the dollar bill are endless. Nicholas Roerich a Russian mystic and Henry Wallace US Secretary of Agriculture in 1933 (the politician most associated with the esoteriv design of the current dollar bill apart from President Roosevelt), were both deeply involved with the Cintamani Stone. Wallace sent Roerich on many missions to Tibet (Shamballa) in the 1930's to fetch and return the stone and intriguingly several of Roerich's famous paintings feature a mystical jewel being transported through a wasteland, some of which inexplicably resemble S. Drechsler's own experiences and begs the question that Kolmer may also have been attempting to return the relic. Roerich later fell from grace with the White House when he was suspected of being a Russian spy and Wallace's career, though not destroyed, was greatly undermined by rumours of unwarranted spiritualism when letters that he had sent to Roerich became public in which he called him his 'guru.' The Cintamani Stone's magical properties are still held in such high regard that it is easy to conclude those with occult objectives might seek to employ its supposed powers. Whether the stone's alchemic capabilities are real or not, it seems that the The Stone and the dollar's histories are so inexorably linked that there has to be something else behind the official story. The US Mint issued the first dollar in 1787 a year after S. Drechsler's account takes place and the '$' sign 'serpent entwining the cross' was incorporated shortly after in 1793. With this in mind is it too far-fetched to assume that what the author had accidentally discovered on his adventures was 'The Birth of The Dollar'? This frightening conclusion would mean that the world's reserve currency would be a creation of the Bavarian Illuminati but with no clarification, hopefully, this part of the mystery will be revealed in future instalments of the memoirs. A piece of The Cintamani Stone is now rumoured to be contained in the cornerstone of the 'Master Building' penthouse built for Roerich in New York on the corner of 53rd Street.

https://www.youtube.com/watch?v=OgdXzZn7sr0

https://en.wikipedia.org/wiki/Nicholas_Roerich

https://en.wikipedia.org/wiki/Henry_A._Wallace

https://www.youtube.com/watch?v=OgdXzZn7sr0

https://robertphoenix.com/the-rite-of-spring-nicholas-roerich-the-manipulation-of-money-and-welcome-aries/

33. **Illuminati & The Kabballah.** (Adam Kadmon: The Man at the end of the Universe). Historians and specialists in Hermetic philosophy will recognise aspects of Illuminati spiritualism within The Ancient Mystery School's occult version of Kabballah. The Kabballah, a complex and little understood religion/belief, the secrets of which are contained within coded layers and originate from the dawn of time, is shrouded in mystery. Adam Kadmon, as the author writes, is the supposed original celestial man at the end of the universe containing the souls of mankind. While he represents 'Above' within the Hermetic tradition, Adam Harishon, the first man of Earth, assumes the opposite symbolic and metaphysical role of 'Below' thus eloquently completing the classical axiom: 'As above so below.' Another interpretation could be found in the equally neat doctrine, 'The universe is a man and man a universe,' describing man's position on the cusp between the macro and microcosmic worlds, enabling him to perceive their respective infinite proportions and, in turn, realise that they are both, in essence, the same. The Godhead, said to be beyond rational or mortal understanding seems to be, in the author's depiction, the location where the soul arrives once freed from the eternal cycle of death and rebirth and, as such, represents Heaven.

https://www.youtube.com/watch?v=HtZhszyUkn4